Microsoft®

W9-BNS-215

Build a Program *Now!*

Microsoft®
Visual C#® 2005
Express Edition

PUBLISHED BY
Microsoft Press
A Division of Microsoft Corporation
One Microsoft Way
Redmond, Washington 98052-6399

Library of Congress Control Number 2005933642

Printed and bound in the United States of America.

1 2 3 4 5 6 7 8 9 QWT 9 8 7 6 5

Distributed in Canada by H.B. Fenn and Company Ltd.

A CIP catalogue record for this book is available from the British Library.

Microsoft Press books are available through booksellers and distributors worldwide. For further information about international editions, contact your local Microsoft Corporation offi ce or contact Microsoft Press International directly at fax (425) 936-7329. Visit our Web site at www.microsoft.com/learning/. Send comments to mspinput@microsoft.com.

Acquisitions Editor: Ben Ryan
Project Editor: Sandra Haynes
Editorial and Production: Custom Editorial Productions, Inc.

Body Part No. X11-50121

Contents

What do you think of this book?
We want to hear from you!

Microsoft is interested in hearing your feedback about this publication so we can continually improve our books and learning resources for you. To participate in a brief online survey, please visit: *www.microsoft.com/learning/booksurvey/*

Introduction

Visual C# 2005 Express and the other Visual Studio 2005 Express Edition products are, in my opinion, one of the best and most intelligent ideas to come out from Developer Division here at Microsoft. I'm applauding and cheering for the people who had this brilliant idea because I believe there is a real need and demand for a world-class and powerful product for the hobbyist programmers, students, and professional developers. And Visual C# 2005 Express Edition answers all of that and more.

Visual C# 2005 Express Edition is a fully functional subset of Visual Studio 2005, suitable for creating and maintaining Windows applications and libraries. It's not a timed-bomb edition, a demo, or a feature limited version; no, it's a key Microsoft initiative to reach more people and give them the ability to have fun while creating cool software.

Who Is This Book For?

This book is for everybody: students, hobbyist programmers, and also for people who always thought programming was a tough task. It's for people who had ideas like: I wish I could build a tool to store all my recipes, I wish I could print them and send them to my friends OR I wish I could build this cool card game that I have never found elsewhere OR I wish I could build this cool software to store my DVD and CD collection OR I wish I could build this software to help me work with matrices and plot graphics for my math class and many more projects that one can think of!

This book is for people who have ideas but don't know how to bring them to reality. It's a good introduction to this art and science that is developing software.

How This Book Is Organized

This book consists of nine chapters, each covering a particular feature or technology about Visual C# 2005 Express Edition. Most chapters build on previous chapters, so you should plan on reading the material sequentially.

Conventions and Features in This Book

This book presents information using conventions designed to make the information readable and easy to follow. Before you start the book, read the following list, which explains conventions you'll see throughout the book and points out helpful features in the book that you might want to use.

Conventions

- Each exercise is a series of tasks. Each task is presented as a series of numbered steps (1, 2, and so on). Each exercise is preceded by a procedural heading that lets you know what you will accomplish in the exercise.

- Notes labeled "Tip" provide additional information or alternative methods for completing a step successfully.

- Notes labeled "Caution" alert you to information you need to check before continuing.

- Text that you type or items you select or click appear in bold.

- Menu commands, dialog box titles, and other user interface elements appear with each word capitalized.

- A plus sign (+) between two key names means that you must press those keys at the same time. For example, "Press Alt+Tab" means that you hold down the Alt key while you press the Tab key.

Other Features

- Shaded sidebars throughout the book provide more in-depth information about the content. The sidebars might contain background information, design tips, or features related to the information being discussed.

- Each chapter ends with an In Summary... section that briefly reviews what you learned in the current chapter and previews what the next chapter will present.

System Requirements

You'll need the following hardware and software to complete the exercises in this book:

- Microsoft Windows XP with Service Pack 2, Microsoft Windows Server 2003 with Service Pack 1, or Microsoft Windows 2000 with Service Pack 4

- Microsoft Visual C# 2005 Express Edition

- PC with a Pentium III-class processor, 600 MHz Recommended: 1 GHz

- 128 MB RAM (256 MB or more recommended)

- Video (800 x 600 or higher resolution) monitor with at least 256 colors (1024 x 768 High Color 16-bit recommended)

- CD-ROM or DVD-ROM drive

- Microsoft Mouse or compatible pointing device

You'll also need administrator access to your computer to configure SQL Server 2005 Express.

NOTE
The CD-ROM packaged in the back of this book contains the Visual C# 2005 Express Edition software needed to complete the exercises in this book.

Code Samples

The code samples for this book can be downloaded from the book's companion content page at the following address: *http://www.microsoft.com/mspress/companion/0-7356-2299-9/*

You'll use the code samples and starter solutions as you perform the exercises in the book. By using the code samples, you won't waste time creating files that aren't relevant to the exercise. The files and the step-by-step instructions in the lessons also let you learn by doing, which is an easy and effective way to acquire and remember new skills. You'll also find the complete solutions if you want to verify your work or if you simply want to look at it.

Installing the Code Samples

Follow these steps to install the code samples on your computer.

 Download the code samples from *http://www.microsoft.com/mspress/companion/0-7356-2229-9/*.

 After you download the code samples file, run the installer.

 Follow the instructions that appear.

The code samples are installed to the following location on your computer:

My Documents\Microsoft Press\VCS 2005 Express

Using the Code Samples

Each chapter in this book explains when and how to use any code samples for that chapter. When it's time to use a code sample, the book will list the instructions for how to open the files. The chapters are built around scenarios that simulate real programming projects, so you can easily apply the skills you learn to your own work.

For those of you who like to know all the details, a list of the code sample projects appears on the next page. Almost all projects have solutions available for the practice exercises. The solutions for each project are included in the folder for each chapter and are labeled **Complete**.

Uninstalling the Code Samples

Follow these steps to remove the code samples from your computer.

 In Control Panel, open **Add Or Remove Programs**.

 From the list of Currently Installed Programs, select **Microsoft Visual C# 2005 Express Edition: Build a Program Now!** and click **Remove**.

 Follow the instructions that appear to remove the code samples.

Project	Description
Chapter 1 & 2	No sample projects
Chapter 3 MyFirstConsoleApplication	Application that takes two numbers and adds them together, then displays the sum in a console window.
MyFirstWindowsApplication	Same application but displays the result in a message box.
Chapter 4 MyOwnBrowser	Simple Web browser application that enables the user to browse on the Internet.
Chapter 5 TestProject	Application that enables you to use the most important features in Visual C# 2005 Express Edition.
Chapter 6 MyOwnBrowser	This is the continuation of the application from Chapter 4. It is the Web browser to which you'll add menus, toolbars, a status and progress bar, and a navigation window with autocomplete.
Chapter 7 Debugger	An application full of problems to help you learn how to debug using features of Visual C# 2005 Express Edition.
Chapter 8 CarTracker	An application enabling the user to track car ads from the Internet using a SQL Server 2005 Express database to store the information.
Chapter 9 WeatherTracker	An application that runs in the system-tray and has a nice UI to display weather data collected by your application from diverse Web services. A deployment package is also created for the distribution of your application.

Prerelease Software

This book was reviewed and tested against the August 2005 release candidate. This book is expected to be fully compatible with the final release of Visual Studio 2005. If there are any changes or corrections for this book, they'll be collected and added to a Microsoft Knowledge Base article. See the "Support for This Book" section in this Introduction for more information.

Technology Updates

As technologies related to this book are updated, links to additional information will be added to the Microsoft Press Technology Updates Web page. Visit this page periodically for updates on Visual Studio 2005 and other technologies.

http://www.microsoft.com/mspress/updates/

Support for This Book

Every effort has been made to ensure the accuracy of this book and the companion content. As corrections or changes are collected, they'll be added to a Microsoft Knowledge Base article. To view the list of known corrections for this book, visit the following article:

http://support.microsoft.com/kb/905040

Microsoft Press provides support for books and companion content at the following Web site:

http://www.microsoft.com/learning/support/books/

Questions and Comments

If you have comments, questions, or ideas regarding the book or the companion content or have questions that are not answered by visiting the sites above, please send them to Microsoft Press via e-mail to

mspinput@microsoft.com

or via postal mail to

Microsoft Press
Attn: Visual C# 2005 Express Edition: Build a Program
    Now! Editor
One Microsoft Way
Redmond, WA 98052-6399

Please note that Microsoft offers no software product support through these addresses.

About the Author

Patrice Pelland

Patrice Pelland is a technical lead at Microsoft working in the Developer Division. He loves .NET and Web services and, for the past four years, he has been working, teaching, evangelizing, and talking about them to everyone.

For the past twelve years, he has been working in software development in various roles: developer, project lead, manager and mentor, and software engineer in QA organizations. He has vast experience spanning multiple technologies and fields: developer tools, fiber optics tele-communication, aviation, coffee and dairy companies, and also three years teaching computer science and software development at a college in Canada.

When not developing great tools for developers and helping customers throughout the world, he enjoys spending time with his family and friends, playing games on XBOX and PC, reading books, reading about Porsche and dreaming about driving one, playing hockey, watching NHL hockey and NFL football, and having great dinners with good food and fine drinks with friends and family. He resides with his family in Sammamish, WA.

Dedication

This book is dedicated to my wife, Hélène. My wife is a breast cancer survivor, and her courage and strength push me to do better things and to face more complex challenges. She's beautiful; she's my idol, my inspiration, my sunshine, my best friend, my love, and an awesome mother! Mon amour, thanks for being who you are and for being there for me! I love you!

Thanks

First of all, thanks to my parents. Mom, Dad, you gave me all the chances to be what I am in life and you gave me the values to be the man I am. Thanks and I love you!

A book is a huge adventure in somebody's life, and it would not be possible without the help of many people. I've always read the thank you sections in other people's books and I was always amazed at how many people are needed to make a book what it is. Now I really understand why!!!

While writing a book is tough, real tough, it's really satisfying at the same time. During the writing process, you sometimes have doubts, and I had my share of--especially those nights at 3:00 a.m. when all other souls in the house are asleep, even my dog, and the product had a bug preventing me from testing something; when I was in front of my laptop with an exception and a white page in Word; when everybody was on vacation this summer while I was working at the library in Sammamish. I can't remember how many times I've said to my friends, "No, I won't be able to be there. I need to work on my book!" But it's an awesome experience to write a book; everybody who has the chance should take the challenge!

With that said, I first need to thank my lovely family. My kids (Laura, 11, and Antoine, 9) and my wife, Hélène, were so great and PATIENT. How many times I heard them say, "Daddy, it's movie night...oh yeah, it's true, you're working on your book again!" But at the same time, they were respecting the space I needed and the time alone!!! You guys are great and I love you!

I have to thank all the people at MS Learning and the publishing team. I would especially like to thank Ben for helping me get in the writing world; Sandra for her constant motivation, help, suggestions, and also for helping me to go through all the hurdles of writing a book; and Megan for all your help getting the job done and a real, tangible product. You guys have my respect for working day in, day out in the crazy world of publishing.

I would also like to thank all the people in the VB, C#, Windows Forms, MSDN and setup teams who helped me by answering all my questions in a dynamic and constantly changing product lifecycle. I would like to thank more specifically Dan Fernandez, Joe Binder, Brian Keller, Brian Johnson, Hong Gao, Jay Roxe, Kavitha Radhakrishnan, Kent Sharkey, Lisa Feigenbaum, Shamez Rajan, Steve Lasker, Aaron Stebner, and Habib Heydarian.

A special thanks to Jeff Prosise for being such a good writer, an awesome trainer, and for writing a blog about the writing process. You were the spark that ignited my flame to write a technical book.

Thanks also to my colleagues from the DDCPX team for always giving me good words of encouragement, to Boris Feldman for sharing his experiences as a writer and, finally, thanks to my good friend, John Cross, for his constructive feedback.

Thanks to my good friends here in the Puget Sound area for the kind words of encouragement and to my family and friends in Canada for understanding why I'm not calling or giving any news. Sorry, Mom and Dad!

And thanks to my good neighbors and friends, Mike and Elizabeth, for their constant encouragement and for letting me use their dog's name, Molly, in my OOP introduction.

Thanks to everybody I might have forgotten!

Patrice Pelland
October 2005
Sammamish, WA

Chapter 1

Introducing Microsoft® Visual C#® 2005 Express Edition

So maybe you've decided you want to try programming and you found yourself with this book. Well, if that's the case, you've come to the right place. This book is all about introducing you to the art, science, and joys of creating software for Microsoft Windows®; yes, the same Microsoft Windows you probably use every day. Throughout the book, I'll show you how to build applications that are very similar to many of the applications you use on a regular basis, such as your Internet browser, your word processor, your e-mail software, and your personal finance application. You're probably wondering how you could possibly do this with no programming experience. By the time you finish this book, you'll believe it. Don't worry. We'll have a blast, and because you'll actually be building the applications as you follow along with each exercise, you'll see for yourself just how easy it can be.

So now, what is that **.NET** thing that everybody is talking about? Maybe you've seen it somewhere online or have come across the term in the jobs section in your Sunday newspaper. For instance, the term might have appeared when you were logging on to Hotmail® or in an online ad where a company is looking for a developer with .NET skills. Look at Figure 1-1 for some examples of where you might have come across a reference to .NET.

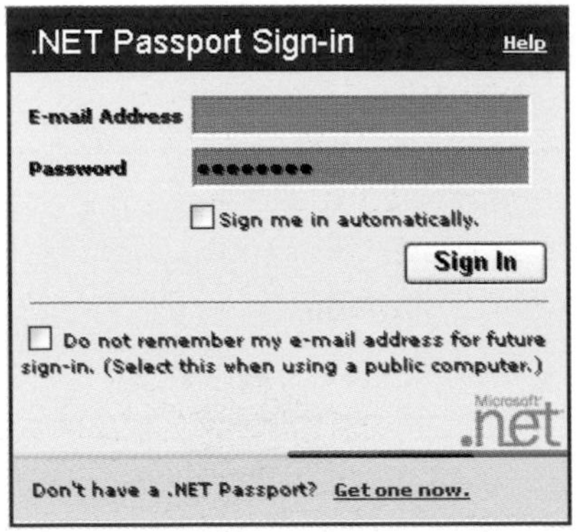

The Platforms SDK team is looking for a strong developer to work on our internal Tools team. The Tools team produces tools and Web sites that track WinFX API development, report metrics on our SDKs, and track the tens of thousands of files that are submitted to our SDKs for WinFX, the .NET Framework, and the Microsoft Windows operating systems.

Figure 1-1
Some examples of where you might have come across a reference to .NET

The term *.NET* by itself does not mean much. You could ask 10 different people in the industry, and you would get 10 different answers. The term is widely used and with a lot of different meanings. In fact, .NET has been used with a lot of market hype attached to it, a little bit like the term *MP3*. So in reality, when you hear or read *.NET*, you really should be thinking about the .NET Framework.

Here is a formal definition of the .NET Framework:

The .NET Framework is a platform that allows you to develop software applications and libraries called "managed applications"; it provides you with the compiler and tools to be able to build, debug, and execute managed applications.

For our purposes, you could say .NET is the platform that gives you everything you need to develop and run managed applications that run on Windows.

We say that applications are managed because their execution is managed by the .NET Framework. In fact, the .NET Framework is *managing* the execution by providing a controlled runtime environment offering a wide variety of services like loading your applications, managing the memory, and finally monitoring and maintaining the security and integrity while the application is executed. Before .NET (and Java), applications were unmanaged because they were not executed by a controlled runtime environment. No other component of the system provided the services .NET offers. The applications had to manage their own services, which sometimes led to erroneous code, security holes, and data corruption. Because of these problems, applications were tough to maintain and debug.

The .NET Framework provides you with a wide variety of tools such as **compilers**, **debuggers**, **programming languages**, an **execution engine** (named CLR – Common Language Runtime), developer tools, and a large number of predefined "building blocks" libraries. Those libraries are named **FCL (Framework Class Libraries)**. You can think of each .NET component as a building block in a house, as illustrated in this image.

I won't put you to sleep with all the definitions for each block of this house, because we're going to use or talk about most of them in our projects; I'll simply introduce the blocks as appropriate. Just consider this illustration and come back to it as needed.

Two notes about this special house are worth mentioning.

First, look at the beige component on the right side of the house. It is not part of the .NET Framework, but it touches the .NET Framework at all levels. The doorknob on this component indicates that through this application, you can develop applications that will allow you touch all the components of the .NET Framework.

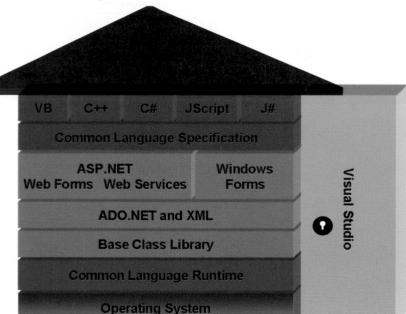

Second, notice that Common Language Runtime (CLR) is the primary part of the house's foundation. It's a crucial part of the foundation because it's the engine that loads and manages the execution of source code. All other services you need to develop applications are on top of the CLR.

What Is C#?

C# is one of the available programming languages that target the .NET Framework. Like any spoken/written language, C# has syntax rules and a series of valid words you can use to create your applications. C# is a popular choice for beginners because some people find the syntax simpler than the syntax of many other programming languages.

Is C# an Object-Oriented Programming (OOP) Language?

C# is a fully fledged object-oriented programming language. Let's talk about what this means.

Object-oriented programming (OOP) is a programming style (or programming paradigm). There are other programming paradigms, such as functional or procedural programming. Languages like C, Fortran, and Pascal are all programming paradigms. But these paradigms focus more on the actions while OOP focuses more on the data itself.

Applications that use the OOP paradigm are developed using OOP languages (OOPL). The first OOPL were introduced in the 1960s, but they really became popular in the late 1970s. They are widely used today because most people agree that they're easy to learn, use, debug, and maintain. For instance, OOPL easily represent real world objects. C# is an OOP language as are Visual Basic .NET, C++, Java, SmallTalk, and Lisp.

Programmers use OOP to write programs that represent the decomposition of real world problems into modules. Those modules represent real world objects and are named classes or types. You can think of an OOP program as a collection of objects interacting with each other. Using OOP, a programmer defines new types to represent real-world objects, such as a plane, a person, a customer, a dog, or a car. Those types or classes create objects

Microsoft Visual C# 2005 Express Edition: Build a Program Now!

or instances. An object is a unit that represents one instance of the real world. It's a self-contained unit because it includes all the data and functionality associated with that object. This means that each object created in an application contains all the information that characterizes it (**data members**) and all the actions (**methods**) that can access or modify that information.

Here is a simple example in C# that defines a person's class:

```
1    using System;
2
3    public class Person
4    {
5        //Data members
6        public string Name;
7        public string Address;
8        public string City;
9        public string State;
10       public string ZIP;
11       public string Country;
12
13       // Methods
14       public virtual void Display()
15       {
16           Console.WriteLine(Name);
17           Console.WriteLine(Address);
18           Console.WriteLine(City);
19           Console.WriteLine(State);
20           Console.WriteLine(ZIP);
21           Console.WriteLine(Country);
22       }
23   }
```

This class includes public data members and a display method to print the object's content to the console. The virtual keyword means that a new class derived from this class will be able to write its own implementation of the display method.

Let's use a different example to go over these concepts. My dog, Chopin, is an instance of the class Dog and the class Dog is a subclass of the Animal class. Because Chopin is a Dog, he has some behaviors and data that are proper for a dog. But because Dog is also an Animal, Chopin also inherits some data and behaviors from the Animal class.

This means that the instance Chopin of the Dog class has data members that characterize him and methods that I can call on that little furry ball. For example, here is the instance information for the Chopin object:

Data

- Breed: He's a Maltese.
- Gender: He's male.
- Weight: His weight is 5.5 pounds.
- Color: He's white.
- Name: His name is Chopin Chabispel.
- Age: He's 1.5 years old.

Actions

- He speaks (barks).
- He eats.
- He moves.
- He sleeps.

All of these data items (breed, gender, weight, color, name, and age) and actions (speak, eat, move, and sleep) characterize him, but they can also characterize any other dog, like my neighbor's dog, Molly. And if you think about it, those items can characterize any animal. This means that the class Dog **inherits** data members and methods from the class Animal.

Let's say you want to develop an application for a veterinary clinic. To cover the cats that come to your clinic, all you must do is create a Cat class that also inherits from the class Animal. Then each class (Cat or Dog) could **override** the functionality from the Animal class as needed. For instance, for the Cat class the speak method would be "meows" instead of barks.

Let's look at the Person class example again. This time, an Employee class that derives from the Person class is added. The Employee class derives from the Person class using the : (colon punctuation symbol) followed by the Person element. The keyword **override** changes the implementation of the **Display()** method.

```
52      public class Employee : Person
53
54      {
55          public int Level;
56          public int Salary;
57
58          public override void Display()
59          {
60              Console.WriteLine(Name + " is at level " + Level.ToString() + " and has a
salary of : " + Salary.ToString() + "$");
61              Console.WriteLine("His address is:");
62              Console.WriteLine(Address);
63              Console.WriteLine(City + "," + State + " " + ZIP);
64              Console.WriteLine(Country);
65          }
66      }
```

TIP
In this book, you'll notice that some code listings include line numbers. If a line does not include a number, it indicates that the code is a continuation from the previous line. Some code lines can get rather long and must be wrapped to be displayed on the printed page. If you need to type in the code in Visual C#, be sure to put continued lines on a single line.

In this case, the Employee class inherits from the Person class and therefore gets all the data fields from that base class. Employee class doesn't have to redefine all fields in its definition because it gets them automatically from Person. So, for the Employee class, you must specify only what is different from an instance of the Person class. For example, an instance of the Employee class would have level and salary whereas not all instances of the Person class would. Plus, the Display method for Employee could add level and salary information to the displayed message when called.

This was just a brief introduction to OOP and some of its concepts. C# supports all of these concepts and many more. Throughout this book you'll see more OOP concepts, and when you do, I'll highlight them in a reader aid information box.

Here's the complete listing used in this section with the addition of another class: the Customer class.

SEE ALSO
In .NET, all class ultimately derives from the Object class, even when it is not specified.

```
1      using System;
2
3      public class Person
4      {
5          //Data members
6          public string Name;
7          public string Address;
8          public string City;
9          public string State;
10         public string ZIP;
11         public string Country;
12
13         // Methods
14         public virtual void Display()
15         {
16             Console.WriteLine(Name);
17             Console.WriteLine(Address);
18             Console.WriteLine(City);
19             Console.WriteLine(State);
20             Console.WriteLine(ZIP);
21             Console.WriteLine(Country);
22         }
23     }
24
25     public class Customer : Person
26
27     {
28         public int ID;
29         public bool IsPartner;
30
31         public override void Display()
32         {
33             string partnerMessage;
34
35             if (IsPartner)
36             {
37                 partnerMessage = " is a partner";
38             }
39             else
40             {
41                 partnerMessage = " is not a partner";
42             }
```

```
43
44              Console.WriteLine("Customer ID: " + ID.ToString());
45              Console.WriteLine(Name + partnerMessage);
46              Console.WriteLine(Address);
47              Console.WriteLine(City + "," + State + " " + ZIP);
48              Console.WriteLine(Country);
49          }
50      }
51
52      public class Employee : Person
53
54      {
55          public int Level;
56          public int Salary;
57
58          public override void Display()
59          {
60              Console.WriteLine(Name + " is at level " + Level.ToString() + " and has a
salary of : " + Salary.ToString() + "$");
61              Console.WriteLine("His address is:");
62              Console.WriteLine(Address);
63              Console.WriteLine(City + "," + State + " " + ZIP);
64              Console.WriteLine(Country);
65          }
66      }
```

This is a simple case, but it illustrates some of the basic concepts of OOP.

What Is Visual C# 2005 Express Edition?

Visual C# 2005 Express Edition is the tool we will use throughout this book to learn how to
develop applications running on Windows.

The Express Editions of Visual Studio 2005 were designed to focus on productivity.
As with their high-end version counterparts, the Express Editions of Visual Studio 2005 are
also what we call Rapid Application Development tools (RAD tools) because their philosophy

is geared toward productivity. These new versions of Visual Studio are easy to use, easy to learn, and streamlined because, although they contain mostly the same components, they lack the full breadth of features found in the higher-end versions of Visual Studio. Most features and components in the Express Editions were simplified to make the learning curve less steep and to fit the needs of the nonprofessional developer.

The Visual Studio 2005 Express Edition family is designed with beginning programmers in mind—people like you who are curious about programming and who are looking for an easy way to build Windows applications while learning how to program. Visual C# 2005 Express Edition is the ideal tool to use to rapidly develop applications for topics you really love or for hobbies you enjoy. It can also be used to help ease your day-to-day job or school tasks. Most importantly, you can have fun with the tool while you're learning to program.

What Kinds of Applications Can You Build with Visual C# 2005 Express Edition?

With this version of Visual Studio 2005, you'll be able to create the following types of applications:

- **Windows Applications** Applications that have a graphical interface with buttons, windows, menus, toolbars, and so on, as in Microsoft Word or Internet Explorer.
- **Console Applications** Applications that have no graphical interface and simply use text to communicate with the user. (Typically, these are a command window or DOS window.)
- **Reusable Components or Class Libraries** A group of tools created to help build other applications.

What you won't be able to build are Web sites and Web services. To create any type of Web application, you will need to get Microsoft Visual Web Developer™ 2005 Express Edition.

NOTE
We will look into the details of what types of applications fall into these categories in Chapter 2.

What Are the Key Features You Need to Know About?

The list below, although not complete, provides the essential features of Visual C# 2005 Express Edition. At this point, don't worry if you don't understand every single feature listed below. I present the features in the list because you'll come across all of them in some way in the fun samples that you will be creating.

Most of the features listed here emphasize the RAD philosophy. Although the idea is to give you an overview of the interesting features that can make your life easier, the feature names alone are not sufficient to understand what they mean. So I include a brief description giving you the essentials and how they should help you to develop applications.

- **Built-in Starter Kits** Fully developed applications with best practices and examples to follow. These applications will give you another example to base your learning on. They will be a good complement to what we are doing with this book.

- **Beginner's Targeted Documentation and Tutorials** A fast and easy way to get the information. They also provide samples.

- **IntelliSense®** Provides real-life syntax suggestions and even finishes your typing for you.

- **Code Snippets** Provide code for various programming tasks to help you complete many common tasks automatically. Code snippets show the recommended way of doing things. They are directly integrated in the development environment, and they are extensible; that is, over time Microsoft will continue to supply new code snippets and members of online communities will contribute their snippets as well. Code snippet extensibility seems to be a really nice feature that will help people share useful things in the online communities.

- **Data-enabled Applications** These applications allow you to connect to Microsoft SQL Server™ 2005 Express Edition and add databases and code to access these data in your applications.

- **Windows Form Designer** With these new tools, you can easily design your Windows application, including features such as snap lines that make sure your controls are aligned in your form and autocorrect to give you real-time syntax analysis feedback.

- **XML Web Services** This product provides easy-to-use tools and wizards that will help you connect to published XML-based Web Services and utilize their functionalities.

- **New Windows Form Controls** These comprise an impressive list of controls—a greater selection than in any previous version of Visual C#. They will help you create user interfaces that have a professional look and feel.

- **Smart Tags** Most Windows Form controls that come with the product include Smart Tags. As in many Microsoft Office applications, a Smart Tag is represented by a little black triangle or an icon and a little black triangle attached to a control. A Smart Tag gives you access to the most common actions you can perform on a control.

- **Refactoring** The Visual C# 2005 IDE now includes robust and powerful refactoring support. Refactoring enables developers to automate many of the common tasks when restructuring code. Restructuring the code is when you want to change some of your source code elements and you want to apply that change to all files and occurrences of that element. For instance you'll be able to rename variables throughout a project, promoting local variables to parameters and many more. It gives you a nice preview feature so that you can see the changes before you make them. You'll be able to get to the refactoring features either by accessing a context-sensitive menu while editing your source code or by using a smart tag. For more information on refactoring, please visit http://www.refactoring.com/ and for more examples on how those features are implemented in the Visual C# 2005 IDE look at http://msdn.microsoft.com/vcsharp/2005/overview/productivity/#refactoring.

- **Click-once Deployment** This features allows you to easily publish your applications on the Internet, on a local area network (LAN), a network share, or on a CD. It also simplifies publishing updates.

- **Edit and Continue** While you are debugging your application, Edit and Continue lets you modify the code, move back and forth in the debugger, re-execute code, add functionality, or fix bugs on the fly without stopping program execution.

- **Debugger Visualizers** While you are debugging your application, the visualizers give you an easy way to get readable representations of your application data. They give you a human-readable representation of the stored data, even for more complex types found in ADO.NET or Extensible Markup Language (XML).

- **Community Access and Start Page** With these features, you can access additional information from online communities and from different sources of online help, including diverse RSS (Rich Site Summary or Really Simple Syndication) Feeds. (RSS is a family of XML file formats; it is widely used by the weblog community and news Web sites.)

- **Simplified Development Environment** Everything in the development environment was created so that you can easily access key functionalities, tools, and objects.

As you can see, Visual C# 2005 Express Edition includes many nice features to help the new programmer develop applications in a fast and fun way. These features will provide guidance even when you're not necessarily sure what syntax or components to use and will greatly expedite your learning of the product.

In Summary...

You now know that .NET is a framework composed of compilers, tools, languages, debuggers, and an execution engine. The CLR, or Common Language Runtime, is that execution engine, and it is responsible for loading and executing managed applications. In essence, .NET is like a house with the CLR as the foundation and all other services built on top of it.

You also learned that C# is an object-oriented programming language. You also started to learn what object-oriented programming is and started to learn the basics of OOP in Visual C# 2005.

This chapter has given you the opportunity to learn the features of Visual C# 2005 Express Edition and how you can create three different types of applications that match your hobbies, job, or school needs. In the next chapter, you'll learn how to install Visual C# 2005 Express Edition.

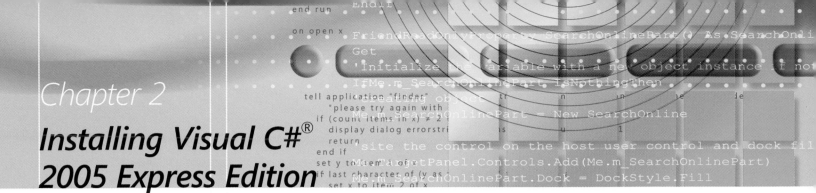

Chapter 2

Installing Visual C#®
2005 Express Edition

Preparing to Install Visual C# 2005 Express Edition, 16

Installing Visual C# 2005 Express Edition, 17

In this chapter, you'll install the product and start getting to know what components are included with it. I'll guide you through all the steps of this installation so that you can be ready to start building applications using Microsoft® Visual C#® 2005 Express Edition right away. I will talk about some common installation scenarios, give you some tips, and I will also cover what to do if the unexpected happens.

The installation process is easy and straightforward, following in the spirit of the Express products.

There are a couple of options for installing Visual C# 2005, particularly if you've had previous versions installed before or if you installed an early version of the product. Before you start the installation, make sure your computer meets the software and hardware recommendations. You can review the Introduction of this book for all necessary information. You will also want to ensure that your computer has been updated with the latest updates from Windows Updates (*http://windowsupdate.microsoft.com*) or Microsoft Updates (*http://update. microsoft.com*). This will confirm that your machine has all the latest security updates along with some installation prerequisites before starting the actual product installation.

If you have an antivirus or an antispyware application installed and running, your antispyware program might prompt you to allow certain setup tasks to proceed. For instance, with the latest Microsoft Windows® AntiSpyware Beta (*http://www.microsoft.com/ athome/security/spyware/software/default.mspx*), I was asked two times to allow certain tasks to proceed and a few other times the antispyware product recognized the source and simply mentioned it and continued. This was the experience I had with the Microsoft product. If you are using another antispyware application, your experience might vary slightly but will bear some similarities to this process. The antivirus and antispyware products are giving you an opportunity to confirm the origin of the product you're about to install. When you're sure it's from Microsoft, allow the setup application to continue its job by allowing the action.

During the installation, if something goes wrong, you're probably not the only person to encounter this problem. The first thing to do is to look at the latest Readme information maintained by the Setup team on MSDN and follow the steps provided to solve installation problems. Here are two links to the MSDN® resources:

- Express Online Readme: *http://go.microsoft.com/fwlink/?LinkId=51322*
- Express Online Known Issues: *http://go.microsoft.com/fwlink/?LinkId=51325*

Side-by-Side Installation If you have a previous version of Microsoft Visual Studio®, say Visual Studio 2002 or Visual Studio 2003, installing Visual C# 2005 Express Edition, or any Visual Studio 2005 product, will be straightforward. This is considered a side-by-side execution, and you can go straight to the section on installing the software.

Previous Versions of Visual C# 2005 Express Edition If you have a pre-release—especially a pre-Beta2 version of Visual C# 2005 Express Edition or any version of Visual Studio 2005 (CTP—Community Technology Preview or a Beta version)—*you must uninstall all pre-release components before installing this new version*. The software components must be uninstalled in a particular order for your new installation to be successful. The most up-to-date information for uninstalling any pre-release versions of the product is available on the following MSDN Help page: *http://go.microsoft.com/fwlink/?LinkId=47062*.

The pre-release (pre-Beta2) versions represent a version of the final product early in the development cycle. They are not officially supported by Microsoft, so when you install early beta or CTP versions, you also understand that the product is undergoing continual changes, which ultimately reflects in the installation process.

When you uninstall a pre-release version of any software, you might encounter problems. At some point, you may have no choice but to reformat your hard drive and reinstall your operating system. This is not an uncommon situation when you work with pre-release software. But this situation has a solution. Before beginning the uninstall procedure, and as a precautionary measure, you'll want to back up all your data before beginning. If possible, a good practice is to avoid installing any pre-release versions of any products on your main computer. Using a test machine (or virtual software) will help you avoid losing any important data and won't slow your productivity in the event something goes wrong. To learn more about the virtual solutions that Microsoft offers, you can look at Microsoft Virtual PC 2004 at *http://www.microsoft.com/windows/virtualpc/default.mspx*.

CAUTION

Please make sure you carefully read this section on the MSDN Help page before starting the uninstall process!

NOTE

Even though the pre-release versions of the software are not officially supported by Microsoft, you will find resources on the Microsoft Web site to help you with installation. In particular, you'll find information on how to uninstall (and in what order to uninstall) the products.

Installing Visual C# 2005 Express Edition

Now that we've addressed a lot of potential issues and now that your machine is ready, you can proceed with the installation. You should find a CD or DVD at the end of this book that contains a full working edition of the product. Simply insert it into any available CD or DVD drive in your system and follow the steps below.

TO INSTALL VISUAL C# 2005 EXPRESS EDITION

 If Autorun is enabled, the installation process should start automatically. If it doesn't start automatically after a few seconds, follow these steps:

a. Click the **Start** button, and then click **My Computer**.

b. Right-click the CD or DVD drive that has the product media and select **Explore**.

c. In the list of files, locate and double-click **Setup.exe** to start the Installation Wizard.

 Within a few seconds, you should see that the setup program is copying all necessary installation files to a temporary folder as shown in Figure 2-1.

Figure 2-1
Copying setup files locally to a temporary folder

Visual C# 2005 Express Edition

Setup is copying required resources to your temp directory.
Copying file 20 of 44.

Copying setup file: lxpvcs.exe

When the Setup program is done copying the files, the setup application loads into memory. While the application is loading, you'll see an initialization progress bar as shown in Figure 2-2.

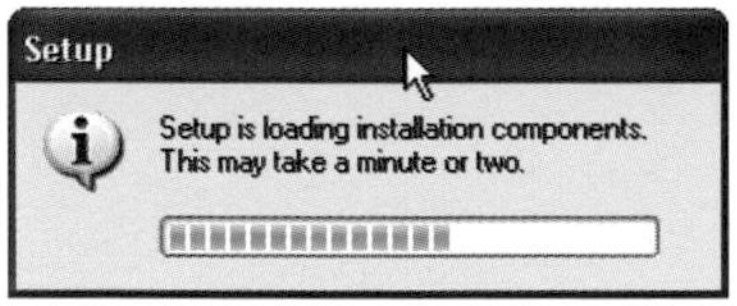

Figure 2-2
Initializing the setup process

Setup

Setup is loading installation components.
This may take a minute or two.

> **NOTE**
> You'll have nothing to do but wait at this point. The wait should not be long—less than a minute in most cases, depending on your computer speed.

4 Next, you'll be greeted by the Welcome page (Figure 2-3), which provides some information about the product and the possibilities you'll have working with it. You'll also be notified if your machine does not meet any prerequisites for loading the software. Click **Next** to continue or **Cancel** to exit the installation program.

Figure 2-3
Welcome page

5 To continue the installation process, you must read and accept the license agreement (Figure 2-4). Please read it carefully to see what you can and can't do with this product. When you're done and you're ready to accept the license agreement, click the check box, and then click **Next** to continue.

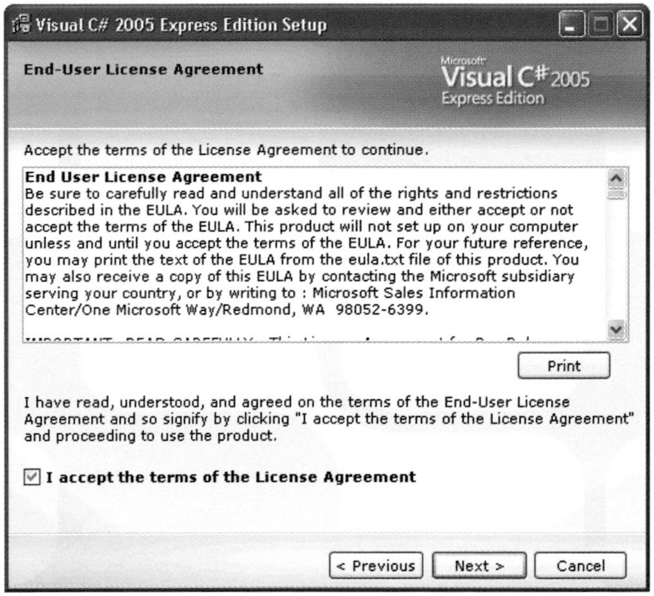

Figure 2-4
License agreement

Figure 2-5
Set your installation options here

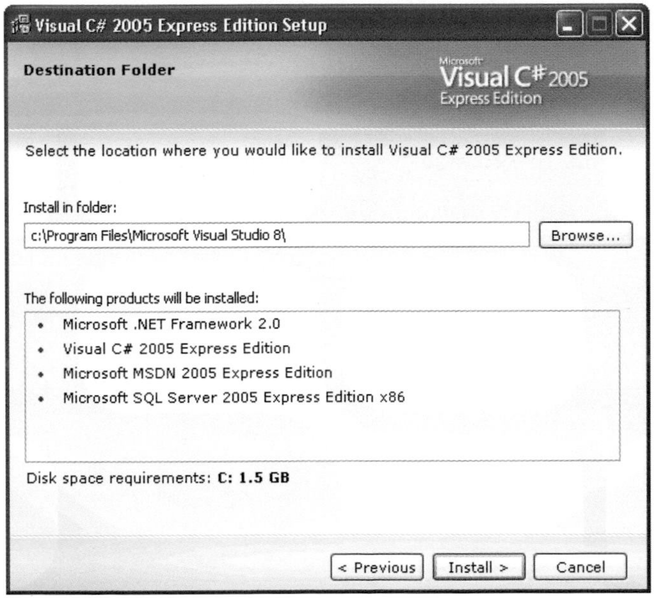

Figure 2-6
Destination Folder

6 The Installation Options page appears, as shown in Figure 2-5. On this page, be sure to specify that you want access to the Help system (MSDN Express Library) and the Microsoft SQL Server™ 2005 Express Edition.

NOTE

> The only reason not to install the local MSDN help or SQL Server 2005 Express Edition is limited hard drive space. Be sure you understand the consequences of your selections. If you don't install MSDN Express Library, you'll need access to the Internet to get help from MSDN Online. If you don't install SQL Server 2005 Express, you won't be able to create applications that must access other sources of data, such as Microsoft Access database information, Extensible Markup Language (XML) files, or other types of RDBMS information. In addition, some sample files from this book won't work automatically, and you'll have to perform some manipulations or re-installations to get them to work.

SQL Server 2005 Express Edition is a relational database management system (RDBMS) that will enable you to easily manipulate data in your application. This is an important step. For example, if you're creating the DVD collection management application, which is one of the Starter Kits, all the data related to your DVD collection will need to be stored in a database using SQL Server 2005 Express Edition.

7 When you're done with your selections, click **Next** to continue.

8 The Destination Folder page appears, as shown in Figure 2-6. This page will ask you where to install the software on your computer. I recommend that you use the default location.

CAUTION

> If you choose to install the software in a folder other than the recommended default, you might have problems working with some of the paths and files mentioned later in the book. If you do install in a different location, rest assured I'll give you some cautionary notes whenever you may run into problems.

9 Click **Install** to start the installation. The installation progress bar appears and the installation is underway (see Figure 2-7)! This might be a good time to get something to drink because installation could take some time.

NOTE

The installation time will vary based on your choices on the previous page. On average, if you selected both MSDN Library and SQL Server 2005 Express Edition, the installation should be around 10 to 30 minutes depending on your computer's speed.

Here is the list of components that will be installed:

■ **The .NET Framework 2.0** This was our house illustrated in Chapter 1.

NOTE

On some computers, depending on the Windows version, when the .NET Framework installation is completed, you might be asked to reboot your computer before the installation continues.

■ **Visual C# 2005 Express Edition** This is the tool itself, which was the beige block representing the door of our house in Chapter 1.

■ **MSDN Express Library** This was described earlier.

■ **SQL Server 2005 Express Edition** This was described earlier.

The Setup Complete page appears (see Figure 2-8), and you are now finished with the installation. Not too painful, was it? Before you click the Exit button, please read the following notes.

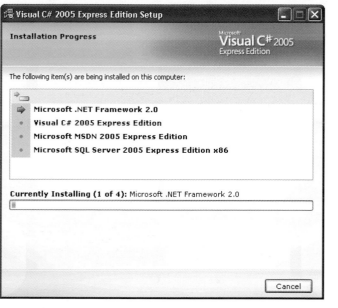

Figure 2-7
Installation Progress

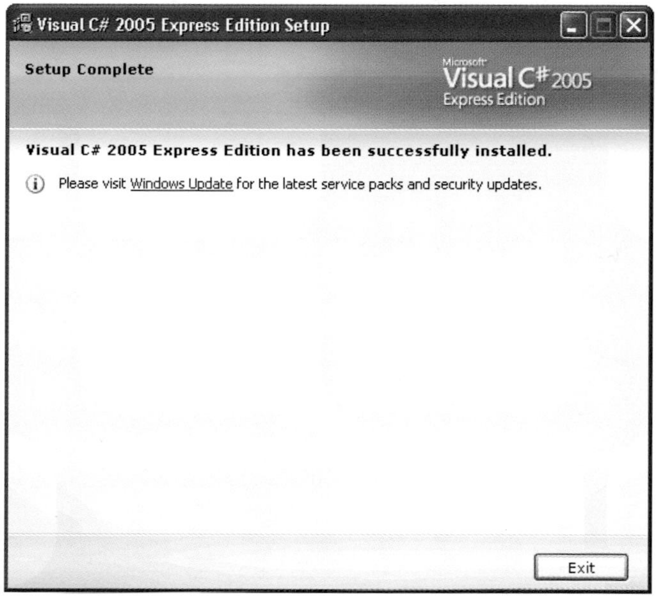

Figure 2-8
Setup Complete

Whenever you install a new application, it's always a good habit to go to Microsoft Update (*http://update.microsoft.com*) or Windows Update (*http://windowsupdate.microsoft. com*) to get all the high-priority updates. Or you can click on the Windows Update hyperlink from the setup application as shown in Figure 2-8. I prefer Microsoft Update because you get all the updates you need for all the Microsoft software already installed on your hard drive. You'll get your Windows, Office, and .NET Framework updates along with your hardware drivers updates, all in one stop!

NOTE
In the future, more products will be added to this list.

It's also important to verify that your antivirus application and its signatures are up to date and that you have updated antispyware installed. One last thing: if you have the latest Service Pack installed on your machine, you should have the Security Center in your Control Panel. If you don't have it, please update your operating system to the latest Service Pack (Only available on Microsoft Windows Server™ 2003 and Windows XP). Open the Security Center and make sure all lights for the Firewall, Virus Protection, and Automatic Updates are green. If not, address those issues to prevent any security hazards.

Click the Exit button when you are done. On exit, the setup application will send some feedback on your installation to the Microsoft servers as shown in Figure 2-9.

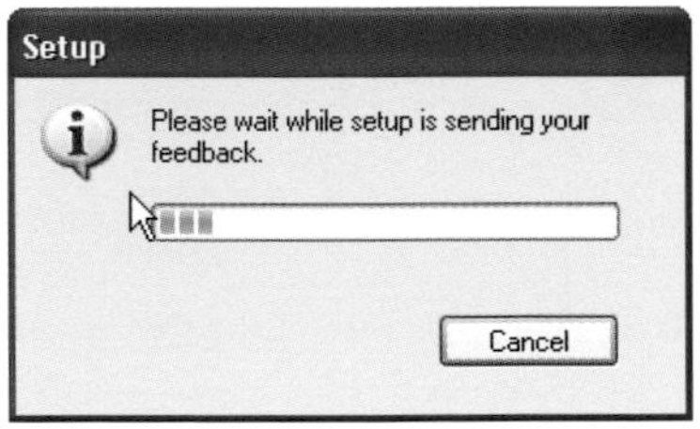

Figure 2-9
The Setup application sends installation feedback to the Microsoft servers

In Summary...

This chapter focused on installing Visual C# 2005 Express Edition. It addressed most issues that you may encounter during the installation, different setup scenarios, and also provided links to MSDN for more help.

After working through this chapter, you should now have the .NET Framework 2.0, Visual C# 2005 Express Edition, MSDN Express Library, and SQL Server 2005 Express Edition installed and ready to go. Your computer should also be up to date with all updates installed and all settings related to security on green.

Whenever you're ready to explore the IDE and write your first two applications, just jump to the next chapter.

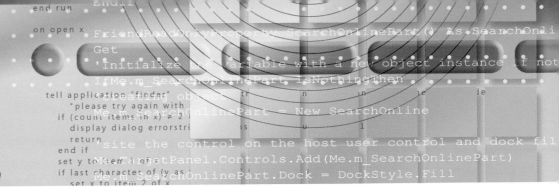

Chapter 3

Creating Your First Application

You've been introduced to Microsoft® Visual C#® 2005 Express Edition; now it's time to create your first application. You'll start this chapter by learning about the differences between a **console application** and a **Windows application**. You'll then look at the **Integrated Development Environment (IDE)**. As its name implies, the IDE is the application that provides all the tools you need to design, plan, develop, and distribute your applications. We could have used any text editor, like Notepad, for example, but in this chapter and for the reminder of the book, you'll be using the IDE to create your applications.

Most programming books usually start with a fairly simple application called Hello World! Your first application will be a simple application as well, but you'll be creating an application that does a little bit more than just say "hello" to the world. In this chapter, you'll learn to create an application that adds two numbers together and outputs a result. With this application you'll also learn about the Solution Explorer as well as the documentation and Help system built into Visual C# 2005 Express Edition.

Two Types of Applications: What's the Difference?

As mentioned on the previous page, you're going to create two versions of the same application: a console application and a Microsoft Windows® application. You might wonder why you even have to worry about this distinction when you're creating a program. Well, sometimes your application can't or doesn't need to have a graphical interface. For instance, some applications need to be executed in a script or a batch file or they can't have a graphical interface because no user interacts with it. In some other cases you don't need a graphical interface for a Windows application. For example, a Windows service is an application that runs on Windows in the background—it doesn't have a user interface, doesn't produce any visual output, starts when Windows starts, and doesn't even require a user to be logged in to start executing.

NOTE

Windows XP SP2 comes with roughly four dozen Windows services. For example, a Windows service validates your user name and password at start up.

In some other cases, you don't want users to interact with a graphical interface you've created. For instance, you could write an application that monitors the available physical memory on a computer then displays that information once it reaches a certain level. The information is displayed in a user interface but does not require any input from the user.

Figure 3-1 shows the result of the famous Hello World! application as a console application.

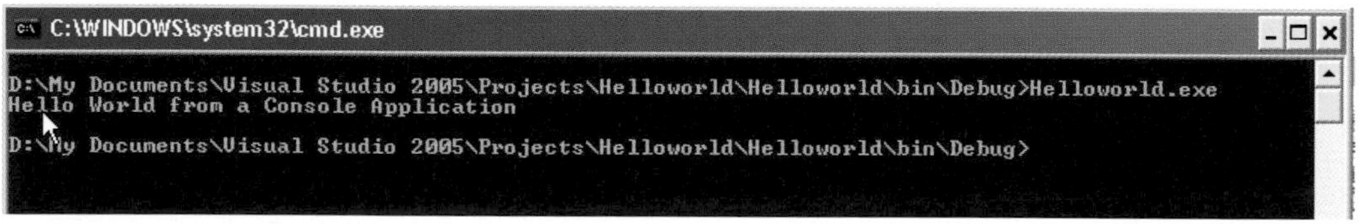

Figure 3-1
Console application

This type of application is called a console application because everything is displayed in a system console window. You may have heard these types of windows referred to by many different names: a DOS window, a command prompt window, or simply the command window. The most common output in a console application is simple text.

Console applications can be as feature rich and as complex as Windows applications. The only difference is that they don't have a graphical interface. Let's look at one possible use for console applications.

In corporate data centers, many applications execute all day and night, producing a large amount of data. It would be time-consuming and problematic to rely on people to verify the data. So data centers are usually highly automated to facilitate this job. Console applications produce, manipulate, and verify the data in scripts or batch files. Console applications can be written in many different programming languages (C, C++, C#, Visual Basic, and so on) and scripting languages (Perl, Python, or JScript®).

Hello World from a Windows Application

In contrast to a console application, a Windows application has a graphical interface, as shown in Figure 3-2. (It is also called a Windows Forms application in .NET).

These applications are usually installed and accessible in the Windows Start menu, and by default they share some common characteristics, such as a Close button, a Maximize button, and a Minimize button.

Close Button   Maximize Button   Minimize Button

Figure 3-2
Windows application

Simple Text and ASCII Characters

Simple text (also called ASCII characters) is the usual output of a console application, but some console applications use ASCII graphic characters. (ASCII stands for American Standard Code for Information Interchange.) An ASCII code is the numerical representation of a character (such as "0" or "#") or an action of some sort. (Pressing Enter in a word processor to move a line of text is an action represented by an ASCII character, for instance.) The ASCII graphic character set, also called extended ASCII characters, includes vertical lines, vertical double lines, corners, and much more. ASCII characters are sometimes used to create boxes around text in console applications.

Getting Started

To get started writing the code for the first version of the application, you'll need to start Microsoft Visual C# 2005 Express Edition. To do this follow these three easy steps: click Start, choose All Programs, then select Microsoft Visual C# 2005 Express Edition.

NOTE

Please note that console applications are still executed in Windows, but in a console context.

The first time you start Microsoft Visual C# 2005 Express Edition, it will take some time to load since the IDE is being configured. You should see a screen similar to Figure 3-3.

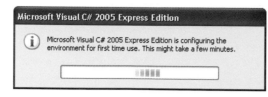

Figure 3-3
Environment configuration for first time use of Microsoft Visual C# 2005 Express Edition

Before we go futher, let's pause and admire the IDE in all its glory. With this version of Visual C#, the IDE got a nice new makeover. Look at Figure 3-4 and feel the excitement.

If you're not feeling the excitement yet, you soon will. The development environment has been designed to make a lot more information available up front and to get you more productive faster. From this screen, everything you need to build an application is available in a couple of clicks. From the IDE you

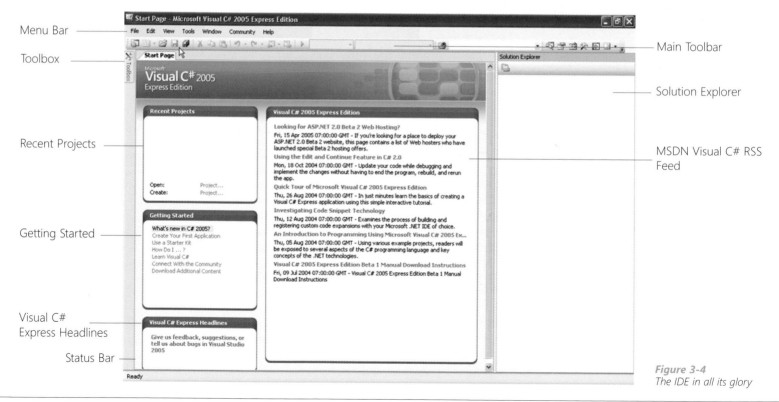

Figure 3-4
The IDE in all its glory

type in your code, compile your code, launch the application, find your mistakes and fix them, get help on the syntax, and many other things. Furthermore, the Visual C# 2005 IDE is designed to help you by generating a lot of code for you so that you have less to type in. If you didn't have the IDE and you wanted to write a Windows Forms application, you would normally have to write a lot more code and it would be more prone to errors. With the new IDE, most of the actions you'll perform will automatically generate a lot of code behind the scenes.

As you spend more time with the program, you'll find that there are many different ways to perform the same actions. For instance, to complete a specific action you can use a series of menu choices, or use a keystroke shortcut, or click an **icon** on a **toolbar**, click on a **hyperlink** in a page, or you can right-click and choose an option from a **context-sensitive menu**. Before diving into our first application and before you write some code, we'll go through each big component of the IDE.

The first page you see is a really useful one: the Start Page. Let's get into what information you see on that page.

- **Recent Projects** Here you'll get the list of projects or solutions that were recently opened. You can also create a new project or open an existing project that is not in the list.

- **Getting Started** I call this useful section Help Central because if you need quick help, this is one of the best places to get answers. Whether you need help with some C# constructs, or you want to see a list of How To articles, or you simply want hyperlinks to communities of programmers, you can often find help in the Getting Started section of the IDE.

- **Visual C# Express Headlines** This is where you find specific news about Visual C# Express coming from Microsoft. These product headlines deliver special messages specific to Visual C# 2005 Express Edition and announce new updates, new releases, new code snippets, or anything that needs special attention on your part.

NOTE
I will show you how and where to look for this generated code in Chapter 5.

TIP
Even when the Start Page disappears, you can always get it back by going to the View menu and selecting Start Page.

The first and only rule of this book is to not be afraid to experiment. Click, look, read, and try whenever possible. This is really the best way to learn. I'll show you some important material, tips, and tricks throughout this book, but my advice to you is to go beyond these examples and just try and try and try . . .

■ **MSDN Feeds** This section of the Start Page includes hyperlinks to articles from one of the **MSDN RSS** (Microsoft Developer Network Really Simple Syndication) feeds. These articles can be configured to any valid RSS feed from the Web. The default is set to the MSDN® Visual C# 2005 Express RSS feed. These articles are different from the Visual C# Express Headlines; occasionally, they might be the same, but the articles from MSDN cover not only C# Express but all topics including Visual Studio Team Systems, Microsoft SQL Server™, Web Services, and so forth. You can modify the feed by selecting Options from the Tools menu, expanding Environment, selecting Startup, and updating the Start Page News Channel field with a valid RSS feed of your choice.

IDE Components

Some important components of the IDE are not part of the Start page.

■ **Menu Bar** This is where you can select and perform almost all possible actions related to your projects, files, and Help. The available options change based on the current context. For example, when you don't have an open project you have fewer menu choices: only File, Edit, View, Tools, Window, Community, and Help. When a project is open, the menu choices will also include Project, Build, Debug, and Data.

■ **Main Toolbar** This toolbar contains icons that are essentially shortcuts to actions that you can also perform by going through the menus.

■ **Toolbox** If you scroll over the toolbox on the left side of the Start Page screen, it will expand. If there is no opened project, the toolbox should be empty. The toolbox contains controls that are used in your applications. At this point you can think of controls as visual elements in Windows applications that possess a graphical interface. For instance, once a project is opened, the toolbox will include buttons, labels, text box controls, menus, toolbars, and so on. These controls are defined and explained in greater detail in Chapter 5.

■ **Solution Explorer** This feature lists the files and components in your project. If no project is open, it should be empty. You'll see more details about the Solution Explorer later in this chapter.

- **Status Bar** The status bar displays a wide variety of information corresponding to the state of certain active operations. For instance, when you load a project you'll see a message on your screen such as "Loading project c:\blabla\blabla.csproj from your hard drive." When you're building an application you'll see something like "build started;" and when the application has finished, you'll see "Build succeeded" or "Build failed" depending on the success of the process.

On to the Projects

From this point on, you'll focus on what you really came here to do: build some projects. So let's start with your first application. First, you'll build the console version of the application.

Building a Console Application

We've been talking about what a console application can do and what it will look like, so why don't we build one? In this section, you'll create a simple mathematic application.

TO BUILD A CONSOLE APPLICATION

1 If Visual C# 2005 Express Edition is not running, start it by clicking **Start/All Programs/Microsoft Visual C# 2005 Express Edition**.

2 You can choose to start building your application either by clicking the **New Project** icon on the toolbar, by selecting **Create: Project** . . . from the Start Page, or by clicking **File/New Project** on the menu bar.

3 In the New Project dialog box, select **Console Application** in the Templates section, and type **MyFirst ConsoleApplication** in the Name box. The New Project dialog box should be similar to the one in Figure 3-5. Click **OK** when you're ready to go to the next step.

TIP

For demos and samples, I recommend that you type in all the source code so you can see and better understand concepts. However, for longer source code listings, you can also download the completed code samples. (*http://www.microsoft.com/mspress/companion/0-7356-2229-9/*)

NOTE

By default in Visual C# 2005 Express Edition, when you click OK, projects are created in a temporary location. When you save or close the project, files are saved in My Documents\Visual Studio 2005\Projects. You can change the default projects location by going to Tools/Options/Projects and Solutions and finding the first text box named Visual Studio Projects location. You'll look into what those files are and what they're content is later in this chapter and also in Chapter 5.

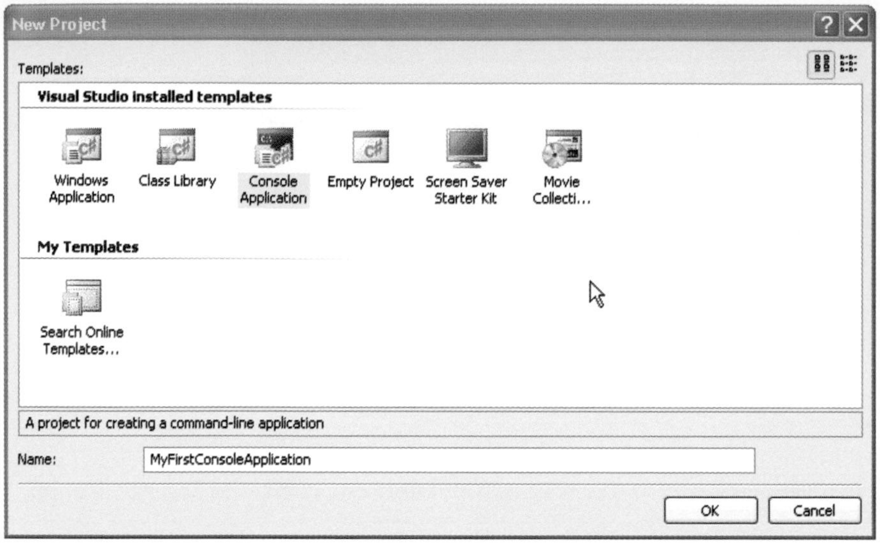

Figure 3-5
Creating a console application using the New Project dialog box

You should now see the IDE in an idle state waiting for you to write the application's code. Your screen should now look like the one shown here in Figure 3-6.

Getting to Know Solution Explorer

Before you write the code, you need to learn about the Solution Explorer. As seen on the right side of the screen in Figure 3-6, the Solution Explorer provides an organized view of your projects and all the files that are associated with them, as well as some useful commands in the form of a toolbar. You'll find all the source code files, the project settings, resource files (like the application icon), configuration files, and so on in the Solution Explorer.

TIP

If the Solution Explorer disappears for any reason, you can get it back by going to the View menu and selecting Solution Explorer.

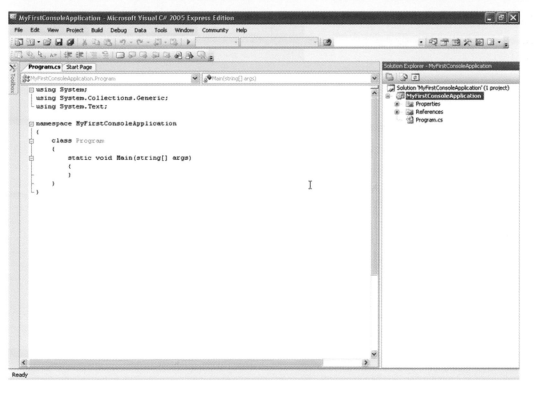

Figure 3-6
MyFirstConsoleApplication without the code

If you want more information about the Solution Explorer you can always do a search in the Help system and product documentation. Before trying to perform a search, please read the next section; you'll learn a lot about all the information that is at your disposition.

Getting Help: Microsoft Visual Studio 2005 Express Edition Documentation

If you want to read more about the Solution Explorer, you need to be introduced to the Help and the documentation systems. You access the documentation by pressing F1 from within Visual C# 2005 Express Edition or by going through the Help menu. The first time you press F1 or go through the Help menu, you'll be greeted with the Online Help Settings screen, as shown in Figure 3-7.

This screen prompts you to choose a primary help source; you can choose online Help as a primary source, local Help as a primary source, or no online Help at all. Think about your options carefully. If you don't have a broadband (cable, DSL, or satellite) Internet connection, I suggest you choose the local Help as a primary source; otherwise choose online Help as your primary source since it is the best source for the latest information.

Once you've made your selection, you'll see the documentation graphical interface, as shown in Figure 3-8.

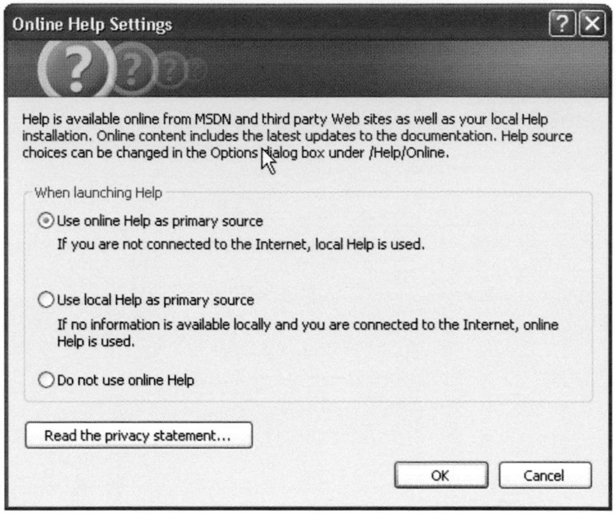

Figure 3-7
Online Help Settings choices

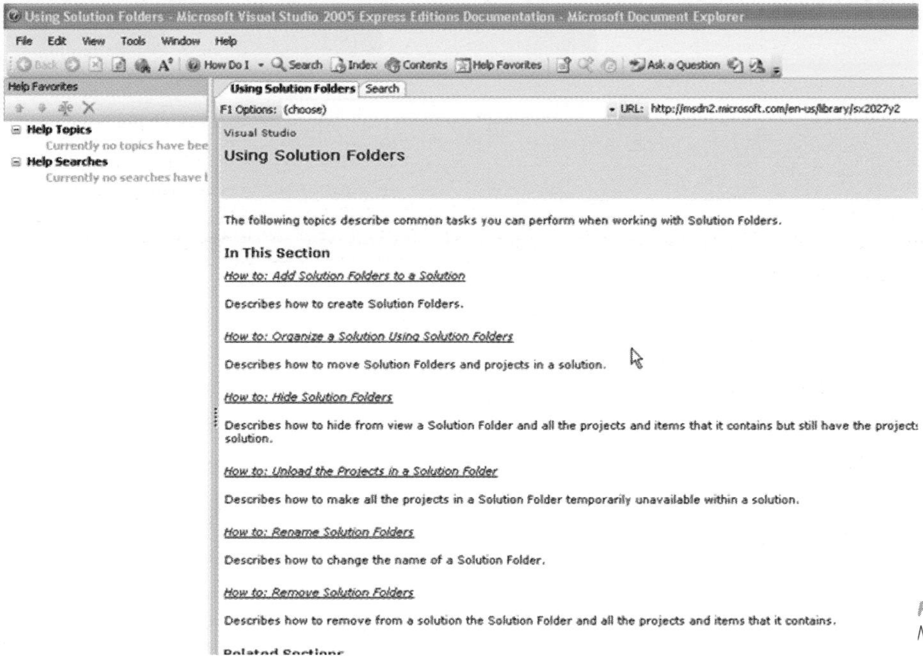

Figure 3-8
Microsoft Visual Studio 2005 Express Edition documentation

The toolbar at the top of the window includes several interesting elements that will help you to get exactly what you need. Figure 3-9 highlights the most important information about the toolbar.

Figure 3-9
Important elements on the toolbar

For example, let's say you want to learn more about the Solution Explorer. Click the Search icon in the toolbar and the search page opens. Enter your search query (in this example, "Solution Explorer"), and either press Enter or click the Search button. The help results come from four different sources. Let's go over each one briefly:

■ **Local Help** This source is fed by the MSDN Library (part of the product installation) and is installed on your hard drive. (If you selected it at install.)

- **MSDN Online** This source contains the most up-to-date information from the MSDN Online Library.

- **Codezone Community** The Codezone Community is a set of Web sites based on Microsoft developer products. To see a list of all Web sites that are researched click Tools/Options and then Online. Figure 3-10 shows what you should look for. Notice the list of Web sites on the right that are part of the Codezone Community. In the future, this list might be expanded to show more sites to provide even better coverage of the community.

On the same screen, you can customize different settings related to the Help system. On the General tab, you can set up how the Help system retrieves and presents information. You can set up the international setting to get local help in the language of your operating system, if available, and get online Help in a predefined list of languages supported by MSDN. Look at the keyboard shortcut mapping for menu commands used throughout the product (for example, notice that the shortcut for Copy is Ctrl+C), or to assign new shortcuts to commands that might not have one already.

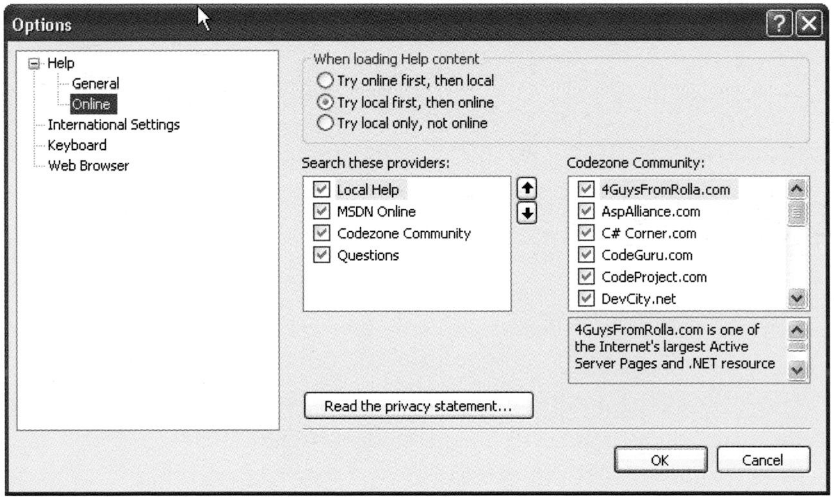

Figure 3-10
Options screen with the Online settings, including the Codezone Community Web sites

- **Questions** This section searches the MSDN Online forums (http://forums.microsoft.com/msdn/). These forums are hosted by Microsoft and are an excellent source of information because they have questions and answers on topics asked by other programmers of all levels and experience. There's a good chance that somebody has had the same problem or the same question as you, so your chance of finding an answer to your problem is much better. You can have confidence in the answers you get because answers on the MSDN forums are often validated by Microsoft employees or MVPs. A check mark in a green circle tells you which answer has been validated as correct.

Coding Your Console Application

Now that you know how to get help if needed, I believe you are ready to code your first console application.

TO CODE A CONSOLE APPLICATION

1 To begin, either type or copy the following code in your code window:

```
1    using System;
2    using System.Collections.Generic;
3    using System.Text;
4
5    namespace MyFirstConsoleApplication
6    {
7        class Program
8        {
9            static void Main(string[] args)
10           {
11               //  Declaring two integer numbers variables that will hold the 2 parts
12               //  of the sum and one integer variable to hold the sum
13               int number1;
14               int number2;
15               int sum;
16
17               //  Assigning two values to the integer variables
18               number1 = 10;
```

Learning to Read Code

Another way of learning about code is to read all the comments in an application source code. I will explain a lot of the source code in this book, but after using some topics more than once (or twice) I might not re-explain each line, but instead explain only the new material. I will try to include helpful comments in the code to guide you as you're learning. At the end of each chapter, I will also include hyperlinks that will point to articles, videos, and white papers. I will often include keywords to help you search for more information in online help. That should help you to progress in your learning in the language and in .NET in general. You have to keep in mind that this book is really showing you all you can do with the product and the steps to get there. It's not a book on OOP or the C# language itself. We are still going to go through 70-80% of the language and most OOP concepts, but it will always be through building applications and never through dry references and explanations.

```
19                  number2 = 5;
20
21                  //  Adding the two integers and storing the result in the sum variable
22                  sum = (number1 + number2);
23
24                  // Displaying a string with the 2 numbers and the result.
25                  Console.WriteLine("The sum of " + number1.ToString() + " and " + number2.
ToString() + " is " + sum.ToString());
26              }
27          }
28      }
```

2 Now that the code is in the window, you can save your work by clicking the **Save** button. This will save the current file. Click the **Save All** button to save all modified files in the project.

TIP

You can also save using the following keystrokes: Ctrl+S to save the current file and Ctrl+Shift+S to save all files.

3 Now it is time to build (or compile) the application. Click the **Build** menu and then click on **Build Solution**.

If you keyed the code exactly as it appears above, everything should be fine and you should see the message "Build succeeded" in the status bar at the bottom of the window. (See Figure 3-11). If everything is not okay, you'll see errors in the Error List window (as shown in Figure 3-12). If you keyed the code and have errors, try copying and pasting the code instead from the completed code samples. (http://www.microsoft.com/mspress/companion/0-7356-2229-9/) Then build the code again.

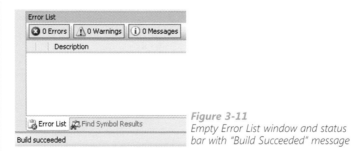

Figure 3-11
Empty Error List window and status bar with "Build Succeeded" message

	Description	File	Line	Column	Project
ⓧ 1	The name 'Consle' does not exist in the current context	Program.cs	24	9	MyFirstConsoleApplication

Figure 3-12
Error List window with errors

In Chapter 7, you'll learn about all the debugging techniques you can use when you get an error.

 To see the execution results of your application, click the **Start Debugging** button in the main toolbar (or hit F5).

Wow! That was fast, wasn't it? You probably saw a command window for a few seconds and then it disappeared. It didn't leave you a lot of time to see if your application displayed the expected output. In the next section, you'll look at a new way of running your application to solve this problem. To do this, you'll need to customize the IDE.

Customizing the IDE

You can easily customize the IDE to fit your needs. Here, you want to execute your application and then have the application pause automatically at the end of the last instruction to allow you as much time as you need to view the output. You'll do this by adding an icon and its attached command to the main toolbar. The name of the command you'll be adding to the IDE is "Starting Without Debugging."

TO CUSTOMIZE THE IDE

 Select the **Tools** menu and then select **Customize**.

 In the Categories area on the left side of the window, select **Debug**.

 In the Customize dialog box, select the **Commands** tab.

4 Scroll down in the Commands area and select **Start Without Debugging**.

Your screen should now look like the one in Figure 3-13.

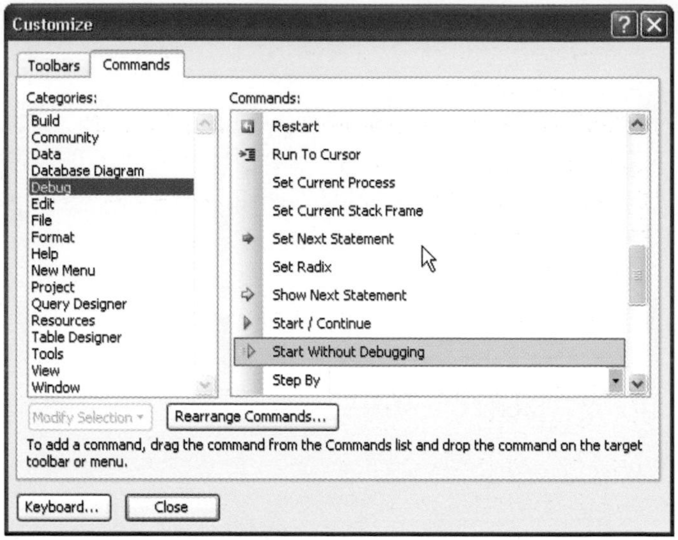

Customize window screenshot:

Customize [?][X]

Toolbars | **Commands**

Categories:
- Build
- Community
- Data
- Database Diagram
- **Debug**
- Edit
- File
- Format
- Help
- New Menu
- Project
- Query Designer
- Resources
- Table Designer
- Tools
- View
- Window

Commands:
- Restart
- Run To Cursor
- Set Current Process
- Set Current Stack Frame
- Set Next Statement
- Set Radix
- Show Next Statement
- Start / Continue
- **Start Without Debugging**
- Step By

Modify Selection ▾ | Rearrange Commands...

To add a command, drag the command from the Commands list and drop the command on the target toolbar or menu.

Keyboard... | Close

Figure 3-13
Customize window with Start Without Debugging selected

Now you must add the command to the main toolbar. To do that, drag Start Without Debugging from the Commands area and drop it onto the main toolbar to the right of the Start Debugging button. (Figure 3-14 shows a before and after view of this process.) When finished, click Close in the Customize dialog box.

NOTE

Both figures have the "before" on the left and the "after" on the right, overlapping the before.

Figure 3-14
Before and after customizing the tool-bar with the Start Without Debugging command.

To make sure the customization worked, click the new icon on the Debug menu or the toolbar. (Or, use the keyboard shortcut Ctrl+F5.) You should see a command prompt window with the expected output, which is the string: "The sum of 10 and 5 is 15." You should also see the message "Press any key to continue . . ." as shown in Figure 3-15.

As you probably realized by now, the effect of the new command is to add the "Press any key to continue..." and pause the execution after the last instruction is executed. Press any key to close the command prompt window and return to the IDE. When you're done, you can close the project by going to File/Close Solution. You'll be prompted to save or discard your changes. Click Save, and then if the name and location are fine, click Save again in the Save Project dialog box.

Figure 3-15
Command prompt window with the expected result and a message indicating a paused execution

Creating a Windows Application

You've just built a console application. The next step is to develop the same application as a Windows application.

TO BUILD A WINDOWS APPLICATION

1 When creating the console application, you saw the New Project dialog box. Open it again by going to the File menu and selecting **New Project . . .** This time, select **Windows Application** from the Templates section and type in **MyFirstWindowsApplication**. Make sure your screen looks like the one in Figure 3-16 and then click **OK**.

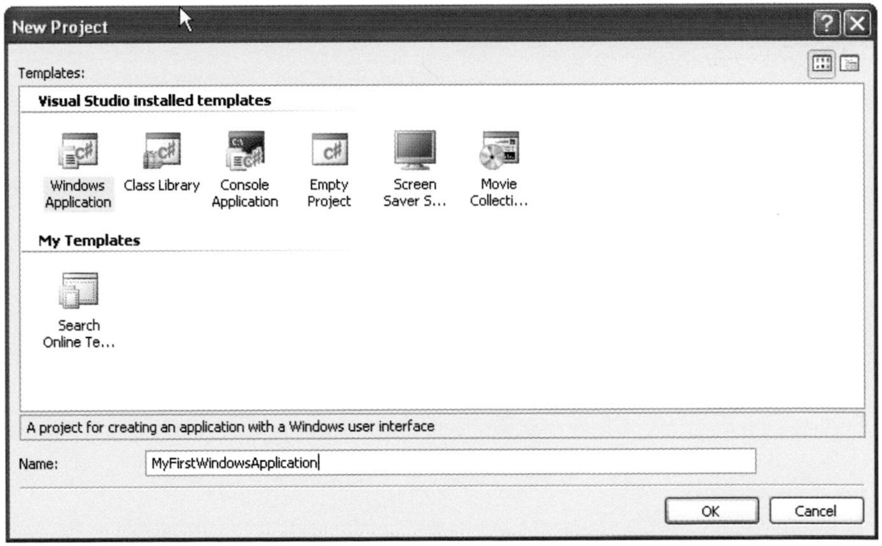

Figure 3-16
Creating a Windows application using the New Project dialog box

You'll immediately see that the result of this operation is quite different for the Windows application process than it was for the console application process. You should see the Windows Form Designer as displayed in Figure 3-17.

Figure 3-17
IDE with the Windows Form Designer and an empty form

2 On the left side of the IDE, move your mouse over the Toolbox tab to open the Toolbox window. Click the plus (+) sign next to the Common Controls. You'll see a list of form controls that are often seen in a Windows application. Select the Button control and drag it onto the Designer surface. You should get a form that looks like the one in Figure 3-18.

Figure 3-18
Windows Form Designer surface with a Button control

Microsoft Visual C# 2005 Express Edition: Build a Program Now!

Maybe you don't realize it but at this moment you already have a full and valid Windows application without having written a single line of code. The application doesn't do anything very useful at this point, but it works! You can easily verify this by running the application. Just hit **F5** and see for yourself. This is part of the "magic" and the beauty of using the Visual Studio® IDE environment for programming instead of using a text editor like Notepad. Visual Studio writes a lot of code for you, and in Chapter 5, we'll take a look at some of the activity that's taking place behind the scenes to make it appear like "magic." When finished, click the Close button on the form to return to the IDE.

Figure 3-19
Button-click method with the code from our previous example

3 Double-click the button on the designer surface. You'll get the familiar source code window but with different content this time. For now, type or copy the code under the Static void Main(string [ ] args) from the console application you created previously in the Button1_Click method as shown in Figure 3-19. (You'll learn more about this method and the whole process behind the double-click in Chapter 4.)

```
private void button1_Click(object sender, EventArgs e)
{
    //  Declaring two integer numbers variables that will hold the 2 parts
    //  of the sum and one integer variable to hold the sum
    int number1;
    int number2;
    int sum;

    //  Assigning two values to the integer variables
    number1 = 10;
    number2 = 5;

    //  Adding the two integers and storing the result in the sum variable
    sum = (number1 + number2);

    // Displaying a string with the 2 numbers and the result.
    MessageBox.Show("The sum of " + number1.ToString() + " and " + number2.ToString() + " is " + sum
}
```

4 In the source code, find the words Console.WriteLine and replace them with the words **MessageBox.Show**. Then build and execute the application by hitting **F5**.

5 When the form comes up, click the button and you'll see the result of your application: a message box with the same string you've seen in the console application. It should look like Figure 3-20. Click **OK** in the message box and then quit the program by clicking the **Close** button on the main form.

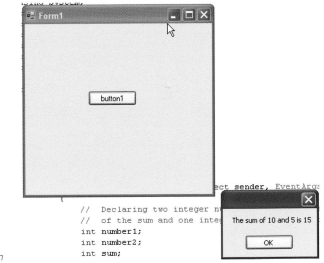

Figure 3-20
Output of MyFirstWindowsApplication

Congratulations! You've just created your first two applications: a console application and a Windows application.

In Summary...

Keywords and Links to More Information

Keywords: *declaring variables; string concatenation*

Another good source of information is the videos from MSDN. These videos were specifically created to cover the Visual C# 2005 Express Edition product. You can find video for Lesson 1 at the following location: http://go.microsoft.com/fwlink/ ?linkid=44030&clcid=0x409

In this chapter, you learned some key information that will help you build on the skills you've started developing in the previous chapters. You learned the differences between a console application and a Windows application. You started the product, went through the IDE, and learned its major components. You created two versions of the same application: a console application and a Windows application. While learning about console applications, you also learned what the Solution Explorer is as well as how to search and use the product documentation and the Help system.

In the next chapter, you'll build on this knowledge and write a simple Web browser. For now, if you want to read more about some topics covered in this chapter, simply create a search query by pressing F1 and then type in the keywords provided in the box to the left. I've also added a link to videos that are a good source of information to continue your learning.

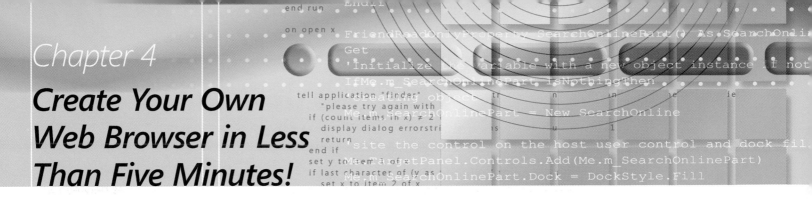

Chapter 4

Create Your Own Web Browser in Less Than Five Minutes!

Now that you've gotten a little experience with creating simple applications in Microsoft® Visual C#® 2005 Express Edition, you'll build a more complicated application in this chapter and finish it in Chapter 6. In this chapter, you'll start with the basic framework of the application; in the next two chapters, you'll continue to learn new features and add them to enhance your project.

In this chapter, you're going to learn how to build your own basic Web browser, and you'll be able to do it in five minutes or less!

What Is a Project?

In the previous chapter, you created a project to hold your source code. I'll now take a moment to explain what a project is and what information it contains. The project is a container for all items in your application, such as forms, source code, and resources. It also stores important configuration data that belongs to the application as a whole: the location of the executable (i.e., binaries) on your hard drive, the version information, and many more settings that affect all of the characteristics of your application. For instance, it's also storing programmer-defined application settings that are very important for the user experience. Users love to customize their software environment to their comfort level and personal style. A typical utilization of those user settings is to make sure the application can preserve user customization from one execution to another. A good example of custom user settings can be seen with your own user preferences in Internet Explorer, such as your home page address, your home page settings, which toolbars are displayed, and whether your toolbars are locked in size and so forth.

In the next chapter, you'll learn about some of the most important settings stored in the project configuration file and how to use them in your application. In the final chapter of this book, you will use programmatic techniques to preserve the user's settings and customizations.

The name you choose when creating your application is going to become your project name. It will also become the default folder name on your hard drive where your application will be stored when you save your application. It will also become the default namespace of your application. A namespace is used to organize the classes in a single hierarchical structure. It does the same for any other types you might define. The creation of a namespace helps prevent naming collisions. What is a naming collision? Let's look at an example to illustrate this concept.

Suppose a company called AdventureWorks wrote a new Windows Forms class named ANewForm. They would create a namespace called AdventureWorks and put their ANewForm class in it to uniquely name their class. The fully qualified name of a class is always composed of the namespace followed by a dot and then the name of the class(es). AdventureWorks's unique class would be AdventureWorks.ANewForm.

Now let's suppose that you are creating a new project using Visual Studio and decide to name your project MyLibrary. Visual Studio would then create for you a namespace called MyLibrary. Suppose that you then define a new class and name it ANewForm. You might not be aware that a company called AdventureWorks also called their new class using the same name. Even though AdventureWorks might be doing completely different things with their class, a problem could arise because the two classes are named the same.

Now suppose that you're trying to use both classes called ANewForm in your new application. If you simply use ANewForm, the compiler will not be able to determine which ANewForm class you want to use--the one from your library or the one from the AdventureWorks library; this is a naming collision. By prefixing the class name with the namespace name, you are then telling the compiler exactly which class you want to use (AdventureWorks.ANewForm).

What Is the Design Layout?

You will soon create a new design layout in the form designer. In doing this, you'll be creating what the application contains and how its content is presented when the user executes the application.

To accomplish this phase of a project, you typically do not need to type a great deal of code; as explained later in this chapter, Visual Studio takes care of that for you. You simply have to worry about how your application looks. When you're done designing all the visual aspects to your liking, your next task usually involves attaching the source code to your visual layout so that your application reacts to and acts upon the user's input.

In this chapter, you will complete the basic layout. You will learn more advanced layout techniques in following chapters. Let's start the next project: a simple Web browser.

TO CREATE A SIMPLE WEB BROWSER

1 Start Visual C# 2005 Express Edition by clicking **Start, All Programs,** and **Microsoft Visual C# 2005 Express Edition**.

2 Create a new Microsoft Windows® Application Project using any of the techniques shown in the previous chapters through either the **File** menu or the New Project icon in the toolbar. Name the new application **MyOwnBrowser**.

3 On the design surface, you'll see the empty Windows Form with a title bar named **Form1**. Click on the title bar once. By default, you don't see the Properties window. To view it, select the **View** menu and then select **Properties Window**. Look over to the Properties window on the bottom right of the IDE, as shown in Figure 4-1.

Figure 4-1
Properties window for MyOwnBrowser application Form control

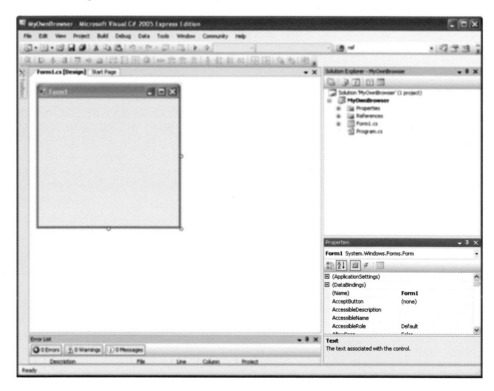

Microsoft C# 2005 Express Edition: Build a Program Now!

We'll be using most of the properties you see listed here! Right now what is important for you to understand is that most of these properties influence how the control you have selected behaves or what it looks like when you execute your application.

For all samples in this book, I suggest that you sort the properties list in ascending alphabetical order; it will be much easier to find properties that I reference in the examples. To sort the properties in alphabetical order, click on the **Alphabetical** button from the Properties window toolbar. The other option is to arrange the controls by categories, but this might slow down your progress throughout this book.

Whenever you select a property, you'll see a brief description of its usage at the bottom of the Properties window. Refer to Figure 4-1 as an example. In this case, the text property was selected. At the bottom of the Properties window, you can see a succinct text message describing the function of the text property.

As mentioned in Chapter 3, my best advice for learning this software is to try, try, and try again. There are a variety of tools in Visual C# 2005 Express Edition and are therefore many possibilities. You will learn to use most of these tools by using this book, but it's impossible to learn all variations and possibilities if you don't do some exploring on your own. With that in mind, to understand the effect of a change on a particular property, try all different possible values. Each time you modify a property, build and check the execution. However, don't make more than one change at a time. It will be difficult for you to know which one of your changes actually triggered a visual modification. By exploring more than one possibility, you'll be able to see the effect of your changes immediately.

4 Make sure you have selected the Form control named **Form1** in step 3 and then modify the following properties using the values in Table 4-1. The property name to modify is located in the left column, and the value to which to set the property is located in the right column. You may have already completed this step, but to facilitate your data entry, verify that you have sorted the properties in ascending alphabetical order.

Property	Value
Text	My Own Browser
Size:Width	640
Size:Height	480

Table 4-1
List of Form properties to change

We're now going to add three Windows Forms controls to your browser application: a text box control in which to enter the destination URL, a button to navigate to the Web page, and a Web browser control in which the Web page content will be displayed.

5 Drag and drop a Web browser control onto the designer surface. The Web browser control is located in the **toolbox** on the left side of the IDE; it's the last control in the **common controls** section. By default, this control will fill the designer surface entirely. As we don't want this behavior for this particular application, you'll click on the following black triangle

which will produce the content of a smart tag. (If you're familiar with Microsoft Office 2003, you've probably encountered smart tags before. Smart tags will be explained further in Chapter 5.) In this particular example, it will help you to undock the control from its parent container (the form). Click on the smart tag and select **Undock in parent container**.

TIP

To add a control to a form, you
need to perform a drag-and-drop
operation. This means you'll move
your mouse to the toolbox, drag
the desired control to the designer
surface, and drop the control
onto it.

6 Expand the control so that it occupies almost the entire designer space. To do this, click on any of the control handles to change its size.

7 To make sure you have the same size as shown in Figure 4-2, select the Web browser control by clicking anywhere on the control. Then go to the Properties window and modify the values for the all the properties listed in Table 4-2.

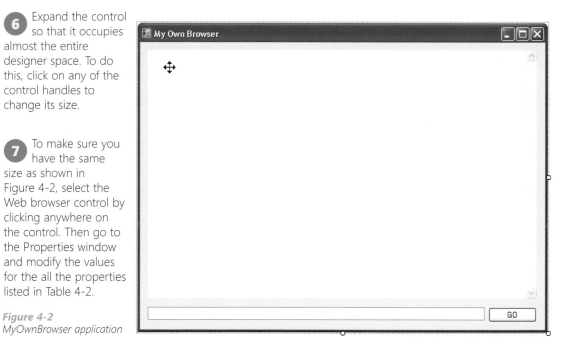

Figure 4-2
MyOwnBrowser application

Property	Value
(Name)	myBrowser
Size:Width	607
Size:Height	385
Location:X	12
Location:Y	12

Table 4-2
Web Control properties to change

8 Drag and drop a text box control and a button control from the toolbox common controls section so that your form looks like Figure 4-2. Change the properties of the controls as you did with the Web browser control in step 7. Select one control at a time and modify its properties with the data in Table 4-3.

Control	Property	Value
Textbox	(Name)	txtURL
Textbox	Location:X	12
Textbox	Location:Y	411
Textbox	Size:Width	526
Textbox	Size:Height	20
Button	(Name)	btnGo
Button	Location:X	544
Button	Location:X	411
Button	text	GO

Table 4-3
Controls, Properties, and Values

9 At this point, we now have a complete application. You can compile and execute your application by pressing **F5**.

If you followed the previous steps exactly, your application should now be running. Because we didn't code any functionality, entering an URL and hitting the GO button will not do anything.

I will use an analogy to explain a fundamental concept. A light bulb by itself is not a useful piece of hardware. To obtain light from it, you need to connect two wires carrying electricity. Similar to what an electrician would do to create this electrical circuit, we need to attach or *wire* the control and the action together by writing code to handle the event of clicking the GO button. Keep this analogy in mind when you see references to the term *wire* or *wiring* used within this book.

Before we try to execute this application, let me explain the line of code you'll add in step 2 on the next page and link it to the OOP concepts previously introduced in Chapter 1.

When you dropped the controls onto the designer surface, you created instances of the **class** represented by those controls. For example, when you dropped the Web browser control, you created an **instance** of the class System.Windows.Forms.WebBrowser that you named myBrowser. The WebBrowser class has many methods, and the Navigate **method** is the one you chose. As its name implies, this method allows the WebBrowser to navigate to an URL. The URL was passed as an **argument** to the Navigate method. An argument, also called a parameter, is used to pass data to a method.

The argument in your case is the text the user entered in the instance of the System.Windows.Forms.TextBox class that you appropriately named txtURL. To retrieve the content of the TextBox named txtURL, you used the Text **property** of that control. A property allows you to set or retrieve the content of a **data member** in a class without accessing the data member directly. That way, the provider of the class (e.g., Microsoft) can modify the implementation of the Text property without concerning the user with implementation details. In OOP, this is called **encapsulation**. You can compare this process to a person driving a car: you don't need to know how the engine and transmission work in order to drive the car. The car example is a good one, but another good example is the Navigate method. You don't need to know how it's implemented, you simply want it to do its job. As mentioned earlier, many things are happening when you design a form with Visual Studio. You have seen that you didn't need to create any of the classes or instances representing your controls because Visual Studio is doing all of that for you!

TO WIRE THE CLICK ACTION TO A BUTTON

 1 Close the running application and go back to the IDE. Double-click the button control. You'll see the code window as shown in Figure 4-3.

If you terminated the execution of your application properly, you should see the source code window with the btnGo click event template. When you double-clicked the button control, you signaled Visual Studio that you wanted to wire the click action to the button control. Typically, each control can trigger multiple events depending on which behavior you want to intercept with your code. Each control has a default event that is triggered by the programmer by using a double-click action on the control on the designer surface. In your case, Visual Studio created the click event template so that you could enter the following code.

```
using System.Windows.Forms;

namespace MyOwnBrowser
{
    public partial class Form1 : Form
    {
        public Form1()
        {
            InitializeComponent();
        }

        private void btnGo_Click(object sender, EventArgs e)
        {
            |
        }
    }
}
```

NOTE

If you try to type some code and it doesn't work, your application is probably still running. If you don't close the application and you go back to Visual C#, you won't be able to modify the source code. A good way to verify that you have closed and terminated the application is to look in the Visual C# Express title bar. If you see the name of your application followed by the word *(running)*, this means your application is still active and you won't be able to add code. If you try to add code, the status bar will report that you are in read-only mode with the following message: Cannot currently modify this text in the editor. It is in read-only.

Figure 4-3
Code window for the btnGo click event

2 Type in the following code at the cursor:

```
myBrowser.Navigate(txtUrl.Text);
```

NOTE

Everything in C# is case-sensitive, so txtURL and txtUrl are two different values.

3 Press **F5** to compile and execute the application. If you named your controls correctly in step 8 in the previous exercise and entered the line of code as shown in step 2, you should now have your own Web browser application. Of course, you won't have all the bells and whistles of Internet Explorer, but be patient—we're getting there. Try going to your favorite URLs to see if it's working as expected. For instance, I went to *www.microsoft.com* and it worked just fine! You can see the result in Figure 4-4.

Figure 4.4
MyOwnBrowser showing the Microsoft.com Web site

Putting It All Together

We've just seen that when you drag a control onto the design surface, you're actually creating an object of that control class. When you're naming the control in the Properties window, you're actually assigning a name to the variable you've just created—which is exactly what we did for the three controls used in your browser. In fact, this is why you want to give your controls meaningful names so that you can use them later programmatically.

As you now know, there was a great deal of activity taking place when you dropped controls onto the designer surface. To better understand what was taking place in the background, we've talked about important OOP concepts behind the line of code you've added to respond to the click event.

Now that you've run the application, here is a list of questions you may have:

- What happens if I put nothing in the text box and hit Enter?
- What happens if I enter an invalid URL?
- What happens if I enter anything I feel like?

My answer to you is simply, "Try it. Try it now." The real deal is that your Web browser will actually behave like any other Web browser and will navigate to whatever URL is typed into the text box. If you don't type anything, clicking on the GO button will have no effect. If you type anything you feel like, the browser control will come back with a Page not found or Code 404 page.

Now is your time to experiment. Remember this book's rule: TRY, TRY, TRY. So go ahead and play with it. Change some of the properties and see the results at run time. Although we haven't used many features yet, you'll add more in Chapter 6. This project is far from over! By adding new features, you'll arrive at a point where your application will start to look much more familiar.

IMPORTANT

Before moving on, I'm inviting you to look at a video from the MSDN® Web site that talks about Object-Oriented Programming, or OOP. You've had a good introduction to OOP both in this chapter and in Chapter 1. To understand the concept from another angle, navigate to *http://go.microsoft.com/ fwlink/?linkid=44030&clcid=0x409* and view Lesson 6, Parts 1 and 2.

MORE INFO

Philosophies differ when it comes to naming the variable that represents controls on the design surface. In this book, I'm going to use up to three letters to describe and identify the control type by looking at its name, such as "btn" for a button control. The variable name then becomes btnGo. I will introduce the list when I talk about common controls in Chapter 5.

In Summary...

In this chapter, you learned how to build a Web browser. You started to:

- Add more than one control to the designer surface
- Set properties in the Properties window
- Wire an event to a control and learn how to add code that will execute when the event is triggered

In this example, you've linked many OOP concepts by using only one line of code. You've added the code to respond to the button click event by calling the Navigate method of your Web browser object. Your Web browser navigated to a URL passed in as an argument to the Navigate method. The argument for the Navigate method was passed in using the text box control Text property. Everything was completed and fully working just by tweaking some properties and adding ONLY one line of code! That's what I call productivity.

In the next chapter, you'll continue this process by learning all of the major features of Visual C# 2005 Express Edition. You'll become more productive at developing applications by learning features such as IntelliSense®, snap lines, code snippets, smart tags, refactoring, and much more.

Links to More Information

Other good sources of information are the videos from MSDN specifically created to cover the Visual C# 2005 Express Edition product. The videos for Lessons 2 and 7 cover some of the topics you have just learned and will provide you with another point of view. You can find the videos for Lessons 2 and 7 by typing in the following hyperlink: http://go.microsoft.com/fwlink/ ?linkid=44030&clcid=0x409.

Chapter 5

Creating Your First Full Windows Application

In Chapter 4, you started building your own Web browser, and in Chapter 5 you'll add to its capabilities. But before you do that, I want to introduce some Microsoft® Visual C#® 2005 features that will help you develop your Microsoft Windows® programming knowledge and skills. We'll look into some of the more useful rapid application development (RAD) features of Visual C# 2005 Express Edition.

NOTE

> You can find all RAD features described in this chapter in every version of Visual Studio 2005. So if you already know how to use these features in the Express Edition and decide to explore any of the other versions of Visual Studio 2005, you'll find it much easier to switch and be productive.

If you already have some programming experience, you'll be pleasantly surprised to find that it's even easier to program using Visual C# 2005 Express Edition.

Snap and Align Those Controls Using Snap Lines

Not being a very skilled user interface designer myself, I've always had problems working on a program with many controls to align. Even more difficult was trying to get the alignment right the first time I dropped the controls onto the form. I've always had to go to the Properties window and align the controls manually by entering their x and y coordinates, which slows down the development process quite a bit! Again, let me reiterate one of the philosophies the Visual C# 2005 team had in mind when creating this awesome new product. They wanted to make sure you didn't have to perform multiple steps at several different places to accomplish a simple task. And they succeeded with a lot of new features; one of these is the new snap lines feature that allows you to easily align objects on the designer surface. Let's do an exercise so you can see the snap lines feature in action.

TO CREATE A NEW WINDOWS FORM USING SNAP LINES

1 Start Visual C# 2005 Express Edition by clicking **Start**, **All Programs**, and **Microsoft Visual C# 2005 Express Edition**. Create a new Microsoft Windows Application project using any of the techniques shown in the previous chapters by using either the File menu or the New Project icon in the toolbar. Name the new application **TestProject**.

2 You should see the designer surface. If you don't, right-click on the filename **Form1.cs** in the Solution Explorer and choose **View Designer**. Then, using the toolbox, drag three labels and three text box controls onto the design surface.

3 Stack the labels vertically. A thin blue line (a snap line) will appear on either the right side or the left side of the labels to help guide the alignment. When the labels are aligned correctly, release the label control.

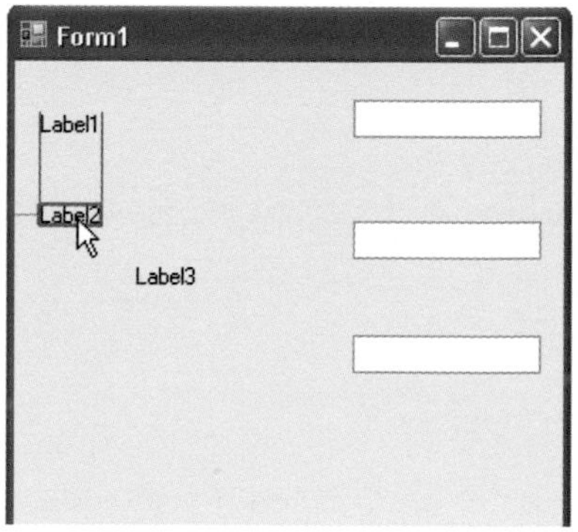

As shown in Figure 5-1, a small blue horizontal line also appears to the left of the label control. This line represents the minimum space between a control and another control or between a control and its container.

Figure 5-1
Snap lines in action with two label controls

4 After aligning the labels vertically, do the same with the text box controls immediately to the right of each label. The designer surface should look like the one shown in Figure 5-2.

5 Notice that the labels are aligned with the bottom of the text box controls. For a cleaner appearance, the labels should align with any text that will be entered in the text box. To align the labels correctly, move each label until you see a horizontal purple line instead of a blue line, as shown in Figure 5-3. In Figure 5-4, Labels 1 and 2 have been properly aligned with the baseline of the corresponding text box contents, but Label 3 is still aligned with the bottom of the text box itself.

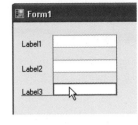

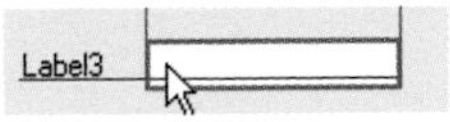

Figure 5-2
All the controls are now aligned

Figure 5-3
Example of alignment with the common text baseline

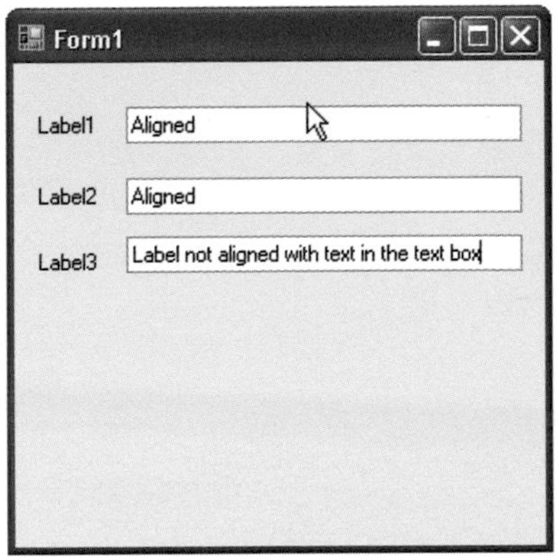

Figure 5-4
Run-time execution of this alignment problem

IMPORTANT

Do not close the test project; you'll need it for the sections that follow. If you close the test project and Visual C# 2005 Express Edition and then re-open them later, you might lose the current view and your form and code might not show up automatically. If you do happen to close the test form, click the View Code button on the Solution Explorer toolbar to get the code of the selected form or on the View Designer button to get the Designer of the selected form. Alternatively, you can right-click on the form filename, in this case *Form1.cs*, and then select View Code to get to the source code or View Designer to get to the design surface.

Using IntelliSense—Your New Best Friend!

IntelliSense® is one of the greatest tools developed for both beginner and experienced programmers. This feature provides contextual language references within the code editor and can even complete the typing for you. This means you can get immediate code syntax help specific to the code you're writing without leaving the code editor. For example, if you're inside a form and you ask IntelliSense for help, you'll get access to code constructs that make sense for that particular form. You've already experienced IntelliSense while doing the previous examples without really knowing that's what you were using.

IntelliSense and Ctrl+Spacebar

One of the easiest ways to bring up the IntelliSense window is to press Ctrl+Spacebar. Figure 5-5 shows an example from the project currently opened in the code editor. You can see in this figure a list of all possible choices based on the context of a form element named Form1.

```
namespace TestProject
{
    public partial class Form1 : Form
    {
        public Form1()
        {
            InitializeComponent();

        }
    }
}
```

#if
#region
_AppDomain
~
AcceptButton
AcceptRejectRule
AccessibilityNotifyClients
AccessibilityObject
AccessibleDefaultActionDescription
AccessibleDescription

IntelliSense and Period/Left Parenthesis

The second way you can get help using IntelliSense is by typing a period (".") after an element. The IntelliSense window will show up whether you are using .NET objects or your own objects. For example, I requested the list of possible constructs involving the variable Form1. In this example, I was looking for the variable textBox1, which represented the first text box on our Form. By typing a period (".") after the keyword *this*, I got the list of all relevant objects in this context. Then by typing the letter *t*, I got the list of all relevant components that have names beginning with that letter. I just had to scroll down to the item I was looking for: *textBox1*. Figure 5-6 illustrates these steps in the code editor (when you insert the button control in the following section). Finally, I pressed the Tab key to insert my selection, *textBox1*, in the code.

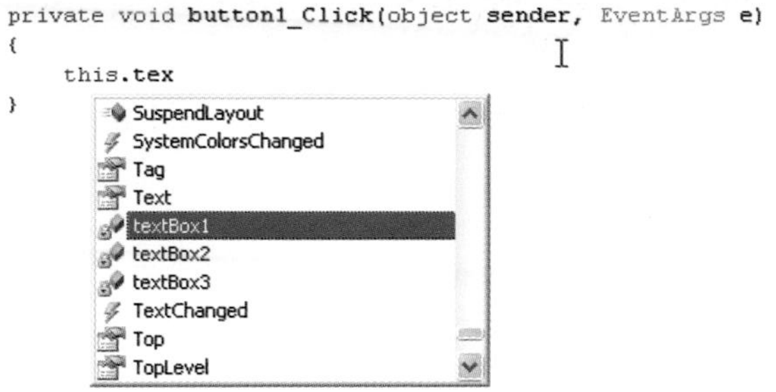

```
private void button1_Click(object sender, EventArgs e)
{
    this.tex                        I
}
```

```
  SuspendLayout
  SystemColorsChanged
  Tag
  Text
  textBox1
  textBox2
  textBox3
  TextChanged
  Top
  TopLevel
```

Figure 5-6
Getting help from IntelliSense by typing in a period (.) after a valid object

TO USE INTELLISENSE

1 From the toolbox, drag a button control to the form.

2 Double-click the button to bring up the button click event handler in the code editor. Then, where the cursor is blinking, press CTRL+Spacebar. The IntelliSense window will open.

3 Type the letter **t**, **h** and normally you should be on *this* in IntelliSense. Press Tab and then period (**.**).

4 Start typing **textbox**. Before you finish the word, IntelliSense should bring up *textBox1*. Press the Tab key to insert the component.

5 Type a period ("**.**") again, type **text**, then press the Tab key or the Spacebar. The code line should look like this one:

```
this.textBox1.Text
```

6 Now add the equal sign (=) and the string literal **"Hello World";** in the end, the line should look like this:

```
this.textBox1.Text = "Hello World";
```

You can now build and execute the application by pressing F5 and verify that it works. When you click the button you created, you should get the string "Hello World" in TextBox1, which normally should be the first one of the three text boxes.

You can also get additional help from IntelliSense if there's more than one available choice for your situation. Typing a left parenthesis ("(") displays a list of all possible choices. For instance, when we did the console application, we wrote to the console using the Console.WriteLine method. We used this method with a string argument, but you can do more with *Console.WriteLine* than just use a **string** as an argument. IntelliSense will indicate if there is more than one option. For Console.WriteLine, IntelliSense indicates there are 19 possible variations, as you can see in Figure 5-7. I was looking for the second variation, which is a Boolean argument. Now it's your turn to try it.

TIP
Know that at any time while you're using IntelliSense, you can press the Tab key to move quickly through the selections Intellisense presents if the item you're looking for is already selected.

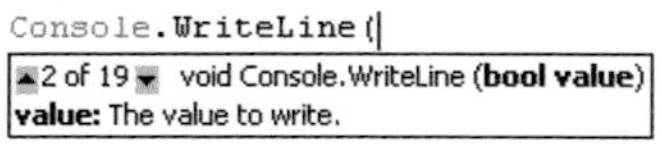

```
Console.WriteLine (|
  2 of 19   void Console.WriteLine (bool value)
  value: The value to write.
```

Figure 5-7
IntelliSense gives you the list of all possible variations of using the WriteLine method

TO SELECT FROM A LIST OF OPTIONS IN INTELLISENSE

 1 If the source code is not visible, just click on the tab over the code editor where you see the filename Form1.cs. Add a new line in the *Button1_Click* event and type **MessageBox.Show** and then type a left parenthesis ("**(**"). The IntelliSense Window opens and shows there are 21 possible variations for MessageBox. Show.

2 Scroll through the list of options using the up or down arrows on your keyboard. Select the option identified by the "1 of 21" in the yellow rectangle, which is called a tooltip.

3 Complete the following line of code so that it looks like:

```
MessageBox.Show("Hello Again");
```

4 Build and execute the application. When you click the button you should see the Hello World string and then a dialog box should show up with the message Hello Again..

IntelliSense Filtering: Pre-Selecting the "Most Recently Used"

You might have noticed that when the IntelliSense window appears, except for the first time you invoke it, you immediately jump to an element in the list. This element has been pre-selected by IntelliSense because it's the most recently used construct. Therefore, to be more productive, IntelliSense picks it up automatically to save you some typing. Another type of filtering is selection based purely on the context you're in at the moment of the invocation. If you're in the code for handling an exception, say in a catch statement in a try-catch block, then IntelliSense will present you the exception types. That's IntelliSense filtering at its best.

IntelliSense Code Snippets: The Time Saver

The next IntelliSense feature is IntelliSense code snippets. Code snippets were invented for only one reason–developer productivity. They are a big part of the new IntelliSense features. The code snippets in C# are related to language constructs but can be extended. In Visual C# you can add code snippets in two ways: you can insert them or, using an existing block of code, you can surround that block of code with a code snippet. Let's look at the first way. At any point in your source code you can right-click and select Insert Snippet... and then select the code snippet that best fits the context. The second way needs a bit more explanation. Let's say you have an existing block of code that reads a line of text in a file and then parses some data. In the process of developing your application you realize that you need the code to read the whole file and not only one line. This means you need to add a looping construct. With Surround With... it's quite easy to add the block of code to do the looping. You just have to select the block of code you want to loop, right-click, and select Surround With... Then you need to select the instruction you want to surround your block of code with. In our example, you would surround the code with a *while* statement. Then you just have to double-click on the *while* statement and your code will be automatically embedded in the *while* block.

Figure 5-8 shows a glimpse of the code snippets first-level menu choices. All code snippets are made with customizable fields, which means that they contain fields that are replaceable with code elements from your own applications. Going forward, you will be able to download additional code snippets from various sources such as Microsoft MSDN® Web site, online communities, and other .NET vendors. You will also be able to add your own code snippets to the code snippets library to fulfill your needs in other projects.

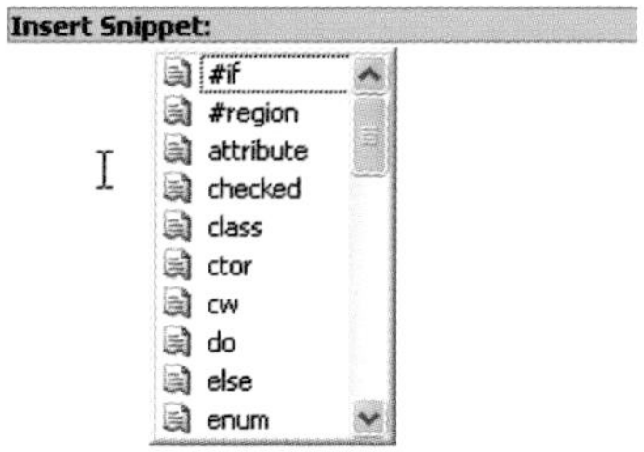

MORE INFO

See the "Additional Information" section at the end of this chapter for more information on code snippets.

Figure 5-8
IntelliSense code snippets menus

How to Invoke Code Snippets

You can invoke the code snippets in the code editor two different ways: by right-clicking and choosing Insert Snippet or Surround With and also by selecting Edit, then IntelliSense and then Insert Snippet... or Surround With... Each way has its own keyboard shortcut: CTRL+K, X for Insert Snippet and CTRL+K, S for Surround With.

TO USE CODE SNIPPETS

1 Using the previous test project, go back to the code editor in the *Button1_Click* event and call up the **IntelliSense Snippet** menu, using either method described above.

2 On the menu, scroll down to the *for* statement. Look at Figure 5-9 to get a feel for which menu choices you should have on your screen. Double-click the ***for*** statement to insert the code in the code editor.

Figure 5-9
Code snippets within the Visual C# language menus

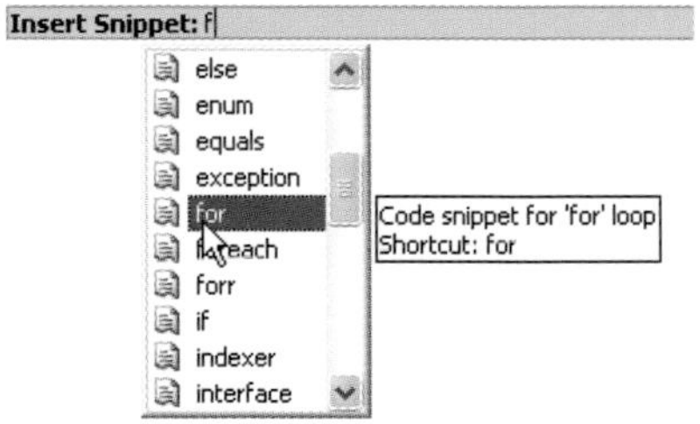

```
Insert Snippet: f|
    else
    enum
    equals
    exception
    for              Code snippet for 'for' loop
    foreach          Shortcut: for
    forr
    if
    indexer
    interface
```

3 Once you select the *for* statement, a generic template for that language construct appears. Refer to Figure 5-10. The green fields in the "before" screenshot are replacement fields pre-populated with some default values that you can modify. Before you go to the next step, edit the code to match the "after" screenshot.

Figure 5-10
Before (left) and after (right) look for the for statement code snippets

```
for (int i = 0; i < length; i++)     for (int i = 0; i < 10; i++)
{                                     {
                                          this.textBox2.Text += i.ToString() + ",";
}                                     }
```

Build and execute your application by pressing F5, then click the button on the displayed form to execute the code snippet you've just inserted. In the second text box, you should see the numbers 1 through 10 separated by commas. This output is the result of the *for* statement looping 10 times, adding the index value string representation and a comma to the text box with each loop. In this sample, the index is "i".

5 Just below the right curly brace (}) of the *for* statement, type the following line of code:

```
this.textBox2.Text += i.ToString() + ",";
```

 Select the line of code you just typed, then right-click and select Surround With... You should see a list of items similar to the Insert Snippet... choices. Double-click the *for* statement from that list. You should have the same type of *for* statement with your line of code embedded in it.

7 Now start your index i at 10 and instead of 1 and instead of increasing, decrease the index by doing **i--**. Look at Figure 5-11 to see the before and after the Surround With...

`this.textBox2.Text += i.ToString() + ",";` **Surround With:**	`for (int i = 10; i > 0; i--)`
#if	`{`
#region	`    this.textBox2.Text += i.ToString() + ",";`
checked	`}`
class	
do	
else	
enum	
for *Code snippet for 'for' loop*	
foreach *Shortcut: for*	
forr	

Figure 5-11
Before (left) adding the code snippet using Surround With and after (right)

8 Now build and execute by hitting F5 and when you click the button you should see the suite of 1 to 9 and then 10 to 1 in textBox2. You might need to resize textBox2 to be large enough to hold the suite of numbers.

IntelliSense Auto-Using Statements

The final IntelliSense feature is auto-using statements. Let's say you want to work with an XML file and you want to load it in memory. The XmlDocument class is in the System.Xml namespace and for IntelliSense to see it, you need a directive on top of your file. The auto-using statements help you continue to type your code without leaving the place where you need the new class. For instance, below the right curly brace (}) of the second *for* loop statement, type the following code:

```
XmlDocument
```

A red smart tag will appear. If you click on it and then click on the drop-down list, you'll see that the first choice you'll have will suggest inserting the using System.Xml directives on top of the file. This will be done automatically without you having to type a single line of code. Great productivity! After the using directives are added, your XmlDocument will change from black to cyan indicating that IntelliSense picked up the using directive and it's a recognized class. Look at Figure 5-12 for the before and after. When you're done experimenting, delete the line of code--you won't need it anymore.

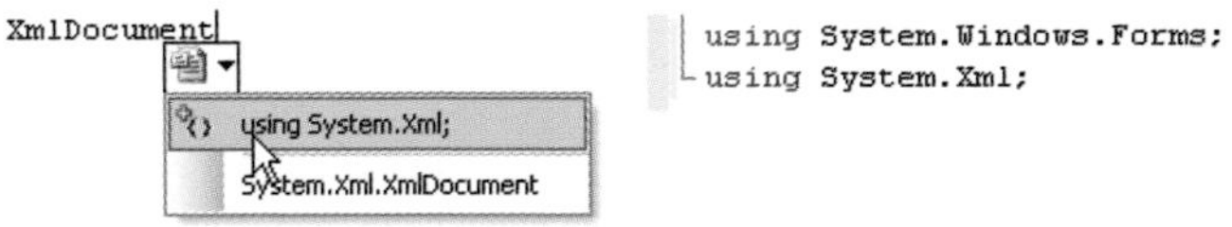

Figure 5-12
Using the auto-using statement and the using directive added on top of the file

Renaming and Refactoring

Visual C# 2005 Express Edition has added a great support for refactoring. Refactoring helps developers to automate many common tasks when they restructure their code. In Visual C# 2005 Express Edition it enables you to do two of those restructuring tasks: rename symbols and extracting method. Let's look at them.

The rename feature found in Visual C# 2005 is quite useful. It provides you, the programmer, with an easy, automatic, and effective way of changing source elements in a selective way, but the symbol is referenced in the code. The variables, controls, comments, strings, and any other items in your applications can be updated to meaningful names using the renaming symbol functionality.

What Can You Rename?

So far in the test project we've worked in, we have not paid attention to the controls' names because we didn't have to write much code and because the project was a quick prototype to test new features. At this point, our controls are all named something like textBox1, textBox2, label1, and so on. That's okay for what we've been doing, but when you develop full applications, you always want to give meaningful names to your controls and variables so that your code becomes self-documented and easier to read and maintain.

How and Where to Use the Rename Feature

So far in our test project, we have defined some text boxes, labels, and other controls, but they all have their autogenerated names (e.g., textBox1 or label1). We can use the rename feature to give meaningful names to these controls. The renaming feature can be used from three different places within the IDE: in the Properties window, directly in the code, and in the Solution Explorer.

The first place we can use the renaming feature is in the Properties window at design time. So far in our test project, we've used the form name Form1. In the next exercise, we'll rename Form1 to TestProjectForm. The expectation is that this change gets propagated throughout the code in the project. But just to see how the functionality works, we'll look into all files where the Form1 symbol is used.

OOP Terminology

Although this book is not an OOP book, we'll certainly use many of those constructs in the real application we'll build. We've talked about OOP in Chapter 1 and Chapter 4, but if you want to learn more about this paradigm, you can go back to the Start Page. If it's not visible, just click the View menu, Other Windows, and then select Start Page. In the Start Page, click on the How do I . . .? hyperlink in the Getting Started section. Once you're in the help system, use the Contents pane to navigate to Visual C# Express\C# Language Primer (Visual C# Express)\Classes. Click and read whenever you want to learn more about OOP and the Visual C# language. It's not a complete OOP book, but it's more than enough for what we are doing in this text.

This is a good point to introduce a new button from the Solution Explorer toolbar. The Show All Files button looks like this in the toolbar:

The Show All Files enables you to see files that are part of the project but that you do not need to work with in most circumstances. For instance the output files of your application. They are important but not in the context of Visual Studio.

1 In Solution Explorer, expand the form1.cs file by clicking the plus sign (+) beside Form1.cs.

2 Right-click the file name *Form1.Designer.cs* and then select **View Code**. Look at Figure 5-13 for a visual representation of what you should see.

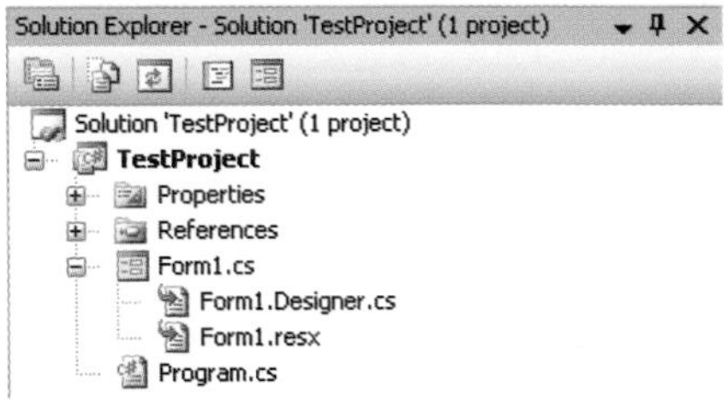

Figure 5-13

3 Now let me introduce you to a useful feature: Search. With the Form1.Designer.cs source code in the code editor, press **Ctrl+F** and then type **Form1** in the Find What text box. Before you click the Find Next button, make sure to select **Current Project** from the Look in list box.

Figure 5-14 shows how the search should be configured.

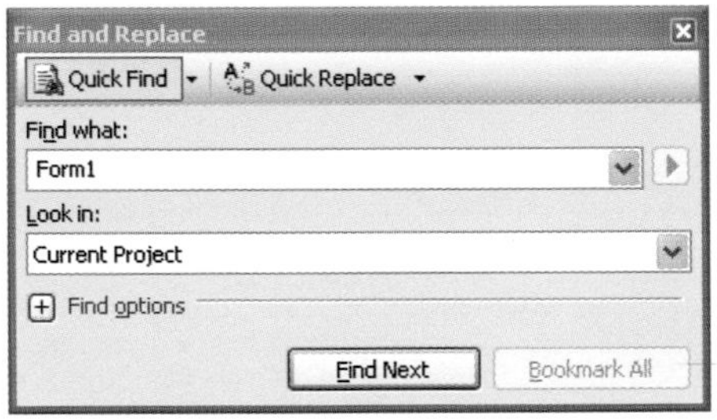

Figure 5-14

4 Search for all occurrences of Form1 in the code by clicking the **Find Next** button. You should see that the search goes through three different files: *Form1.cs*, *Program.cs*, and *Form1.Designer.cs*.

Once all instances of Form1 have been found, a dialog box will display a message saying that the search is complete and that there are no more occurences left based on your search criteria.

5 Now that all instances of Form1 have been identified, we can rename it *TestProjectForm*. To do that, select the **Form1.cs [Design]** tab to return to the designer surface. Then click the title bar to select the form.

In the Properties window, be sure the form control named *Form1* is selected. Modify the (Name) property by changing *Form1* to **TestProjectForm**. Press **Enter** to begin renaming. A small hourglass should be displayed while the renaming is in process.

 Now repeat the search from Steps 3 and 4 and you'll see that the only occurrence left is a string that corresponds to the Form control text property (i.e., title bar name).

8 You can also rename a symbol directly in the code. In Form1.cs, place the cursor anywhere in the word *textBox1* in the following line of code:

```
this.textBox1.Text = "HelloWorld";
```

9 Right-click and select **Refactor** and then **Rename**; a dialog box like the one in Figure 5-15a appears. Replace *textBox1* with *txtMessage*; the dialog box should now look like the one in Figure 5-15b. You have three check boxes that can control how deep your rename will go.

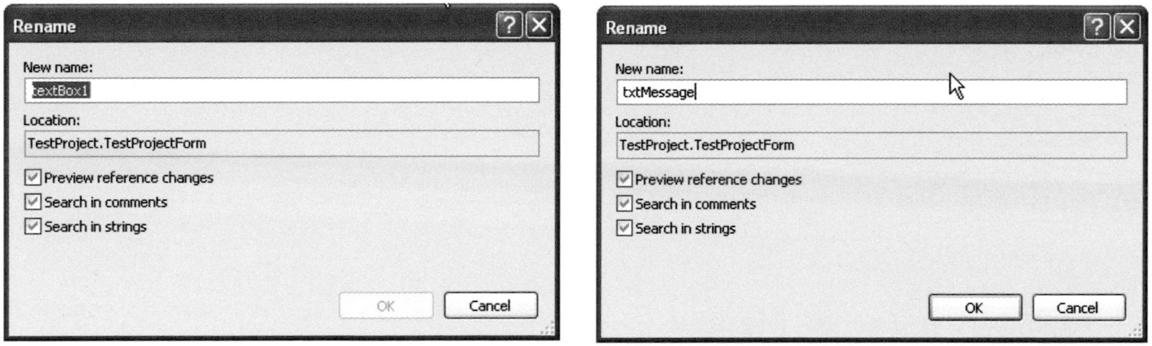

Rename ? X	Rename ? X
New name:	**New name:**
textBox1	txtMessage
Location:	**Location:**
TestProject.TestProjectForm	TestProject.TestProjectForm
☑ Preview reference changes	☑ Preview reference changes
☑ Search in comments	☑ Search in comments
☑ Search in strings	☑ Search in strings
OK Cancel	OK Cancel

Figure 5-15

10 Click **OK** to start replacing all occurences of *textBox1* with txtMessage. You should see a dialog box that will give you a preview of all the changes that will be done by the Refactoring. The upper section shows you where the string was found and the bottom portion shows you what the change will look like if applied to the selected item. The check boxes allow you to select only the changes you really want to perform. The neat thing is that they are organized by type of change: one for the code elements, one for the comments, and finally one for the strings. Look at Figure 5-16a to see the Preview Changes dialog box upper window completely scrolled and Figure 5-16b for the first selected change preview.

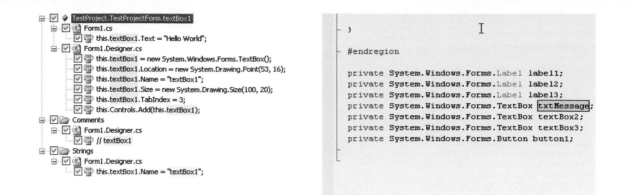

Figure 5-16

Click Apply to perform the renaming. It's that easy. Imagine how much time you would save using the Rename feature if you had 10 files with hundreds of lines of code. Not only would you be sure to find every occurrence, the code would be a lot easier to read.

11 The third way to rename a symbol, and in this case only for project elements, is to do it directly in Solution Explorer. Even though earlier we changed the Form1 variable into something more meaningful, the file name Form1 hasn't changed because it's not in the source code; it's in the Solution Explorer and contained in the project, so it's still Form1.cs. For consistency, right-click the filename Form1.cs in the Solution Explorer, then select **Rename** and change the filename to **TestProjectFormOtherName.cs**. Two things will happen: first, you'll see that the filename and all dependent filenames are automatically changed to the new name; and second, you'll see that all references to TestProjectForm are now changed to TestProjectFormOtherName. You can verify this renaming change by pressing Ctrl+F and performing a search on the old name (form1.cs).

Refactoring–Extract Method

It's common when you develop an application that a block of code turns into a mega method that does a lot more than the original functionality it was supposed to provide. Therefore you need to re-organize your code and maybe break the problem into smaller pieces. That's where the refactoring–extract method will become your friend. With this refactoring functionality you just have to select a block of code within a method, right-click, select Refactor, and then select Extract Method... Visual C# 2005 Express will then create a private method with the selected block of code and call that method where the code was. If the block of code uses local variables from the original method they will be automatically passed as argument to the new method. Look at Figure 5-17a and b to see what it looks like before the refactoring, during and after the refactoring.

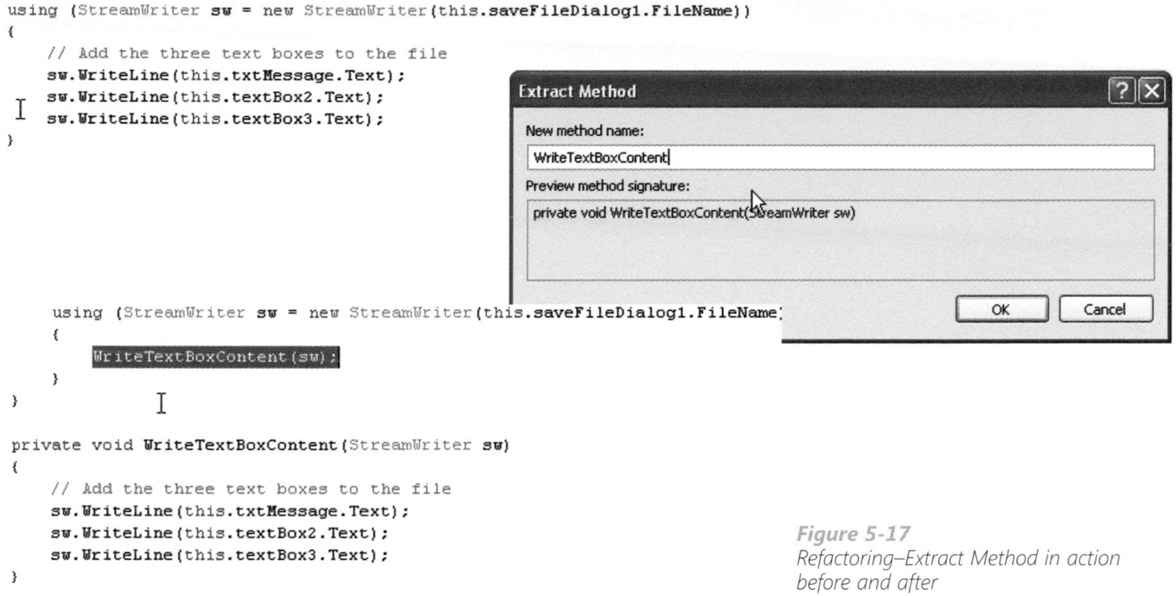

```
using (StreamWriter sw = new StreamWriter(this.saveFileDialog1.FileName))
{
    // Add the three text boxes to the file
    sw.WriteLine(this.txtMessage.Text);
I   sw.WriteLine(this.textBox2.Text);
    sw.WriteLine(this.textBox3.Text);
}
```

Extract Method   [?][X]

New method name:

| WriteTextBoxContent |

Preview method signature:

private void WriteTextBoxContent(StreamWriter sw)

[OK]   [Cancel]

```
    using (StreamWriter sw = new StreamWriter(this.saveFileDialog1.FileName)
    {
        WriteTextBoxContent(sw);
    }
}
        I

private void WriteTextBoxContent(StreamWriter sw)
{
    // Add the three text boxes to the file
    sw.WriteLine(this.txtMessage.Text);
    sw.WriteLine(this.textBox2.Text);
    sw.WriteLine(this.textBox3.Text);
}
```

Figure 5-17
Refactoring–Extract Method in action
before and after

Common Windows Controls

I will not spend a lot of time here explaining all the details and properties of each control in the toolbox. This book is not a reference about Windows Forms programming. Other books do a great job with that topic. However, Table 5-1 provides a quick introduction to the most common controls you will find in most Windows Applications.

There are many more controls than those shown here. But this table should make it clear that there are a plethora of controls available to perform many tasks. To save time and effort, you can usually find a control to provide the results you want with very little effort. It is especially desirable if the control you pick can restrict choices or how the data is selected without having to perform any other validation. In software development, always keep the 80/20 rule in mind: 80 percent of results for 20 percent effort.

Table 5-1
Common Windows applications controls

Visual representation	Name	Description
Button1	Button	Indicates that the user makes a decision and wants to communicate his action. In your application, a button clicked by the user triggers an event that your code needs to handle.
	TextBox	The text box is used to get user input. On the screen it can be a single or multi-line control. It can also provide password character masking if you need this behavior in your application. It's a good choice to input information that is not restrictive in choices, for instance a Boolean decision like yes/no, on/off, or a list of specific choices like a list of country names. It's good for names, addresses, phone numbers, URLs, etc.
Label1	Label	The label is usually simple text used to describe other controls. It is not an inter-active control.
○ Grayscale ○ Color	RadioButton	Multiple choices are offered but the user can only pick one from the list. Let's say you have an application and you want to provide the option to print in grayscale or color. You could use two radio buttons to select the desired method.

Continued on next page

Continued from page 72

Visual representation	Name	Description
☐ AC ☐ CD Changer ☐ Metallic Paint ☐ ABS	CheckBox	A check box is great for Boolean choices (e.g., on/off, yes/no, etc.). It can also be used in a group of check boxes to indicate characteristics of a single entity. For instance, in a car ordering tool that is part of a dealership application you could have check boxes for all the car characteristics (AM/FM radio, CD changer, heated seats, metallic paint, etc.).
Alabama Arkansas California Connecticut Washington	ComboBox	A combo box is a combination of a text box and a drop-down list with valid choices. It's great to display an editable text box with a list of permitted values. You can have autocomplete and the values can be sorted. The values can come from static entry or from other sources of data like a database. For instance, a good example is selecting a state. You can either enter the state name or select it from the list of possible values.
Joe John Brad Mark Jim	ListBox	A list box is a short list of valid choices for the domain this component represents. This control is great when there is a list of possible choices that is not too big in number. It does not allow the user to enter text but lets the user select one or more than one choice by using CTRL or SHIFT.

Continued on next page

Continued from page 73

Visual representation	Name	Description
Name [ ] Customer Name	ToolTip	The ToolTip control is helpful for displaying information about a control when a user holds the mouse over the control.
1971	NumericUpDown	This control is really useful when you want the user to select a numerical value from a predefined set of numbers. It allows the user to select a single numerical value from the list using the up and down button to increment and decrement the number. It could be perfect to force the user to pick up a numerical value for a year component of a date.

What Happens When an Event Is Triggered?

All Windows applications are event-driven. This means that whenever you select a menu item, click a button or even move from one text box to another, you are generating an event. Blocks of code attached to each of your actions execute as you work. Events are generated not only by your actions, but also by the surrounding environment, namely Windows itself or by other external sources. To understand what "other external sources" means, think about any Internet messenger application like MSN Messenger. When you chat with someone and exchange data back and forth, you are actually generating events. In nontechnical terms, data incoming from your friend over the Internet is an event.

These events exist for a multitude of actions you usually do without realizing they are events. Some events are handled for you by autogenerated code like clicking the red X in the right corner of an application and some others need to be handled by your code.

With this section, we'll start to work on wiring source code to events. For practice, we will wire two objects from our test project. Before beginning, use what you've learned so far to make the test project look like Figure 5-18.

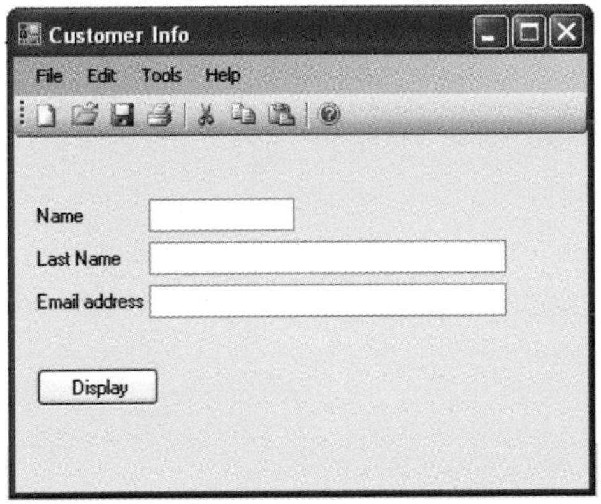

NOTE
To add the menus and toolbar buttons, go to the toolbox in the Menus & Toolbars category and add a MenuStrip control and a ToolStrip control to the form. Next, select each control, open the smart tag menu, and select Insert Standard Items.

Figure 5-18
Customer Information Form

When an event is triggered, the code that is wired to handle the event is executed. If there is no code attached to a particular event, then nothing happens. Our application is basically in that stage right now. (Except for the button that was doing some work for us as shown previously.) We will add some functionality to our test project application by wiring the Save menu choice and the toolbar Save button to the source code that will save all the content of the text boxes to a simple text file in the current directory. Because the save and open file dialogs are standard and also to get a consistent feel to applications, the Visual C# development team decided to write save and open controls and make them available to you. We'll take advantage of this shortcut in our exercise.

TIP

If you want to look at all the possible events that can be fired for a particular control, you can click on the yellow lightning icon that is located at the top of the Properties window as seen in the graphic from the previous tip. To come back to the properties, you just have to click the little sheet symbol to the left of the yellow lightning icon.

Using Comments in Your Code

One good habit you should start embracing when writing code is to comment your code. Right now, the code for the problems we are solving isn't too complicated. But keep in mind that adding comments serves the following purpose: first, your code becomes much more maintainable because you can come back six months later and, if the comments are good, you will be able to understand what you developed. It also makes your code more readable and facilitates getting help from somebody. Write your comments in normal English without too many jargon words. Another

Continued on next page

TO WIRE SOURCE CODE TO EVENTS

1 Drag the **SaveFileDialog** control onto the form from the toolbox dialogs category. This control has no design time representation, it will appear only in the component tray, the gray section below the designer surface. See Figure 5-19 for the location of the SaveFileDialog.

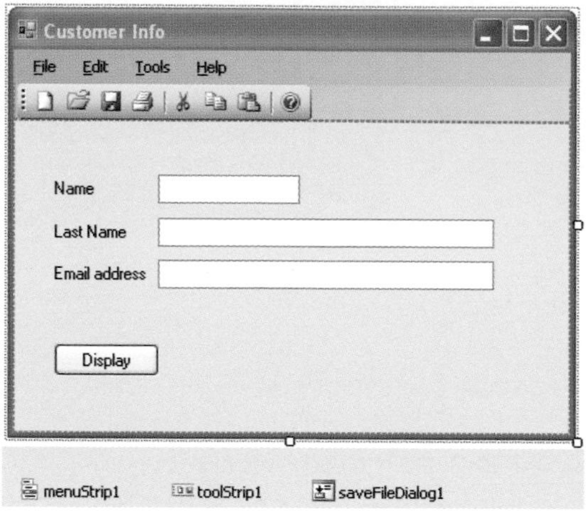

Figure 5-19
Design time representation of the SaveFileDialog

We'll use the SaveFileDialog to wire the click event to both the Save button on the toolbar and to the Save choice in the File menu. To have the same operation performed when either event occurs, we'll write a block of code called an event handler. The block of code will perform the same operation whether it is triggered by the button on the tooolbar or the by the menu selection.

2 Click the little blue disk icon on the toolstrip to select it. Check the Properties window to be sure you have the correct control:

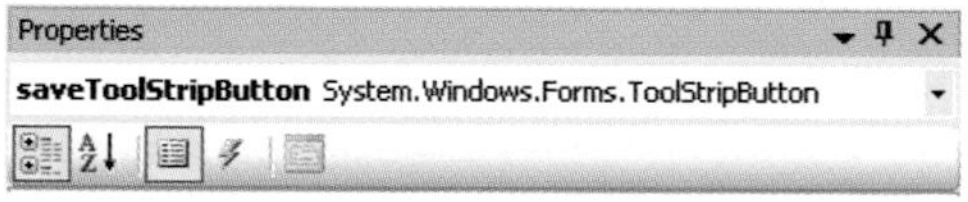

Verify that the name and type of control is the one you intend to work with.

3 Double-click the blue disk on the designer surface and you will be presented with the default event template for this control, which is the click event.

4 Add the following line of code to the saveToolStripButton_Click event procedure. (I will explain what it does below.)

```
this.saveFileDialog1.ShowDialog();
```

 5 This block of code displays the SaveFileDialog1 by calling the ShowDialog() method on it. At this point, if you want to see the effect of the change, just build and execute the application by pressing **F5** and click the **Save** icon to see that the save dialog will show up.

6 In every SaveFileDialog, there is a save button and a cancel button. The cancel button is automatically taken care of for us. But we need to wire what is going to happen when the user clicks on the save button of that new dialog.

7 To wire the save button, select the **saveFileDialog1** icon in the component tray and double-click it to get to the most common event, which is the FileOk event in this case.

8 Whenever the user clicks the Save button, your application will take the content of the three text boxes and write them into a file on the hard drive. When finished, your code should look like the listing below. Examine the comments to understand what we are trying to accomplish. You can use the Insert Snippet and use a using snippet.

SaveFileDialog1_FileOk Method

```csharp
private void saveFileDialog1_FileOk(object sender, CancelEventArgs e)
{
    // By using the using statement, not to be confused with the using
    // directive on top of the file, we are making sure that if an
    /* exception is happening that a finally is executed to close the
     * file.  The using is in fact a try - finally block. */
    using (StreamWriter sw = new StreamWriter(this.saveFileDialog1.FileName))
    {
        // Add the three text boxes to the file
        sw.WriteLine(this.txtMessage.Text);
        sw.WriteLine(this.textBox2.Text);
        sw.WriteLine(this.textBox3.Text);
    }
}
```

9 Add the following using directive to the top of the code file:

```csharp
using System.IO;
```

Continued from page 76

thing to remember is that the comments are never compiled in the application you execute so they will never slow down the performance of your application.

As you can see in the listing in step 8, you can comment your code by inserting two forward slashes (//) for a one line comment or using /* and */ on the same line or on a separate line for a multi-line comment. Your comment should appear in green; if not, then your line is not seen as a comment by the compiler. Another good way to comment your code is to use two buttons from one of the toolbars. Let's say you decide that all the previous code in the FileOk event is not the code you want to execute because you want to test something else. You do not want to delete all the text but you can comment out the code by selecting it and then clicking on the Comment Out the Selected Lines button. And if you want to uncomment a block of code, you just have to select the code you want to uncomment and then click the Uncomment the Selected Lines button.

10 Now we just need to attach the same event code to the File/Save menu choice. Double-click the Save choice in the File menu and add the same code as in step 4. Build the application and execute it by pressing F5. Type some text in the text boxes and then save the content to a file by using the Save menu or the Save toolbar button. You should check that the content of the file your application saved is really what was on the form. To verify that it worked properly, open the file with Visual Studio by selecting the File/Open File menu, browsing to the location of the saved file, and then opening it to view its contents.

We just handled two events, but I want to point out that we already handled events previously by coding the Button1_Click and modifying properties of other controls. For instance, we modified the Text property of our TextBox controls when we handled the button click. And we were able to do that by using the control's name property.

In Summary...

Finding Additional Information

Even though it's a bit outdated, there is a really good article on extending the IntelliSense Code Snippets that you'll find at the following URL: http://msdn.microsoft.com/ vcsharp/default.aspx?pull=/ library/en-us/dnvs05/html/ codesnippets.asp

Another good source of information is the videos from MSDN specifically done to cover the Visual C# 2005 Express Edition product. I suggest you

Continued on next page

Wow, that was a big chapter with a lot of new features. These features will definitely help you write your applications. We went over some IDE features such as the snap lines to help you to align the controls on the form. We went on to the rich features of IntelliSense that help you with typing of your code by either suggesting appropriate choices, completing code sentences for you, or providing you with code snippets. In the end, IntelliSense is there to reduce the amount of typing you do so that your productivity can increase. On top of that, it is a great tool for beginners.

We then saw the benefits of the new refactoring feature to rename elements in your source code, elements such as: code elements, comments and even string literals. Then the refactoring-extract method lets you restructure your code by extracting blocks of code and automatically creating new methods and all the supporting code. It is especially useful to replace autogenerated variable names with more meaningful variable names. We examined the most common controls you will find in every Windows application with some graphical examples and justification on their usage. Finally, we ended the chapter with how event-based programming is performed.

78   Microsoft Visual C# 2005 Express Edition: Build a Program Now!

In the next chapter, you'll put into practice everything you just learned in this chapter. You'll also take a look at some new features, controls, and concepts that you'll use as we continue with the Web browser project.

Continued from page 78

watch the following two lessons as a complement; they will reinforce a lot of topics covered in this chapter.

Lesson 2 video: http://go.microsoft.com/fwlink/?linkid=44030&clcid=0x409

Lesson 3 video: http://go.microsoft.com/fwlink/?linkid=44030&clcid=0x409

Those two lessons will be a pretty good visual live summary to this chapter.

Chapter 6

Modify Your Web Browser Now!

After reading the avalanche of new concepts presented in the first few chapters, you're ready to apply them and take your Web browser to the next level. In this chapter, you'll add rich features to your browser such as a splash screen, an About box, tool strips, menu strips, a tool strip container that will give you a rich user experience "à la Internet Explorer," a status strip control, a progress bar, professional-looking toolbars with "déjà vu" icons, and new Microsoft® Visual C#® 2005 Integrated Development Environment (IDE) features, like the Document Outline window. You'll also learn to respond to events coming from the Web Browser control.

When you load an application, you often see something called a **splash screen**. Some good examples of splash screens are the opening information boxes you see for Microsoft Office, Visual Studio® 2005, and most other programs. Although they're often very nice looking, those screens aren't there just to display the software version and appealing artwork or to make sure you're not bored. These screens serve a function. Once you've started an application, a lot of processing is happening; for instance, the application is connecting to databases, populating controls with data from the database, getting saved configurations for the user interface (UI) preferences, and so on. Displaying the splash screen while all of this processing is happening helps inform the user that the application is working.

You'll now add the splash screen to your project. Remember that a splash screen is only a regular form that you bring up at the start of a program. It can have two different usages: to simply display information and a logo or to serve the same purpose but with a lot of processing happening in the background. In your case, you'll add the splash screen simply to introduce your browser.

NOTE

In this chapter, I've created a starting browser application that is the same as the application you created in Chapter 4. If you installed the companion content to the default location, it should be at the following location on your hard drive: My Documents\Microsoft Press\VCS 2005 Express\Chapter6\. Look for a folder named Start under the Chapter6 folder. Double-click the MyOwnBrowser.sln solution. If you want, you can also start from your own Chapter 4 browser project.

Figure 6-1
Add New Item dialog for the creation of the splash screen

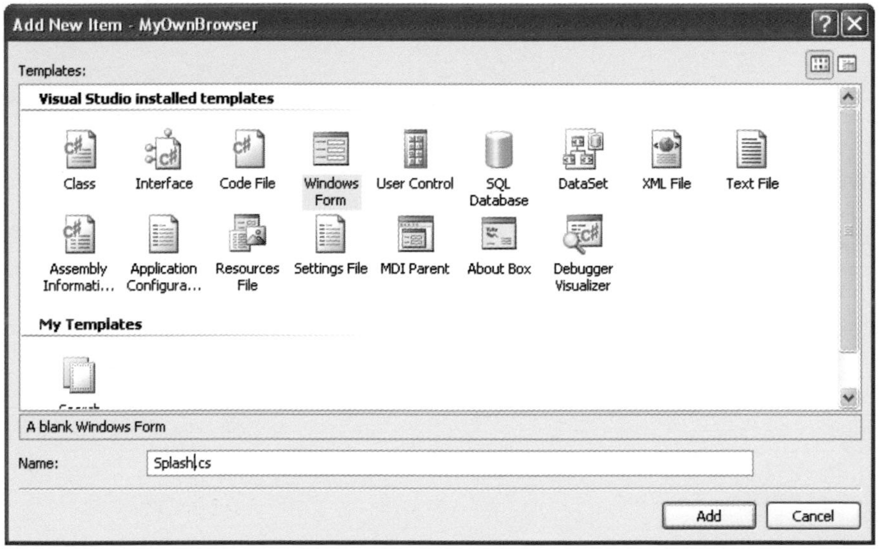

TO CREATE A SPLASH SCREEN

1 To start, you'll give Form1 a more meaningful name. (Keep in mind that everything in your application needs to be meaningful for readability and maintainability.) In the Solution Explorer, rename Form1.cs to **Browser.cs**. When asked if you want to rename all references to Form1 in the project, click **Yes**.

2 To add a regular form to your project you can either go to the Project menu and select **Add Windows Form . . .** or go to the Solution Explorer, right-click the project name (in this case, MyOwnBrowser) select **Add**, and then select **Windows Form**. The Add New Item dialog box will appear and ask which type of form you want to add.

3 Select Windows Form and name the file Splash.cs. Look at Figure 6-1 for the Add New Item dialog to see what it should look like.

4 A splash screen has particular properties since you're not suppose to interact with it, it is purely informational and should not appear in the task bar, should not be resizable and more. Now make sure you select your new form in the Properties window and set those particular form properties using the table to the right.

The image for the background is located in the Images folder under Chapter 6 where you've installed your companion content. (If you installed the companion content at the default location, then it should be at the following location on your hard drive: MyDocuments\Microsoft Press\VCS 2005 Express\)

Properties	▾ ਧ ×
MainLayoutPanel System.Windows.Forms.TableLayoutPa ▾	
ApplicationTitle System.Windows.Forms.Label	
Copyright System.Windows.Forms.Label	
DetailsLayoutPanel System.Windows.Forms.TableLayoutPan	
MainLayoutPanel System.Windows.Forms.TableLayoutPanel	
splash System.Windows.Forms.Form	
Version System.Windows.Forms.Label	

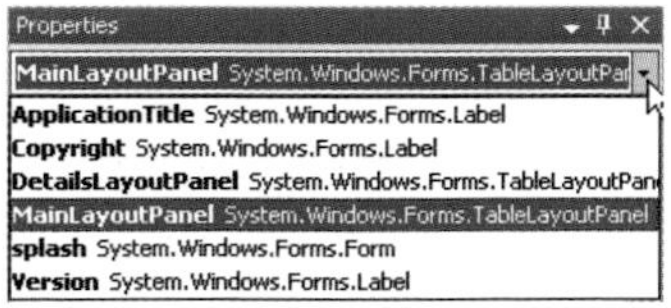

Figure 6-2
Finding all the controls on a selected form

Control Name	Control Type	Property	Value
Splash	Form	FormBorderStyle	None
Splash	Form	ShownInTaskbar	False
Splash	Form	StartPosition	CenterScreen
Splash	Form	Size:Width Size:Height	450 375
Splash	Form	BackgroundImage	www.jpg
Splash	Form	BackgroundImageLayout	Stretch
lblApplicationTitle	Label	Text	Application Title
lblApplicationTitle	Label	BackColor	Web:Transparent
lblApplicationTitle	Label	Font	Microsoft Sans Serif, 20pt
lblApplicationTitle	Label	ForeColor	Web:White
lblVersion	Label	Text	Version
lblVersion	Label	BackColor	Web:Transparent
lblVersion	Label	Font	Microsoft Sans Serif, 12pt
lblCopyright	Label	ForeColor	Web:White
lblCopyright	Label	Text	Copyright
lblCopyright	Label	BackColor	Web:Transparent
lblCopyright	Label	Font	Microsoft Sans Serif, 8.25pt
lblCopyright	Label	ForeColor	Web:White

5 Add three label controls to the form and name them **lblApplicationTitle**, **lblVersion**, and **lblCopyright**. Use the Properties window to set the properties specified in the previous table.

6 Look at Figure 6-3 to see where the three labels are located and place them there in the designer. The text in the image is for reference only; the application title, version, and copyright information are all obtained dynamically. This means the form will get the values from a variable or a setting somewhere in your project. In fact, at run time those three pieces of information are obtained when the splash screen is loaded by looking up application settings stored in the Project Designer Application pane.

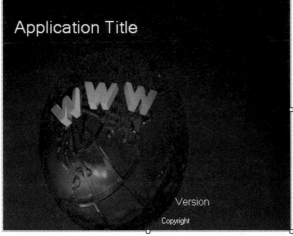

Figure 6-3
*Splash screen with the background
and the labels location*

7 Now you'll have to hook up the splash screen to the application and to do this you have to modify the browser form constructor. Open the code for the browser form (not the splash screen form) and modify the constructor so that it looks like the following:

```csharp
public partial class Browser : Form
{
    Splash splashScreen = new Splash();

    public Browser()
    {
        InitializeComponent();
        splashScreen.Show();
        Application.DoEvents();
    }
}
```

8 The previous step will display the splash screen but you need to close it and make it disappear whenever the other form is ready to be displayed. The last event before the form is displayed is the Activated event. So you need to select the Browser form in Design View and then go in the Properties window. Then click on the Events button (yellow lightning) at the top of the Properties window and double-click the Activated event. The Browser_Activated event handler is displayed in Code View. Add the following code:

```csharp
private void Browser_Activated(object sender, EventArgs e)
{
    Thread.Sleep(3000);
    splashScreen.Close();
}
```

9 Place your cursor within the "Thread" text. You should see a familiar yellow and red smart tag. This smart tag is there to let you know that the Thread class is in the System.Threading namespace and that you don't have it in your using directives on top of the file. Move your mouse over the smart tag, click the down arrow and then select **using System.Threading;** to add it to your list of using directives.

TO VIEW THE APPLICATION TITLE, VERSION, AND COPYRIGHT PROPERTIES

1 Select **MyOwnBrowser** from the Solution Explorer, right-click, and choose **Properties**.

The Project Designer page opens. The Project Designer has a series of information tabs (as shown in Figure 6-4). You'll work mainly in the first tab for now, which is the Application pane. You'll configure several elements in this pane. All the elements you'll modify will affect how the application looks.

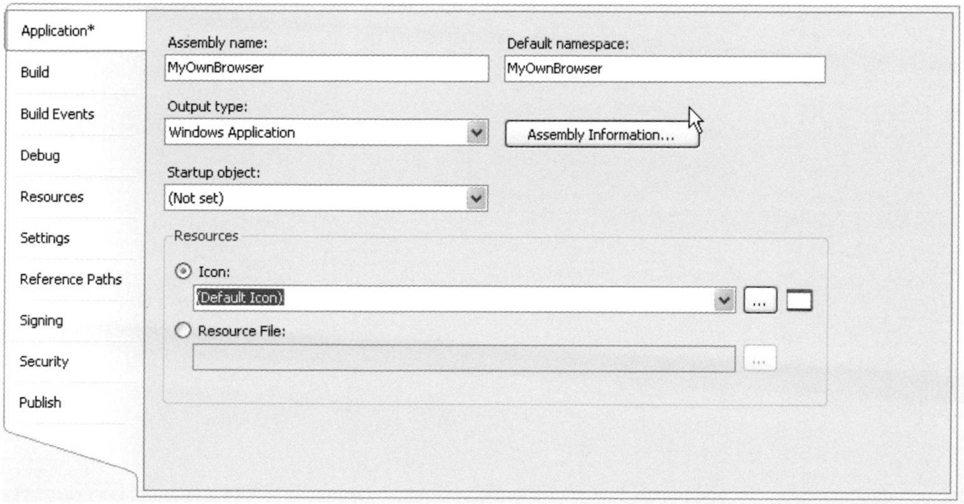

Figure 6-4
Project Designer page

2 To change the application icon, select the Icon option, and then click the Ellipsis button (...). Find the Chapter 6 directory where you've installed the book's sample files and look for the **globe.ico** file in the Images folder. (If you installed the companion content at the default location, then it should be at the following location on your hard drive: My Documents\Microsoft Press\VCS 2005 Express\.)

You've changed the icon of your application assembly or, in other words, you've changed the icon of the executable binary (.exe) file itself. If you build the application and look on your hard drive where the application is compiled (as you learned in a previous chapter, all your projects are by default located at My Documents\Visual Studio 2005\Projects\MyOwnBrowser\MyOwnBrowser\bin\Debug or \bin\release), you'll find that your application, MyOwnBrowser.exe, has the globe icon that you've just selected instead of a default icon.

> **NOTE**
> You're not changing the icon of the main form when doing this application icon change. In order to do this, you need to change the form icon's property by assigning a bitmap image. You're going to change the main form icon in the last section of this chapter.

Assembly Information

Title:	MyOwnBrowser
Description:	
Company:	Microsoft
Product:	MyOwnBrowser
Copyright:	Copyright © Microsoft 2005
Trademark:	
Assembly Version:	1 · 0 · 0 · 0
File Version:	1 · 0 · 0 · 0
GUID:	1ba194b0-8cd0-4f4c-82da-3c88d98eb9c1
Neutral Language:	(None)

☐ Make assembly COM-Visible

OK   Cancel

Figure 6-5
Assembly Information dialog box

3 Click the **Assembly Information. . .** button. You should see a dialog box that looks like the one in Figure 6-5.

4 Change the Copyright information: replace the word *Microsoft* with your name and keep the rest of the information as it is. (If it's not already filled with your information, change it to match your name or company info.)

5 Insert spaces between the words *MyOwnBrowser* in the Title text box. (This string is used to display the application title on the splash screen.) Insert two spaces to get the following title: **My Own Browser**.

6 Click **OK** to close the Assembly Information dialog box.

> **NOTE**
>
> The assembly version information that you see here is also what the application will display in the splash screen you're creating. You'll see the source code that will display the information on the splash screen later in the chapter.

Now that you have all your assembly data entered in the Project Designer application pane you need to get it onto your splash screen form and in the correct labels. You need to do this in the splash screen constructor to obtain the information from where it was entered. The idea here is to make the splash screen generic enough that you could reuse it in another project. I've used the same methods that are found in the about box template as you'll see in a minute. Open Splash.cs in Code View and modify the code so that it looks like the following. (If you don't want to type all of this code, you can copy it from the completed application in the Chapter6 folder.)

```
1 using System;
2 using System.Collections.Generic;
3 using System.ComponentModel;
4 using System.Data;
5 using System.Drawing;
6 using System.Text;
7 using System.Windows.Forms;
8 using System.Reflection;
9
10 namespace MyOwnBrowser
11 {
12     public partial class Splash : Form
13     {
14         public Splash()
15         {
16             InitializeComponent();
```

```
17          this.lblApplicationTitle.Text = AssemblyTitle;
18          this.lblCopyright.Text = AssemblyCopyright;
19          this.lblVersion.Text = "Version: " + AssemblyVersion;
20      }
21
22      #region Assembly Attribute Accessors
23
24      public string AssemblyTitle
25      {
26          get
27          {
28              // Get all Title attributes on this assembly
29              object[] attributes = Assembly.GetExecutingAssembly().GetCustomAttributes(
30                  typeof(AssemblyTitleAttribute), false);
31              // If there is at least one Title attribute
32              if (attributes.Length > 0)
33              {
34                  // Select the first one
35                  AssemblyTitleAttribute titleAttribute = (AssemblyTitleAttribute)attributes[0];
36                  // If it is not an empty string, return it
37                  if (titleAttribute.Title != "")
38                      return titleAttribute.Title;
39              }
40              // If there was no Title attribute, or if the Title attribute was the empty string, return the .exe name
41              return System.IO.Path.GetFileNameWithoutExtension(Assembly.GetExecutingAssembly().CodeBase);
42          }
43      }
44
45      public string AssemblyVersion
46      {
47          get
48          {
49              return Assembly.GetExecutingAssembly().GetName().Version.ToString();
50          }
51      }
52
53      public string AssemblyDescription
54      {
55          get
56          {
57              // Get all Description attributes on this assembly
```

```
58          object[] attributes = Assembly.GetExecutingAssembly().GetCustomAttributes(
59              typeof(AssemblyDescriptionAttribute), false);
60          // If there aren't any Description attributes, return an empty string
61          if (attributes.Length == 0)
62              return "";
63          // If there is a Description attribute, return its value
64          return ((AssemblyDescriptionAttribute)attributes[0]).Description;
65      }
66  }
67
68  public string AssemblyProduct
69  {
70      get
71      {
72          // Get all Product attributes on this assembly
73          object[] attributes = Assembly.GetExecutingAssembly().GetCustomAttributes(
74              typeof(AssemblyProductAttribute), false);
75          // If there aren't any Product attributes, return an empty string
76          if (attributes.Length == 0)
77              return "";
78          // If there is a Product attribute, return its value
79          return ((AssemblyProductAttribute)attributes[0]).Product;
80      }
81  }
82
83  public string AssemblyCopyright
84  {
85      get
86      {
87          // Get all Copyright attributes on this assembly
88          object[] attributes = Assembly.GetExecutingAssembly().GetCustomAttributes(
89              typeof(AssemblyCopyrightAttribute), false);
90          // If there aren't any Copyright attributes, return an empty string
91          if (attributes.Length == 0)
92              return "";
93          // If there is a Copyright attribute, return its value
94          return ((AssemblyCopyrightAttribute)attributes[0]).Copyright;
95      }
96  }
97
98  public string AssemblyCompany
99  {
```

```
100              get
101              {
102                  // Get all Company attributes on this assembly
103                  object[] attributes = Assembly.GetExecutingAssembly().GetCustomAttributes(
104                      typeof(AssemblyCompanyAttribute), false);
105                  // If there aren't any Company attributes, return an empty string
106                  if (attributes.Length == 0)
107                      return "";
108                  // If there is a Company attribute, return its value
109                  return ((AssemblyCompanyAttribute)attributes[0]).
110                      Company;
111              }
112          }
113          #endregion
114      }
115  }
```

7 Save the application (Ctrl+Shift+S saves all files and Ctrl+S saves the current
file) and press F5 to run it. Look at Figure 6-6 to see the splash screen in action
with the dynamic information collected from the Project Designer Application pane.

Figure 6-6
The splash screen in action

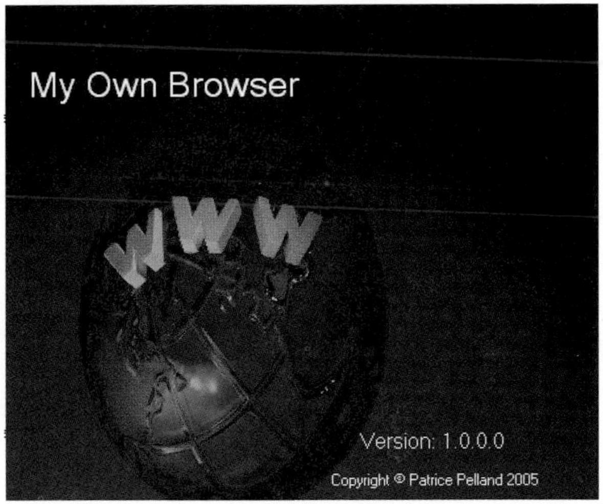

Interacting Through Dialog Boxes

The dialog boxes you create help the user interact with the software. They are additional
forms that you add to your application. In this section, you'll add two dialog boxes to your
Web browser: an About box and a Navigate dialog box.

Adding an About Box Dialog

The first dialog box you'll add is an About box, which exists in most Windows applications.
This dialog box essentially contains the same information as the splash screen, but sometimes contains more legal, system, and version information. You'll also prepare the application for a transformation into a more feature-rich Internet browser.

TO ADD AN ABOUT BOX DIALOG

1 On the Browser form, delete the **txtURL** and the **btnGo** controls. Delete the **btnGo_Click** event handler by removing its signature and content from the Browser.cs file.

2 On the Browser form, select the **Web Browser** control, and using the smart tag, select **Dock In Parent Container**.

3 As you did for the splash screen, add a new item to your project, but this time when presented with the templates, choose the **About Box** template and name it **AboutBox.cs**.

Similar to the splash screen, the About box will be populated with information from the project settings from the Project Designer window. At this point, if you run the application, there is no link between your About box and the rest of your browser, so it won't show up anywhere. Usually, the About box shows up when you request it from the Help menu, so you'll add this missing link now.

TO LINK THE ABOUT BOX TO THE HELP MENU

1 Select the **Browser.cs [Design]*** tab to return to the Browser Form Design view. Drag a **MenuStrip** control from the toolbox onto the design surface to add a Menu Strip control to the Browser form. An empty menu appears on the form and a component appears in the component tray. Name it **msBrowser**.

2 To add the Help menu, select the menu strip on the form, click the smart tag, and then select **Insert Standard Items**. You'll get a familiar Windows application menu strip and its menu choices with their submenus, icons, and keyboard shortcuts.

3 Delete all menu choices *except* the Help menu and the About. . . menu choices under the Help menu. To perform this clean-up, select any menu choice, then right-click to bring up the contextual menu and select **Delete** to remove it. Also remove the menu separators (that is, the lines separating menu choices).

4 To wire the new About box form with the About. . . menu choice, double-click the **About. . .** menu choice to get to the AboutToolStripMenuItem_Click event handler.

5 Add the following line of code to the Browser.cs file just above the browser constructor, i.e., public Browser(). Adding this line of code will let you exchange data with this form if needed.

```
AboutBox myAboutBox = new AboutBox();
```

Then add the following code to the AboutToolStripMenuItem_Click event handler.:

```
myAboutBox.ShowDialog();
```

6 Save the application and then run it. Select **About. . .** from the Help menu. The screen should resemble Figure 6-7. The ShowDialog() method brings up the form in the middle of the executing application, and nothing else can happen until you click one of its buttons or the red **X** to close the dialog box. In this case, it has only the OK button.

NOTE

I modified the Assembly Information fields in the Project Designer to come up with the information displayed in the About box. You can do the same. You simply add or modify the content in the Description, Company, Product, and Copyright fields.

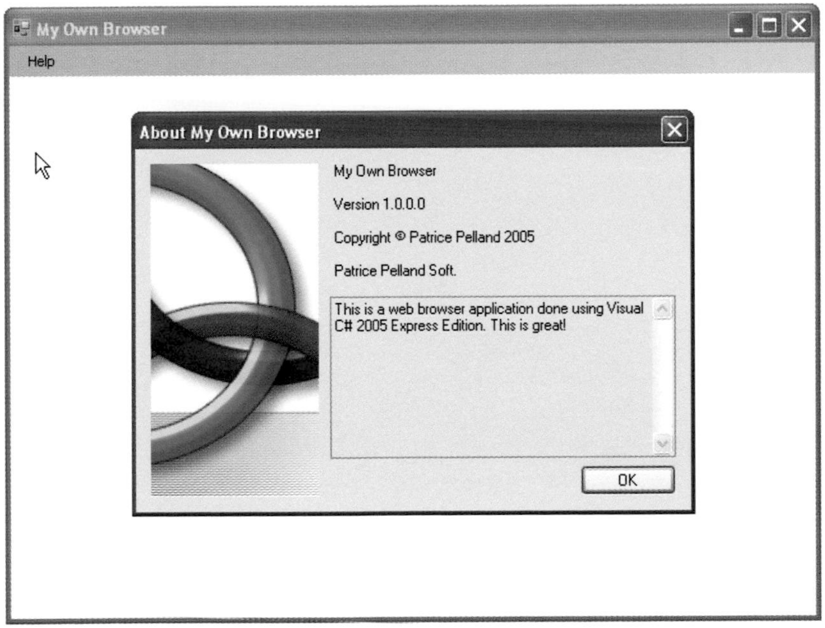

Figure 6-7
About box dialog showing up in your newly refined browser application

You're probably wondering why the application worked when you clicked the OK button even though you didn't write any code to handle this event. This is an example of the productivity gains you'll get when using templates. The template includes the code to handle the click button event. Review the source code for the dialog box by right-clicking the AboutBox.cs filename in the Solution Explorer and selecting View Code.

Now that you've added the About box dialog, it should be easy to add another that will allow your users to navigate to Web pages.

Adding a Navigate Dialog Box

You saw earlier that deleting the button and the address controls removed the ability to navigate to a Web page. This, of course, is not useful for a Web browser. Now you'll add a dialog box that will give your user another way to navigate to Web pages.

TO ADD A NAVIGATE DIALOG BOX

1. As you've done for the About box and the splash screen, add another new item to your project. Using the templates, select a **Windows Form** template and name it **Navigate.cs**.

2. You'll now add the components for the Navigate form. These are pretty generic to any dialog box form that you would want to create.

3. First add a table layout panel control with one row and two columns. Use the smart tag to adjust the rows and columns.

4. Add one button in each column of that table layout panel control. Name your buttons btnOk and btnCancel, respectively.

5. Using the following table, set the various properties on the form, table layout panel, and buttons.

Control Name	Control Type	Property	Value
Navigate	Form	AcceptButton	btnOk
Navigate	Form	CancelButton	btnCancel
Navigate	Form	FormBorderStyle	FixedDialog
Navigate	Form	MaximizeBox	False
Navigate	Form	MinimizeBox	False
Navigate	Form	ShowIcon	False
Navigate	Form	ShownInTaskbar	False
Navigate	Form	Size:Width Size:Height	450 150
Navigate	Form	StartPosition	CenterParent
tableLayoutPanel1	TableLayoutPanel	Anchor	Bottom,Right
btnOk	button	Text	Ok
btnOk	button	DialogResult	Ok
btnCancel	button	Text	Cancel
btnCancel	button	DialogResult	Cancel

That's it; those are the properties that you will find in any dialog box.

 Add a label and a text box:

■ Name the label **lblInfoUrl**, set the Text property to "Type an Internet address and My Own Browser will open it for you."
■ Name the text box **txtUrl**, set the AutoCompleteMode property to **SuggestAppend,** and set the AutoCompleteSource property to **AllUrl**. Next set the Modifiers property to **Public**.

 Size and position the controls so that the Navigate form looks like the one in Figure 6-8.

Figure 6-8
Creating a new instance of the form Navigate

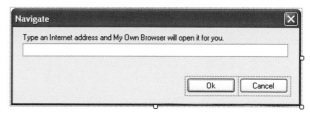

You've set some of the autocomplete properties of the text box to behave the same way they do in Microsoft Internet Explorer. This means that the text box will suggest and append URLs based on the letters the user types in. You'll now wire this form to the application using a new menu called Navigate.

TO WIRE THE FORM TO THE APPLICATION USING THE NAVIGATE MENU

1 Return to the Browser form in Design view and look at the top of the Browser form. You already have a menu strip with the Help menu; now add a new menu to your menu strip by clicking beside the Help menu and typing **&Navigate**. The & in front of the *N* will create an underscored N so that the user can press the keystroke combination Alt+N to fire the click event on the Navigate menu.

2 Once it's created, you'll see that the Navigate menu shows up to the right of the Help menu. To move a menu choice, simply select it and drag it where you want. In this case, select it and drop it to the left of the Help menu.

3 Before adding the code for the event itself, you need to add an important line of code. Remember that in C# everything is an object, and if you want to manipulate another form and exchange data between the two forms, you first need to create an object of that type that is visible to your main form (Browser form)—in this case, an object of type Navigate. Create an instance of the Navigate form outside the source code of any event handler by writing the following line of code in Browser.cs:

```
Navigate navigateWindow = new Navigate();
```

Look at Figure 6-9 to see where to insert it.

```
namespace MyOwnBrowser
{
    public partial class Browser : Form
    {
        // The about box and navigate form
        AboutBox myAboutBox = new AboutBox();
        Navigate navigateWindow = new Navigate();
        Splash splashScreen = new Splash();

        public Browser()
        {
            InitializeComponent();
            splashScreen.Show();
            Application.DoEvents();
        }
}
```

Figure 6-9
Creating a new instance of the form Navigate

Now that you have an instance of the Navigate form class, you can write code to exchange data back and forth with the browser form. And that's exactly what will happen. When the Navigate form displays and the user clicks the OK button with a URL in the text box, the browser control will navigate to the specified URL. Also note that the URL textbox will clear after navigating to the URL to make sure it's empty the next time the user accesses it.

4 On the browser form, double-click the **Navigate** menu to add the navigateToolStripMenuItem_Click event handler.

5 Add the following code to the NavigateToolStripMenuItem_Click event handler.

```
If (navigateWindow.ShowDialog() == DialogResult.OK)
{
    this.myBrowser.Navigate(navigateWindow.txtUrl.Text);
}
navigateWindow.txtUrl.Text="";
```

6 Build and execute the application by pressing **F5**. The form should resemble Figure 6-10 when the user selects the Navigate menu.

7 Now, test the application with all the modifications you've made. Verify every new aspect:

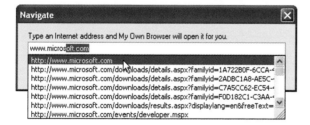

Figure 6-10
Execution of My Own Browser using the navigate form with autocomplete

■ Does pressing Alt+N take you to the Navigate form?

■ Can you hit Cancel with/without content?

■ Can you navigate to a good URL/bad URL?

■ Is the text box empty when you come back to the Navigate form (that is, after you've performed all other steps above and pressed Alt+N to come back)?

NOTE

If you don't get IntelliSense when typing navigateWindow.txtUrl.Text, be sure you set the Modifiers property on txtUrl to Public as described earlier.

MORE INFO

It's important for you to start learning how to test your own code by doing what's known as black box **testing**. At a high level, this consists of testing what the user can do and what is presented to the user. This means that you need to test every little detail in the UI as well as the situations the UI offers to the user. When you perform a task like this, I suggest you create a spreadsheet that contains a matrix of all test cases. Then fill it in as you test. This will give you a visual representation of all tests and features. You're now doing this manually because your application is small in scope, but you'll quickly realize that with a bigger application or an application you might sell, you'll need some sort of automated mechanism to make sure that the tests are all executed and you're not forgetting any. You'll then require a UI testing tool, and in most situations you'll need to build your own tools. But that's out of context for this book; I just wanted to emphasize the importance of testing your application.

In this section, you'll continue to add functionality to your browser using components that you might have seen in other Microsoft applications. You'll add appealing and professional touches to your application in a fast and easy way.

Adding a Tool Strip Container and Some Tools

A tool strip container is a new control that ships with this release of Visual C# 2005, and it allows you to let your users customize the application you wrote in a way similar to how they customize the toolbars in Microsoft Office Outlook® or Word. The tool strip container has five panels, one on each side of the screen, and a content panel in the middle. You can have all of them on the screen enabled at one time or choose them selectively at design time. You can also control them with source code. You can put a tool strip and a menu strip in a tool strip container at design time, and at run time your users have the opportunity to arrange their workspace the way they like. The tool strip container gives your application the same look and feel as Outlook (see Figure 6-11). For instance, I was able to put two tool strips on the left of my screen. This means those tool strips are embedded in the tool strip container left panel. But I could easily move any visible toolbar back to the top, the right, or to the bottom. With a tool strip container, you give your users control of the layout of their tool strips and menu strip, which is a great feature to have.

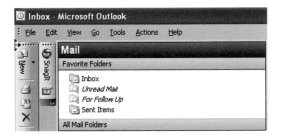

Figure 6-11
Tool Strip Container example in Outlook

TO ADD A TOOL STRIP CONTAINER

1 Drag a tool strip container onto the Browser Form design surface.

2 Rename toolstripcontainer1 to **mainFormToolStripContainer**.

3 Use the smart tag from the tool strip container to select **Dock Fill In Form**.

Wait a minute . . . where is the Web Browser control? Don't worry, it didn't disappear. The control's z-order has changed. The Web Browser control is visually under the tool strip container, and its parent is not the tool strip container but the browser form.

The Document Outline view is a valuable tool that can help you solve this problem and save you a lot of time. For those of you familiar with previous versions of Visual Studio, this view existed before for HTML and ASPX documents only. With Visual Studio 2005, it has been extended to Windows Forms. To have the Document Outline view in your IDE, simply go to View/Other Windows/Document Outline or press Ctrl+Alt+T. This view lets you manage all controls on your form. It shows how the controls are arranged on the screen and which control(s) belongs to another control. For instance, right now you cannot see the Web Browser control, but if you enable Document Outline view, you'll see that the Web Browser control is at the same level as the newly added tool strip container (see Figure 6-12). To rearrange the order and change how the controls are displayed, follow the next steps.

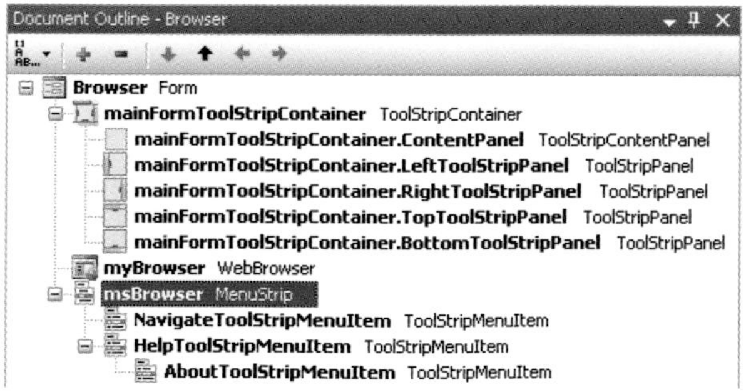

> **NOTE**
>
> The z-order is the control's position relative to the other windows or controls on the screen; think of it as the third dimension or being on top of or beneath other controls.

Figure 6-12
The Document Outline window for the My Own Browser project

TO REARRANGE THE ORDER OF CONTROLS

1 In the Document Outline window, select the Web Browser control called **myBrowser** and drag it just below the tool strip container content panel called mainFormToolStripContainer.ContentPanel. (When you drag the Web Browser control, a black line indicates where the control will be dropped if you release the mouse button.)

2 Now display the form again. The Web Browser control is in the middle of the form. But as you can see, the Menu Strip control is not in the tool strip container. Repeat step 1 for the Menu Strip control, but instead of dropping it in the content panel, drop it in the top panel of the tool strip container (mainForm-ToolStripContainer.TopToolStripPanel).

MORE INFO

If your application design demands it and if you want to constrain the user in any way, you can also hide panels and prevent users from docking any tool strip or menu strip in a panel. Let's use the current application as an example. If you want to do this, select the tool strip container control named mainFormToolStrip-Container. You can either select it from the Properties window or the Document Outline. Then modify the visible property of the panel you want to hide. For instance, if you would like to hide the bottom panel, set the BottomToolStripPanelVisible property to false.

Now the only thing missing from the new menu strip is a dotted grip like the one in the Outlook figure. Without this grip, a user is unable to select the menu strip at all; it is fixed in the top panel.

TO ADD A DOTTED GRIP TO THE MENU STRIP

1 From the Document Outline window, select the menu strip called **msBrowser**, go to the Properties window, and set the GripStyle property to **Visible**.

2 Run the application by pressing **F5**. Move the menu strip from one panel to the other. You now have an application as cool as Outlook.

Adding a Status Bar to Your Browser

Your application is becoming rich in features, but to get it closer to most Windows applications, you need a status bar to report information about what's going on at any moment during the execution. To accomplish this in your browser, you'll add a Status Strip control and, within this status strip, you'll add a progress bar.

TO ADD A STATUS STRIP CONTROL AND A PROGRESS BAR

 On the tool strip container, click the bottom panel handle to expand it. (Note that the glyph arrow direction reverses when you click it.) The tool strip container's bottom panel appears as a blue strip.

 Drag a Status Strip control to the tool strip container's bottom panel. After you drop it onto the bottom panel, it should expand to cover the whole panel surface.

 Rename the Status Strip control from StatusStrip1 to **sscBrowser**.

 Change the **RenderMode** property of the Status Strip control to **Professional**. This will allow the application to present a status bar to the user using the operating system colors. For instance, if the themes in Windows XP are blue, then the status bar will be blue as well.

5 Add a Label control to the status strip by clicking on the down arrow of the Status Strip Add control button and then selecting StatusLabel.

6 Rename the control from ToolStripStatusLabel1 to **lblApplicationStatus**.

7 Add a progress bar to your status strip just as you did for the Label control.

8 Rename the control from ToolStripProgressBar1 to **pbStatus**.

When the status strip and the progress bar are displayed to the user, they usually bring important information about events that are occurring during execution. Think of it like a letter arriving at your house. You hear the mail truck and realize the mail has arrived. This is the event that is raised. You open your mailbox and the envelope to learn that it's your credit card bill. The bill is one of the pieces of information that comes along with the event. To analagously populate the controls in the status strip, you'll have to configure your application to extract this information from all controls (i.e., envelope) when events are happening (i.e., mail truck arriving). And you'll do that programmatically by writing code in event handlers.

TO POPULATE CONTROLS WITH INFORMATION

 On the design surface, select the **My Own Browser** form by clicking its title bar. Look in the Properties window to make sure the Browser form is selected and click the **Event** button (yellow lightning) in the Properties window. Find the **Load** event and double-click it to bring up the default event handler: Browser_Load. (The form Load event is raised just before the form displays to the user. So, it's a good place to change properties that affect the visual aspects of a form.)

2 Add the following code to the event (Browser_Load) to modify the status message label (lblApplicationStatus) in the status strip.

```
this.lblApplicationStatus.Text = "Ready";
```

You'll now attach some code to the progress bar and modify the label on the status strip to indicate where the user is navigating to. When the page is fully downloaded to the client PC, you'll reset the label content in the status strip to the word "Ready". You'll also modify the browser title to include the URL where the user navigated to. Whenever the OK button is clicked in the Navigate form, the Web Browser control named myBrowser raises the Navigating event. That's where you'll start writing code.

3 Select the **myBrowser** control and then go to the Events list in the Properties window. Double-click the **Navigating** event and enter the following code:

```
//Modifying the label in the status strip with the URL entered by the user
this.lblApplicationStatus.Text = "Navigating to: " + e.Url.Host.ToString();
```

Once the user enters a URL and the document is being downloaded the progress bar will need to update. Periodically, the Web Browser control raises the ProgressChanged event. That's where you'll update the progress bar in the status strip.

4 Make sure you have the **myBrowser** control selected in the Properties window and then go to the Event list. Double-click the **ProgressChanged** event. Enter the following code (*look at the comments to understand the source code*):

```
/* The CurrentProgress variable from the raised event
 * gives you the current number of bytes already downloaded
 * while the MaximumProgress is the total number of bytes
 * to be downloaded */
if (e.CurrentProgress < e.MaximumProgress)
{
    // Check if the current progress in the progress bar
    // is >= to the maximum if yes reset it with the min
```

    Microsoft Visual C# 2005 Express Edition: Build a Program Now!

```
    if (pbStatus.Value >= pbStatus.Maximum)
        pbStatus.Value = pbStatus.Minimum;
    else
      // Just increase the progress bar
      pbStatus.PerformStep();
}
else
      // when the document is fully downloaded
      // reset the progress bar to the min (0)
      pbStatus.Value = pbStatus.Minimum;
```

When the user's document is fully downloaded, the browser will raise the DocumentCompleted event. When this event is raised, the application title needs to be updated to the current URL and the application status label in the status strip will need to change to the "Ready" state.

 In the myBrowser event list, double-click the **DocumentCompleted** event. Then add the following code to it:

```
// The about box is retrieving this information in a nice clean method so let's reuse it
// If you don't have an about box you can just create this method using the code from
// the about box. We don't need to validate if the title is empty the method is doing it.
// if it's empty it will use the .exe name
this.Text = myAboutBox.AssemblyTitle + " - " + e.Url.Host.ToString();

this.lblApplicationStatus.Text = "Ready";
```

As you can see, in this code you've just reused similar source code used in the About box and the splash screen dialog sections.

 Save all files and run the application now. You should have a working progress bar, and all new information should be displayed: modified title window and status strip label.

Personalize Your Application with Windows Icons

In this section, you'll continue to personalize your browser by adding some icons that come from known Microsoft applications. After this section, you'll have a working Internet browser with most navigational features fully implemented—maybe not with all the functionality of Internet Explorer, but you should be proud of yourself. Look at Figure 6-13 to see what you will have accomplished after this section.

Figure 6-13
Your browser at the end of this section

As you can see, you'll implement a nice list of features in this section. Here's what you're going to accomplish:

- Link all buttons to browser functionalities
- Manage the Go button and the Enter key on the address text box in the tool strip
- Change the browser form icon to the same globe icon that you've set for the application icon on the hard drive

First, you'll add two new tool strips and all their buttons. You'll also add the code to handle all those new buttons. Each time you add a button, rename it before writing the event handling code. You should do this to make sure you have the correct variable names. It's just a matter of consistency and good practice.

MORE INFO

I suggest that you rename your buttons immediately when you add them to make sure the event handling code has the correct name. It is possible to rename the buttons later, but it's more tedious because you have to perform extra steps, which takes more time. It's just easier, cleaner, and faster to do it as soon as you create the controls.

TO ADD TOOL STRIPS AND BUTTONS TO YOUR BROWSER

1 Start by adding two new tool strips to the browser's form right below the menu strip. Name the first one **tsIcons** and the other one **tsNavigation**. Use the **Document Outline** to make sure they are under the top panel of the tool strip container.

NOTE

If you see only events in the Properties window, click the Properties button at the top of the Properties window.

2 Select the **tsIcons** tool strip. Then, using the **Add Tool Strip Item** drop-down list, add six buttons, and name them **tsbBack**, **tsbForward**, **tsbStop**, **tsbRefresh**, **tsbHome**, and **tsbSearch**.

3 To modify the image for each button, change the Image property of the Tool Strip Button control by clicking the Ellipse button (...) to browse on your hard disk for the icon. Or you can right-click the icon in the tool strip and select **Set Image. . .** You'll then have the same dialog to import the image files from your hard disk. The images for these buttons are all located in the Images folder under Chapter 6 where you've installed your companion content.

4 For the tsbSearch button, right-click the button, select **Display Style**, and set it to **ImageAndText**.

5 Modify the Text property of the tsbSearch button to **Search**.

6 For each button, add the respective functionality. (You'll see how easy it is to add the desired functionality because the Web Browser control was well designed.) Double-click one button after the other and you'll get to the Click event for each one. In each Click event, add the following code. See below for the corresponding button name and event source code.

tsbBack	`myBrowser.GoBack();`
tsbForward	`myBrowser.GoForward();`
tsbStop	`myBrowser.Stop();` `lblApplicationStatus.Text = "Ready";`
tsbRefresh	`myBrowser.Refresh();` `lblApplicationStatus.Text = "Ready";`
tsbHome	`myBrowser.GoHome();`
tsbSearch	`myBrowser.GoSearch();`

7 Run the application and determine if the buttons are working. Everything should be working except for the navigation buttons.

You'll now modify the behavior of the two navigation buttons in the tsbIcons tool strip to make sure they're enabled only when they should be—that is, when there are pages in the browser's history. When you start the application, the buttons should be disabled. The best place to put this code is the Load event of the Browser form. It's a good place because the event will happen right before the user actually sees the form. Next, you need to think about where you should put the code that will enable and disable the two navigation buttons. The ideal place for the validation code is where the navigation occurs because you know at that moment the browser will navigate to a new URL.

TO MODIFY THE BEHAVIOR OF NAVIGATION BUTTONS

 In Browser.cs, add the ModifyNavigationButtons method and modify Browser_Load and myBrowser_DocumentCompleted to look like the following:

```
private void Browser_Load(object sender, EventArgs e)
{
    this.tsbBack.Enabled = false;
    this.tsbForward.Enabled = false;
    this.lblApplicationStatus.Text = "Ready";
}


private void ModifyNavigationButtons()
{
    // Add the code to enable or disable whenever there are URLs
    // in the browsing session's history
    if (myBrowser.CanGoBack)
        tsbBack.Enabled = true;
    else
        tsbBack.Enabled = false;

    if (myBrowser.CanGoForward)
        tsbForward.Enabled = true;
    else
        tsbForward.Enabled = false;
}

private void myBrowser_DocumentCompleted(object sender, WebBrowserDocumentCompletedEventArgs e)
{
    // The about box is retrieving this information in a nice clean method so let's reuse it
    // If you don't have an about box you can just create this method using the code from
    // the about box. We don't need to validate if the title is empty the method is doing it.
    // if it's empty it will use the .exe name
    this.Text = myAboutBox.AssemblyTitle + " - " + e.Url.Host.ToString();

    ModifyNavigationButtons();
    this.lblApplicationStatus.Text = "Ready";
}
```

2 Run the application to determine if the buttons behave correctly now.

Next, you'll add the names and controls to the tsNavigation tool strip as you did for the previous tool strip. However, this time instead of just adding some tool strip buttons, you'll add different types of controls.

For instance, you'll modify the browser to navigate to the URL specified in the text box when the user clicks Enter. You'll also modify the behavior of clicking the Go button to make sure it does the same thing.

TO ADD NEW CONTROLS TO THE TSNAVIGATION TOOL STRIP

1 Use the **Add Tool Strip Item** drop-down list on the tsNavigation toolstrip and add the following controls to the toolstrip: Label, TextBox, and Button. Name the controls **tslblAddress**, **tstbUrl**, and **tsbGo**.

2 Use the table below and set the properties of the controls.

Control name	Type	Properties	Value
tslblAddress	ToolStripLabel	Text	
tstbUrl	ToolStripTextBox	Size:Width	350
tsbGo	ToolStripButton	Text	Go
tsbGo	ToolStripButton	DisplayStyle	ImageAndText
tsbGo	ToolStripButton	Image	Go.bmp

The tsNavigation tool strip is not a dialog box with an OK button or a Cancel button, so you cannot use the AcceptButton or CancelButton properties. Therefore, you need to capture another event that will be triggered whenever the user presses Enter.

The KeyUp event is triggered whenever a key is released by the user. For instance, whenever the user types in a letter, he presses down the key of the desired letter. When he releases the key, the KeyUp event is triggered. The code you'll add in the next exercise will determine if the key the user just released was the Enter key. If it was, a new method called NavigateToUrl will accept a string representing the URL as a parameter and navigate to the URL.

You'll use the same method for the Go button. When you develop an application, you never want to duplicate two pieces of code that differ only by a literal. You always want to re-use the source code whenever possible. The way to do that is to create methods that are generic enough to be used by more than one component. Since the NavigateToUrl method has only one line of code, you might be tempted to say that if it's almost the same one line of code, why use a method? The answer is simply that in the future you might have to add some validation. If that one line of code is repeated throughout the source code, you'll have to update it in multiple places. However, if there is only one place where you have to modify the code, your solution is less prone to errors and a lot less tedious.

TO CONFIGURE THE BROWSER TO NAVIGATE TO THE URL

1 Select the **tstbUrl Tool Strip** text box.

2 In the event list in the Properties window for tstbUrl, double-click the **KeyUp** event. Below is the code to determine if the user pressed and released the Enter key and also the method NavigateToUrl that will enable you to use the same code in more than one place. Add this code to tstbUrl_KeyUp and add the NavigateToUrl method.

NOTE

By the way, there's more than one event that is being triggered by pressing the Enter key, but the one that you'll trap is the KeyUp event.

```
private void tstbUrl_KeyUp(object sender, KeyEventArgs e)
{
    // e is of type KeyEventArgs and contains all the
    // information that triggered the event. The KeyCode
    // is one those information.
    if (e.KeyCode = Keys.Enter)
        this.NavigateToUrl(tstbUrl.Text);
}

private void NavigateToUrl()
{
    myBrowser.Navigate(Url);
}
```

3 Double-click the **Go** button on the tsNavigation tool strip and add the following code to the tsbGo_Click event procedure. (Notice that this is the NavigateToUrl method.)

```
private void tsbGo_Click(object sender, EventArgs e)
{
    this.NavigateToUrl(tstbUrl.Text);
}
```

You can now modify another piece of code, the Navigate menu click event. You simply have to modify the code so that it calls the NavigateToUrl method, as shown below:

```
private void navigateToolStripMenuItem_Click(object sender, EventArgs e)
{
    if (navigateWindow.ShowDialog() == DialogResult.OK)
    {
        this.NavigateToUrl(navigateWindow.txtUrl.Text);
    }
    navigateWindow.txtUrl.Text = "";
}
```

Finally, you'll modify the Browser Form icon so that the user sees a globe when the browser is running or minimized.

TO MODIFY THE BROWSER FORM ICON

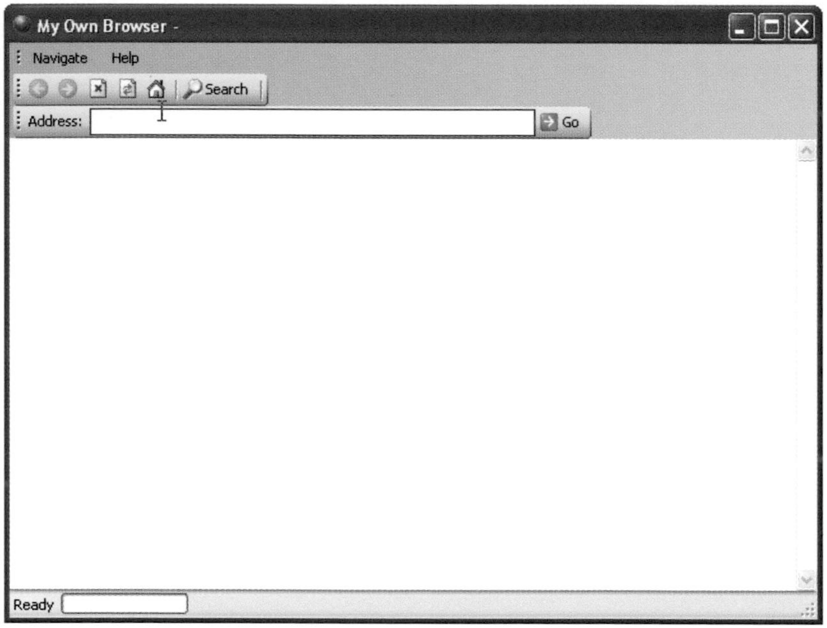

1 Select the **Browser** form and then look for Icon Property in the Properties window. If you only see events in the Properties window, click the Properties button at the top of the Properties window. Click the **Ellipsis** button (...) to browse for the **globe.ico** in the Chapter 6 directory in the Images folder under the Chapter 6 directory.

The result of your hard labor is the finished product—the My Own Browser application, as shown in Figure 6-14.

Figure 6-14
Finished product—the My Own Browser application

In Summary...

In this chapter, you took a simple application and upgraded it to create a professional-looking application with many nice features for your users. You learned to add a splash screen to your application and to work with dialog boxes. You created an About box and a Navigate dialog box to allow your user to navigate to a URL; you added an autocomplete feature to your text boxes and the autosuggest/append feature using the browser's URLs history. You then added tool strips, progress bars, and icons from Windows. You dynamically managed controls, and you learned a lot about new events and how to handle them using event arguments.

In the next chapter, you'll learn techniques to use when things don't go too well; that is, learn the art of debugging code. You'll also learn about the Edit and Continue feature, the new data visualizers, tips and tricks, and much more.

Chapter 7

Fixing the Broken Blocks

As you'll discover more and more, when you develop an application, you rarely succeed on your first attempt. Most of the time (and especially when you start developing applications), the process goes like this: brainstorm on paper, look at the users' needs (often yours), perform some analysis, proto-type, design, develop, test, fix bugs, test the product again, and finally release it to people. This is a high-level view of the process; it can be much more complicated or simplified. It all depends on the complexity of the proj-ect, the number of people involved, and so on. One thing is certain: you always need to debug your applications, and Microsoft$^{®}$ Visual C#$^{®}$ 2005 provides many tools to help you fix your bugs faster.

To learn the tools and techniques to debug your applications, I've created a sample application that you'll use for this chapter. If you installed the companion content at the default location, it should be at the following location on your hard drive: My Documents\Microsoft Press\VCS 2005 Express\Chapter7\. Look for a folder named DebuggerStart under the Chapter 7 folder. Double-click the DebuggerStart.sln solution.

This solution contains new items that you have not seen yet, with the first one being a solution with more than one project. This is a common practice while developing applications. In this case, the solution (named **DebuggerStart**) contains two projects: a Microsoft Windows® Forms application named **Debugger** and a managed library named **MyLibrary** (managed **DLL**). The acronym DLL stands for Dynamic Link Library. A DLL is a library of functions that are called dynamically and as needed by an application. A DLL doesn't contain a main entry point and cannot be executed by itself. Also, a DLL can be used by multiple applications at the same time.

The second new thing is that the project Debugger has a type of file that you haven't seen yet: a text file. You can have multiple different files in your projects, and a text file is not uncommon. In this case, the text file is used by one of the methods called by the debugger.exe application. The text file will be used by this application, so to have it in the output folder, you need to select it in the Solution Explorer and then change the Copy To Output Directory property to Copy If Newer.

Using a DLL in an Application

When you design an application, you usually have more than one component. In many cases, the components are new classes (types). It is good practice to have those types in a separate source code file instead of keeping them with the user interface code. Often, the classes are grouped in a single library or DLL.

When you want to use a type from a library, you need to make your application aware of all the types and methods contained in that library by adding a **reference** to it in the application.

Adding a Reference to Your Application

To add new references to your application, follow the steps here.

TO ADD A REFERENCE TO YOUR APPLICATION

1 Select the project where you want to add the reference; in this case, select **Debugger**.

2 Right-click the project name (i.e., Debugger) and then select **Add Reference...**. Look at Figure 7-1 to make sure you're at the right place.

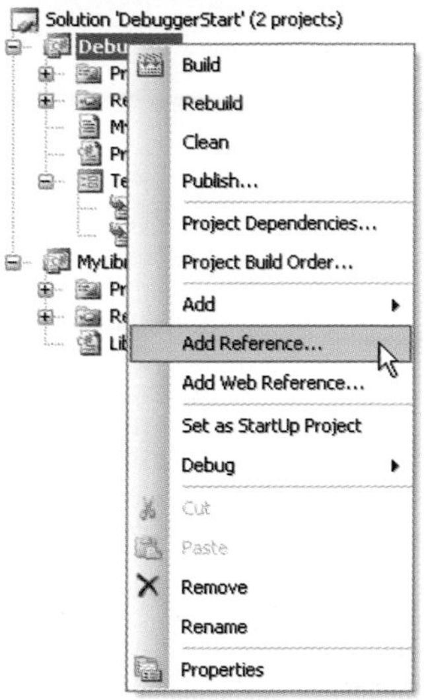

As you can see from the tabs on the dialog box that appears, the references can come from multiple sources.

3 Select the **Projects** tab and then select the **MyLibrary** project, which contains the managed DLL. Press **OK** to add the reference to your project.

Because the DLL is in the same solution and you just added a reference of that DLL to your application, Microsoft Visual Studio® now knows there is a dependency between the two and will always build the DLL first so that your application builds the executable with the most up-to-date DLL possible.

You can verify that the reference has been inserted using the following technique.

In the Solution Explorer expand the References node and look for the MyLibrary reference. Click on it to see the details in the Property window. By default, when you create a Windows Form project plenty of references are automatically added to the project during its creation. Figure 7-2 shows the references and Property window for information pertinent to MyLibrary.

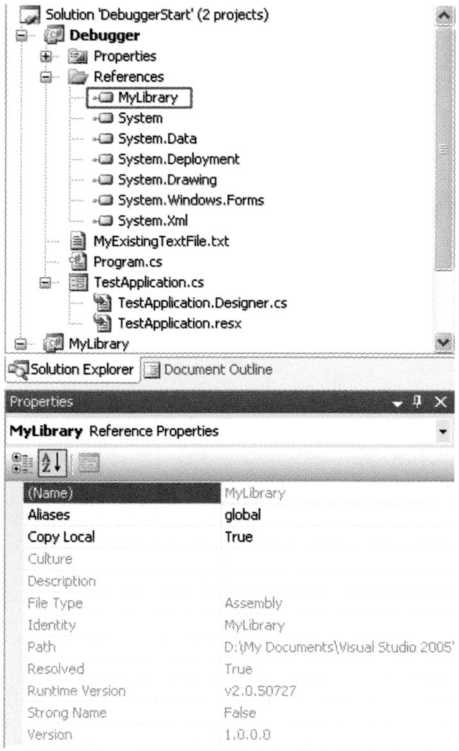

Figure 7-2
All references for this project.

Figure 7-1
Add Reference. . . menu choice from the Debugger project

When you're done adding the reference, your application can create instances of the new types that are built in the DLL and use them appropriately. The build process (compiler and linker) will now accept the use of those new types, but for Visual Studio to have those new types available via IntelliSense® and for the compiler to know about those new types, one more step is required. You might already have seen the first line of code in the TestApplication.cs file. The line reads *using MyLibrary;*.

You create a *using* directive to use the types in a namespace without having to specify the fully qualified namespace name. For instance, Console.WriteLine() comes from the System namespace; by adding it on top, you don't have to type System.Console.WriteLine(). It saves time and it's easier to read. By adding this line of code, you're telling Visual Studio to look into that assembly for the metadata that will enable IntelliSense to be populated with the public/protected elements. After adding this line, you'll have access to those items whenever you have an instance of one of the types built in the library.

NOTE

A *using* directive does not give you access to any namespaces that are nested in the namespace you specify.

Breakpoints, Locals, Edit and Continue, and Visualizers

There is no better way to dive into this subject than by looking at and going through the code. If the TestApplication.cs source code file is not already open, open it by right-clicking on the TestApplication.cs file and selecting View Code. You should see red dots on the left-hand side of the screen; those red dots are **breakpoints**. Figure 7-3 shows the source code and the breakpoints.

TIP

If the breakpoints don't appear, you can add them by clicking in the left margin.

```
private void button1_Click(object sender, EventArgs e)
{
   Library myObjectLibrary = new Library();
   string myString = "Helloworld";

   MessageBox.Show(myObjectLibrary.Divide(5, 3).ToString());
   MessageBox.Show(myObjectLibrary.Divide(3, 3).ToString());

    MessageBox.Show(myObjectLibrary.ReadFile("MyExistingTextFile.txt"));
    myObjectLibrary.ManipulateStrings(ref myString, 20);
    MessageBox.Show(myString);
    myObjectLibrary.ManipulateStrings(ref myString, 1);
    MessageBox.Show(myString);
    MessageBox.Show(myObjectLibrary.Divide(6, 4).ToString());
    MessageBox.Show(myObjectLibrary.ReadFile("MyNotExistingTextFile.txt"));
}
```

Figure 7-3
Source code and breakpoints from the TestApplication Windows form

When the debugger encounters a breakpoint, it stops executing the application. In this source code, one of the breakpoints is on the call to the *MessageBox.Show(myString);*. There is another breakpoint in the Library.cs in the first line of code of the Divide method. In the following procedure, you will execute the code and go through a debugging session.

To debug an application, you can do one of two things:

■ Press F5 or the Start Debugging button.

 The program will start executing normally. If there is a breakpoint in the source code, the execution will stop there. Otherwise, the program will continue to execute unless there is an unhandled exception, or error.

■ Alternatively, you can debug the application by stepping through the code line by line. To do this, press F11 or the Step Into button.

For now, you'll jump to the first breakpoint and execute the code in the sample program using the first technique.

TO BEGIN DEBUGGING AN APPLICATION

1 Press **F5** or the **Start Debugging** button.

2 You will see a button that says **Try Me!** Click it. The code should stop executing at the first breakpoint in the Divide method, and you should see what is shown in Figure 7-4. The yellow highlighted line means it is the next statement to be executed.

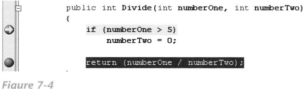

```
public int Divide(int numberOne, int numberTwo)
{
    if (numberOne > 5)
        numberTwo = 0;

    return (numberOne / numberTwo);
}
```

Figure 7-4
Execution stopped at the first breakpoint in the Divide method

You're now in debugging mode, and you have access to a plethora of tools and data elements about your application to help you understand what is happening when your application is executed. You can see the content of local variables, parameters, exception messages, the console window, and many more items you'll discover in the next few steps. All of that information is useful when an application is not behaving the way it should and you're trying to understand why. With all the information the debugger provides, you can try to uncover where the problem lies and see why you have a bug. You can also use the debugger for learning purposes as you are doing right now. The debugger is an excellent teacher when you're new to a technology, language construct, or when you're simply trying to understand a new element. It is also common to use the debugger to understand someone else's code. It is especially helpful when you need to make modifications to existing code.

You'll now look at the first series of data elements offered by the debugger while you're stepping through your code. At the bottom of the Visual Studio screen, you can see a series of tabs, which can include **Locals, Watch, Call Stack, Immediate Window, Output,** and **Error List**. If you don't see these tabs, you can open these windows by selecting them on the View and Debug menus. Most of these are not visible when in editing mode. You saw in Chapter 3 that the Error List is only there to show the results of the real-time compilation. While you're debugging, the Locals tab is usually on top and shows the current variables and object information, and beside it you'll see the Call Stack that displays all methods that have been called, enabling you to follow the execution of your application at any given point during the debugging. Look at Figure 7-5a and Figure 7-5b to see the two windows.

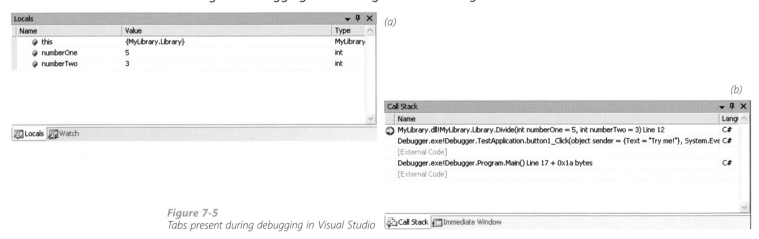

Figure 7-5
Tabs present during debugging in Visual Studio

In the Locals tab section, you can see three elements of data from your Divide method: this, numberOne, and numberTwo. Those are, in order, the instance of the current object and the two parameters. The debugger detects all elements that are in scope in that method and displays them in the Locals tab. The elements in scope are all the elements that are visible from where the instruction pointer is located. In this case, it could be either local variables or static variables. This means that throughout the execution of the Divide method, you'll be able to follow the values that those items will have. Now it's your turn to see this for yourself.

TO CONTINUE DEBUGGING THE APPLICATION

1 Press **F11** or the **Step Into** button to get to the division operation.

While debugging, you can always hover the mouse over program elements to get the information you otherwise find in the Locals tab. For instance, if you hover your mouse over the numberOne element, you'll see the same value that is shown in the Locals tab, as illustrated in Figure 7-6.

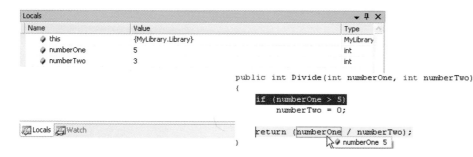

Figure 7-6
Getting the value of the numberOne local variable in two different ways

2 Execute the next line of code by pressing either **F11** or the **Step Into** button on the toolbar or in the Debug menu.

At this point, you can see the results of the division by selecting the operands in the return statement and hovering the mouse over the selection. Verify that it's 1. Now let's say it is a more complex operation and you would like to see the outcome of a change in the source code or a change in the content of a variable. Previously you would have to stop the debugging process, change the values, recompile, and see the outcome. But now there is a new feature in Visual C# 2005 that allows you to modify your code and verify immediately if the change you make solves the problem. This feature is called **Edit and Continue**. As its name implies, the Edit and Continue feature lets you edit an element in the application and continue the execution. In fact, not only can you do this, but you can also modify the next instruction to execute, change the value of a variable, and re-execute the instruction again. This is a huge time saver in some cases because you don't have to stop the execution, make the change, rebuild, and re-execute the new code. You can see the changes right away.

3 Go to the left-hand side, where the yellow arrow indicates the next instruction to be executed. When you hover your mouse over the yellow arrow, you should see a transparent arrow indicating that you can move the arrow. Click and hold the yellow arrow and slide it up and back over the *if* statement.

4 Change the value of numberOne to -5 by hovering your mouse over the variable, clicking on the number 5 in the tooltip that appears, and then modifying it to **-5**. You can also modify the values in the Locals tab at the bottom of the IDE. Then re-execute the instruction by pressing **F11** or clicking the **Step Into** button.

5 Step into the code until you see a message box with -1 for the first division. If you don't see the message box, you might need to switch to it on the Windows Taskbar. Click **OK** in the message box. Continue stepping into the code until you return to the Divide method with a new set of values and you're pointing at the first instruction in the method.

When you're back to the Divide method, you will not re-execute every instruction. Instead, you'll step out of the code using the Step Out function. Stepping out doesn't mean that you'll skip the execution; stepping out simply means that the debugger will execute all instructions of the current method and go back to the calling point. If you do it on a single instruction that is not part of a function source code, it will simply execute it. To see this in action, follow these steps.

TO STEP OUT OF THE CODE

1 In the Library.cs file, click the red dot in the first breakpoint of the Divide method. By clicking the red dot, you actually remove the breakpoint. The breakpoint should now be gone.

2 To disable the second breakpoint, you can use three different methods.

- The first one is simply to right-click the line of code that has the breakpoint, then select the **Breakpoint...** menu choice, and finally select the **Delete Breakpoint** choice. Look at Figure 7-7 to see this in action.

- The second method is to select the **Debug** menu and then select **Toggle Breakpoint** or press **F9**.

- The third method is to right-click the red dot indicating the breakpoint and select **Delete Breakpoint**.

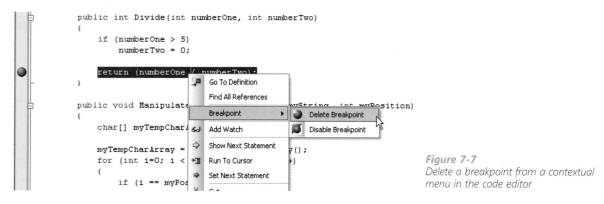

Figure 7-7
Delete a breakpoint from a contextual menu in the code editor

 3 You should be at the first line of code in the Divide method. Press **Shift+F11** to step out of the Divide method or you can press the **Step Out** button. This will execute all the instructions in that method and go back to the caller.

MORE INFO

The using block guarantees that you're going to dispose of the resources you're using when you exit the block. You can read more about this by doing a search in the Help system in the Look For text box using the using statement as keywords.

4 Press **F5** to execute all methods up to the next breakpoint.

You should see another message box with the result 1. Click **OK** and then you should be stopped in the source code of the ReadFile method.

 5 The ReadToEnd method reads the content of the opened file and puts it in a string variable. Press **Shift+F11** and then **F11**. A message box should display the string variable content. Click **OK** in the message box. You should now be back at the caller.

6 Step into the code until you get the string Helloworld in a message box. Pay attention to the order of execution and look into the variables and into the content in each of the tab sections.

7 Step into the code again to get into the ManipulateStrings method.

The first instruction in the ManipulateStrings method is taking the string received in argument and converting it to an array of characters. The reason this is done is because strings are immutable in .NET, and therefore you have to work with them in read-only mode once they're created. Methods modifying a string are actually returning a new string object that contains the modification applied to it.

MORE INFO

As you can see in the source code, one of the ManipulateStrings arguments, myString, is passed with the ref keyword. When you have an argument that is passed to a method by reference, the called method is receiving a reference to the same memory location used by the caller. Therefore, if the method is modifying the content of that argument, it is modifying the content at this memory location and thus modifying the variable from the caller. In this case, anything that is done to the myString argument will modify the value of the variable in the calling code. The other argument is myPosition, and it is passed by value. When you have an argument that is passed by value, the method is receiving a copy of the variable from the calling code and thus can't modify the original value from the caller. Therefore, the content will get lost when the method ends and execution flow returns to the caller.

Therefore if you want to modify a string character by character or if you want to access one single character in a string by using an index, you first need to convert the string into an array of characters.

TO BEGIN STEPPING OUT OF THE MANIPULATESTRINGS METHOD

1 Press **Shift+F11** to step out of the ManipulateStrings method, or you can press the **Step Out** button.

The application stops abruptly. What just happened is an unhandled exception. An unhandled exception happens whenever an error occurs that is not anticipated or handled explicitly by your application. In that case, the execution of your application is halted because there is no way the application can continue in that state without potentially corrupting the memory or opening security holes. One of the .NET runtime (CLR) principles is to make sure that neither ever happens. Therefore, the CLR crashes your application to prevent your application from continuing to execute in an unknown state. Even though the CLR is taking those precautions, it is less probable to have insecure code executing in .NET, but still possible.

To help you find the bug that raised that unhandled exception, Visual Studio includes another useful tool: the **Exception Assistant**. This assistant replaces the previous Exception dialog box, and it's helpful because, based on the context of the exception, it provides more information than before, such as: the type of exception, troubleshooting tips, and corrective actions that may be applied through the Exception Assistant. Look at Figure 7-8 to see what it looks like for the current exception.

When you look at the exception name, the troubleshooting tips, and the data visualizers, it can become apparent why an unhandled exception was raised. The exception name alone is self-explanatory: IndexOutOfRangeException. The first troubleshooting tip displayed asks you to make sure the maximum index on a list is less than the list size. Arrays in .NET are 0 based; this means that the first element starts at index 0. The length of the string received as argument is 10, as shown in Figure 7-8.

The intent of this method was to modify the last character of the string when the position in the array is equal to a position passed by value to the method. In this particular case, the position passed by value to the method is 1.

Therefore, in the "for loop" at the second character of that string, the "if" statement will return true and then the index *i* will get the value of the string length. This means that *i* is now equal to 10. When the application tries to modify the character at index 10, an exception will be generated because index 10 is outside of the range of the array. The array has 10 characters with index from 0 to 9. Figure 7-9 uses a new visualizer to look at the char array content.

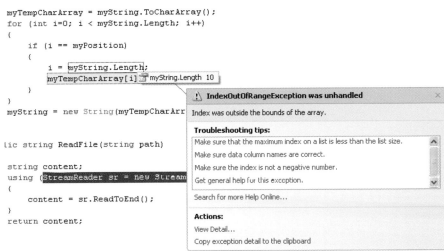

Figure 7-8
Exception assistant

When you move the mouse over program elements, you'll sometimes see a magnifier. If you click the drop-down list, you will see a list of visualizers that display the information in a way that is meaningful to the data type you're looking at. For instance, if you're working with Extensible Markup Language (XML) or Hypertext Markup Language (HTML) content, the XML or HTML

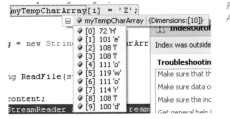

Figure 7-9
Array visualizer

visualizer will allow you to see the content as if you were using Microsoft Internet Explorer or any other XML/HTML tool. You'll use one of the visualizers soon when you debug the ReadFile method.

TO FIX THE OUT OF RANGE PROBLEM

1 Modify the ManipulateStrings method. Subtract 1 from the string length when you assign a new value to i. The source code should look like this after you modify it:

```
if (i == myPosition)
{
    i = myString.Length - 1;
    myTempCharArray[i] = 'Z';
}
```

2 After modifying this line of code, move your next execution pointer to the "for" statement so that index i starts at 0. Step through the code or step out. This time there should be no exception. Continue to step through the code; you should now see another message: HelloworlZ. The string has been modified because it was passed by reference.

Continue to step through the code and soon you'll get a second exception, which is a Division by 0 error. Of course, an exception is raised because the Divide method assigns 0 to the denominator when the numerator is greater than 5. Using a visualizer, you can see that the numerator is 6, therefore 0 will be assigned to the denominator.

Again, the first displayed troubleshooting tip helps by suggesting that you make sure the denominator is not 0. To solve the problem, you could add an "if" statement; but before you do that, consider another .NET principle.

A good practice in .NET is to use the exception mechanism to catch those corner cases instead of coding special conditional instructions which bloat the code. The exceptions are an integral part of the .NET framework and they're everywhere. Let's see the logic behind this decision.

In a real application, your application would not purposely assign 0 to the denominator; therefore, most divisions would result in a correct operation. Adding an "If" statement would result in a conditional instruction executed for every single division. And because most divisions would be valid, you would automatically slow down your application. Using an exception-handling mechanism to catch those corner cases is a much better solution because the exception-handling code will get executed only when necessary, so your application should be faster.

When you insert exception-handling code in your application, it is best practice to always catch exceptions from the most precise to the least precise. In this case, you know that the DivisionByZeroException is the one most likely to occur; therefore, it's the first one you want to catch.

When you catch an exception, the exception is "handled." You then need to do something about it; either you handle it by mentioning it to the user or you throw the exception back. In this case, you want the user to know that an exception was raised but you don't want the program to crash. Here's an example that demonstrates this form of handling that I'm sure you already know. If you try to divide by zero in Microsoft Office Excel®, Excel won't crash; it will simply indicate that your entry results in a division by zero and display the #DIV/0! message in the cell.

An older way of doing things was to make your method return an integer to indicate success or failure. And that's where people met with trouble because between two applications, and sometimes between two functions, the same integer code meant two different things. You received an integer that was supposed to tell you why your application failed, but the originating code had two meanings, and it was a nightmare to figure out which one was the valid error code. In addition, when people used error codes, their code was ugly because they either had a switch case or a series of nested ifs.

In .NET, you should never design your methods to return an integer to indicate success or failure, nor should you use a Boolean for the same purpose. This is a bad practice that was used when exceptions did not exist or when people didn't know or want to use them appropriately. *You should never do this.* Instead, use exceptions.

TO ADD CODE TO HANDLE DIFFERENT EXCEPTIONS

1 Click the Stop Debugging button or press Shift+F5 to stop debugging mode. In TestApplication.cs, modify the button1_Click method to look like the following:

```
Library myObjectLibrary = new Library();
string myString = "Helloworld";
string myFile = "";

try
{
  MessageBox.Show(myObjectLibrary.Divide(5, 3).ToString());
  MessageBox.Show(myObjectLibrary.Divide(3, 3).ToString());
  MessageBox.Show(myObjectLibrary.Divide(6, 4).ToString());
}
catch (DivideByZeroException ex)
{
  MessageBox.Show(ex.ToString());
}

try
{
  myFile = "MyExistingTextFile.txt";
  MessageBox.Show(myObjectLibrary.ReadFile(myFile));
  myFile = "MyNotExistingTextFile.txt";
  MessageBox.Show(myObjectLibrary.ReadFile(myFile));
}
catch (FileNotFoundException)
{
  MessageBox.Show(myFile + " doesn't exist!");
}

myObjectLibrary.ManipulateStrings(ref myString, 20);
MessageBox.Show(myString);
myObjectLibrary.ManipulateStrings(ref myString, 1);
MessageBox.Show(myString);
```

2 Remove all the breakpoints in TestApplication.cs and Library.cs and execute the code. Look at the different message boxes. If a DivideByZeroException or FileNotFoundException occurs, a message box will be displayed.

There are some useful tabs that you didn't use in this debugging session. For instance, the Watch tab is important because you can enter variables and expressions that you want to follow and monitor during the execution of the application.

Another useful tab is the Immediate window, where you can type anything and the compiler verifies, compiles, and executes it on the fly! Any effect on the application under debug is immediate. Any piece of code that can be evaluated by the compiler and does not require a block of code can be entered into the Immediate window. You could enter a loop, for instance. You also have full access to IntelliSense in this window just as if you were in the code editor. Let's look at a simple example.

TO USE THE IMMEDIATE WINDOW

1 Put a breakpoint at the first instruction in your application and run the application by pressing **F5**.

2 If you don't see the Immediate window, just select the **Debug** menu and then select **Windows** and **Immediate**. You should have an empty Immediate window in the bottom of your screen.

3 Type the following line and press Enter: **int i = 5**

4 Now type this line and press Enter: **MessageBox.Show(i.ToString());**

The message box that appears should show a 5. You can test code in real time during the execution without executing a single line of code from your application. But beware if you use variables that are in your application; remember that if you modify them in the Immediate window you modify them for the application as well.

5 Click the **Stop Debugging** button to stop executing the application.

You're now not only able to build new applications, but you're aware of the techniques and tools available to debug them.

In Summary...

In this chapter, you learned how to use breakpoints; about different techniques to step into, step over, and step out of the source code; and about data visualizers to see the data in the most pertinent way based on its content or context. You also learned how to work with a DLL.

You discovered that you can use the Edit and Continue feature to modify variables at run-time and continue the execution.

You learned how you can move the next instruction pointer to re-execute some lines of code. You also started to deal with exceptions and learned the dos and don'ts of debugging. You've seen how subtle bugs can find their way in—usually due to distractions and sometimes simply because you don't possess all of the knowledge and experience—but that's okay. Don't worry; you're in a process called learning.

In the next chapter, you'll learn about databases, ADO.NET, and manipulating data to and from a Microsoft SQL Server™ Express database. You'll also learn how to use this data to populate controls on a Windows form. You'll learn to create an application to add, modify, delete, and visualize rows in the car tracker application.

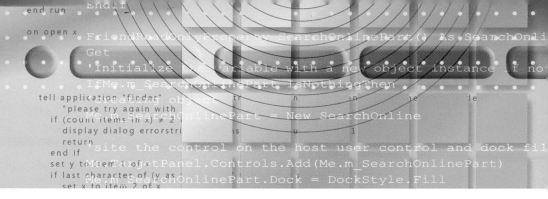

Chapter 8

Managing the Data

So far, you've seen how to build a Windows Forms application and what characteristics those applications contained, but you have not managed a great deal of data. Managing data is always a concern, whether at home, at the office, at school, or even for recreation. For instance, I have many recipes and ideas for great dinners, but when I want to prepare a nice meal, it takes me so much time to find them that usually I change my mind. If I had this information in my computer, it would be easy to quickly access my recipe for "rack of lamb with herb crust" and prepare a fabulous meal. I could also add other pertinent information to the recipe file, such as what side dishes were served with it or what wines went well with this recipe. I could even add a picture of the finished meal.

You could manage data using a word processing program, such as Microsoft Word, but it could become unmanageable as soon as you collect a lot of recipes and need to search for information within that file. Using a spreadsheet, such as Microsoft Excel, is also problematic. The fact is that trying to find information quickly when using more than one variable is close to impossible. Using the recipe example, suppose you want to retrieve all of the recipes that can serve at least six people and that have lamb stew meat but no mint in the ingredients because one of your guests is allergic to mint. Imagine the time it would take to find that information in either a Word file or an Excel spreadsheet. That's where databases come to the rescue.

In this chapter, you'll learn what a database is; how to create a database; how to add, delete, and update data; how to search or query a database; and how to use a database in a Windows Forms application. Accompanying Visual C# 2005 Express Edition is SQL Server 2005 Express Edition, which is a fully workable version of its bigger brother, SQL Server 2005, but with fewer features. SQL Server 2005 Express Edition is free, easy to use, and geared toward building simple and dynamic applications.

What Is a Database?

A database is a collection of data that is stored in files on disks using a systematic structure. The systematic structure enables users to query the data using management software called Database Management System (DBMS). SQL Server 2005 is a Relational Database Management System (RDBMS). It is based on a relational model because its data is structured using sets (the sets theory in mathematics) and logical relations (predicates). Most commercial database products are based on the relational model. In fact, it's been one of the most popular models for the last 20 years. Apart from Microsoft SQL Server, you may have also heard of the following product names: Oracle or IBM DB2.

What's In a Database?

NOTE

You'll learn about some of the other elements contained in a relational database later in this chapter.

A relational database, such as SQL Server 2005, contains multiple tables that are related together. A database can also contain views, stored procedures, functions, indexes, security information, and other elements. In this section, you'll learn about the basic element of a relational database, which is a table and its components.

A table contains columns and rows. A column defines the type of data, and a row contains the actual data. Because the relational model has strict rules, a RDBMS that uses the relation model must implement them.

MORE INFO

In reality, no popular RDBMS is fully implementing the pure relational model as it was first created in the 1970s.

Data Normalization and Data Integrity

The rules defining the relational model are called normalization rules. Normalization is a process that data architects must apply whenever they are at the design phase. Normalization rules exist to reduce the chance of having the same data stored in more than one table; in other words, they exist to reduce the level of redundancy and also to preserve data integrity in the database. Logically, the normalization process exists to help split the data into its own table so that there is no duplication of information in more than one table. For example, having an application in which the customer's address, city, state or province, zip or postal code, and country are duplicated in two different tables is a bad idea. There should be only one link from the customer table to the other table referencing additional customer information. Having duplicate data would make updates and deletions more problematic and would also pose the risk of having modified data in one table and not the other. This example demonstrates a data integrity problem.

Let's look at another data integrity problem. Suppose you have both a product table and a table containing customer order details. Although you normalized your data, data integrity does not exist (for this example). Now let's say you decide to delete product1, which means removing a row from the product table that corresponds to product1. If the RDBMS would let you do this, it would mean that suddenly all rows in the customer order details table that contained this product would not be able to show which product was ordered because the product would no longer exist. Those rows would be orphaned, which could have disastrous results for the company.

As you can see, data integrity is a very important concept that is related to the accuracy, validity, and correctness of the data. To better understand some of these concepts, let's look at another example.

Suppose you are the owner of an online store and want to manage your company using a software application. To use a software application, you must start thinking about using a database. Any company, both small or large, typically has a great deal of data to store. Also, because data is all around us, people want more access to this data so as to create reports and conduct analysis. That is why databases are so useful. Returning to your online store, at a minimum you would like to store information about your customers, products, invoices, purchasing, and inventory. To summarize all of those areas, let's take a look at the Product, OrderHeader, and OrderDetail tables.

> **NOTE**
> The following tables have purposely been kept simple (some columns are missing) and are used to illustrate the concepts you've just learned.

Column Name	Data Type	Allow Nulls?
ProductID (PK)	integer	Not Null
ProductNumber	nvarchar(10)	Not Null
Name	nvarchar(50)	Not Null
Description	nvarchar(200)	Null
Photo	image	Null
Price	money	Not Null
Taxable	bit	Not Null

Table 8-1
Product Table

Column Name	Data Type	Allow Nulls?
OrderID (PK)	integer	Not Null
OrderDate	datetime	Not Null
DueDate	datetime	Not Null
CustomerID (FK)	integer	Not Null
TaxAmount	money	Not Null
Total	money	Not Null

Table 8-2
OrderHeader Table

Column Name	Data Type	Allow Nulls?
OrderID (PK) (FK)	integer	Not Null
LineDetailID (PK)	integer	Not Null
ProductID (FK)	integer	Not Null
Quantity	integer	Not Null
LineTotal	numeric(38,6)	Not Null

Table 8-3
OrderDetail Table

Your Product, OrderHeader, and OrderDetail tables could also be represented graphically, as shown in Figure 8-1. This is a common way of looking at databases.

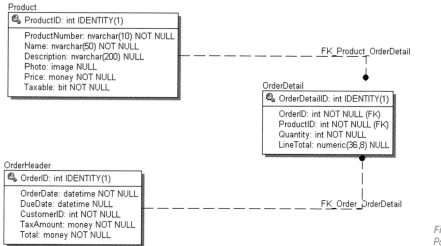

Figure 8-1
Partial database diagram of a small online company

What Is Null?

One of your first observations is that there's a column in the tables titled Allow Nulls?, which is also reflected in Figure 8-1. When designing a table, you need to consider what's absolutely necessary (Not Null) and what's not (Null). For instance, when you insert a new row into the Product table, it may not matter whether the product has a photo, but it might be a problem to have a product without a product number. Now let's correlate how allowing null is related to data integrity. Whenever a table is designed with a column that doesn't allow null, the RDBMS will reject any insertion of a new row that has a column set to null when it is not supposed to. When you pay attention to those columns that cannot contain null when designing your tables, you automatically add another data integrity layer by making sure that all necessary data is present before the record is inserted into the database.

What Are Primary Keys and Foreign Keys?

You'll see in Figure 8-1 that some columns have the letters (PK) for primary key in the tables or a yellow key for primary keys. Some columns also contain (FK) for foreign key. Let's start by talking about the primary key.

Primary Key

A primary key is a value that is used to uniquely identify a specific row in a table. A primary key:

- Can be composed of one or more column names. When it's composed of more than one column, it's called a composite key.

- Is often a numeric field.

- Is often generated by the RDBMS, in which case it's called a surrogate key. A surrogate key is frequently (but not always) a sequential number. A surrogate key is also called an identity in SQL Server 2005. An identity starts at a set number, called the identity seed, and increments by another set number, called the identity increment. For example, if you create a table named Product, you can have a column named ProductID that is set as an identity, and you can set the identity seed to 1 with an identity increment to 1. When the first row is created in the Product table, the ProductID will be generated by the RDBMS and set to 1. The following row will have a ProductID that is set to 2 and so forth.

- Should be as short as possible, but long enough to support the number of rows it will represent.

- Is immutable, meaning its value should never change.

- Is also a natural key when the key has a logical relationship with the rest of the columns in the table. For example, if you had a book table, the ISBN number could be used as a primary key because it uniquely identifies only one book. It would be an advantage compared with a generated key because it would take less space and has to exist anyway!

- Is also used to relate two tables together.

In our Product table example, the ProductID is the primary key. At design time, it will also be an identity. You can claim that the product number could be a primary key and you could be right, but in certain scenarios a product number could be used twice. For example, suppose you have product #FG-001 with a revision 1.0. In time, you change the product because of customer complaints and give it a revision 2.0. You want your customers to continue to order the same product number for many business reasons. In your database, you would retire the product revision 1.0 by perhaps changing a column named Active, then add another row in your table with the new product details, including revision 2.0, and set it to Active. Why can't you use the same row? Let's assume that six months after creating the new product revision, you want to create a graph to determine whether your changes to the product meant that you had fewer returns from your customers. It would be difficult to come up with good data if you had only one row for the product, but it would be fairly easy to do if you have two rows because they would be unique in the database, with each one having a different ProductID.

In the OrderDetail table, you have a composite primary key that is a combination of the OrderID and OrderDetailID. This means that these two columns would ensure the uniqueness of a row in the OrderDetail table.

In the OrderHeader table, the OrderID is the primary key.

Foreign Key

A foreign key is a column in a table that relates to a column in another table. It also enables you to create relations between tables. A foreign key in a table is always a primary key in another table. Foreign keys are used to enforce data integrity by being part of foreign key constraints. Foreign key constraints are created to make sure referential integrity is preserved and not violated. There are two foreign keys in the order details. The first is the ProductID foreign key in the OrderDetail table, and it's related to the primary key named ProductID in the Product table. The second is the OrderID foreign key in the OrderDetail table, and it's related to the primary key named OrderID in the OrderHeader table. Concerning the naming of foreign keys, it's a good practice to define them using the same name as their primary key counterpart; otherwise, it may lead to problems for those looking at your logical data model.

I introduced you to data integrity at the beginning of this chapter. In doing so, I cited an example that could create similar problems to the one in the Product and OrderDetail table example. Adding a foreign key constraint between these two tables would prevent a user from deleting a product in the Product table that could potentially create a large number of orphaned rows in the OrderDetail table. If you look at Figure 8-1, the foreign key constraint between Product and OrderDetail is shown as a line between the two tables that can be found by looking at the name FK_Product_OrderDetail. Naming constraints is an easy way to understand what they are for. We only have three tables in our example, but you can imagine that constraints without names that exist between numerous tables would quickly become unclear.

Another foreign key constraint exists here, which is the one between the OrderHeader and OrderDetail tables that would prevent an order from being deleted before all of its matching OrderDetails have been deleted. You can see in Figure 8-1 that the OrderHeader table has another foreign key called CustomerID. Therefore, another foreign key constraint would exist between the Customer and OrderHeader tables. Following the same principles found with other foreign key constraints, this would prevent a customer from the Customer table from being deleted before all of its matching orders in the OrderHeader table and all detail rows in the OrderDetails table that match the orders have been deleted.

If there were no foreign key constraints in this database, data integrity would be easily violated. The database would be left with a big problem: a time bomb of orphaned rows that take up space and slow down all queries. By adding this foreign key constraint, the RDBMS would ensure that all rows in the OrderDetail table that reference this product have been deleted before the product row could be deleted in the Product table.

How Do You Interact with a Relational Database?

So far, I've talked about tables in which you can update, add, or delete rows or query the database to get particular results. Perhaps you've been asking yourself: But how do I talk or interact with the database? How does it return the answers to my queries? And how do you create those tables? I'm sure you've been asking yourself many other questions as well. The answer to all of these questions is SQL Server 2005 Express Edition.

SQL stands for **S**tructured **Q**uery **L**anguage and was invented in the 1970s. The acronym is pronounced SEQUEL and was also introduced using that same spelling, but because of a trademark dispute in the UK in the 1970s, the name was shortened to the now well-known SQL acronym. Back then, the SEQUEL acronym meant **S**tructured **E**nglish **Qu**ery **L**anguage. SQL is an English-based language and is very similar to human language questions. That's why it's easy and fast to learn basic SQL programming. Let's look at two examples:

1. SELECT * FROM CUSTOMER

2. SELECT COUNT(*) FROM PRODUCT

The first example can be translated in English to give me all (*) rows in the Customer table or give me the list of customers in English. The second example can be translated as a request to give me the total of all rows contained in the Product table or to count how many products this company has.

When you issue an SQL query to a relational database, the database returns a result set that simply contains the rows with the answers to your query. Using SQL, you can also group or aggregate the results of a query. You also use SQL to create tables or delete (drop) tables. You've learned about primary keys, foreign keys, and constraints, but you probably didn't know that they're also created using SQL.

It's also good to know that SQL is an ANSI/ISO standard; therefore, any RDBMS producer needs to obey a set of rules. Basic SQL is a base programming language and as such is usually not sufficient to solve all possible problems or analysis needs that an application may demand. It has a rather limited set of keywords. Because its first goal is to query data from a database, the most popular RDBMSs on the market have added extensions to SQL to permit the addition of procedural code. These additions turn SQL into a full-fledged programming language that helps solve more complex problems. The following is a list of popular extensions and their manufacturers: Microsoft Transact-SQL (or T-SQL for short), Oracle PL/SQL, and IBM SQL PL. Recently, in addition to these extensions, RDBMS manufacturers have added the support of other programming languages. Microsoft is adding .NET language support into the database with all SQL Server 2005 Editions, while Oracle and IBM have added Java support.

There are more database concepts and theories than those listed and explained here, but we have covered the immediate database needs of this book. You'll now apply those concepts concretely in a Windows Forms application that will use a SQL Server Express 2005 database.

SQL Server 2005 Express in Visual C# 2005 Express Edition

In this section, you will develop a Windows Forms application. This will be a car tracker application that will enable the user to track the prices of cars over time and determine where the listing was observed. You will first use Visual Studio to create the database and the tables, then add some data and validate some of the concepts you've learned in the first part of this chapter. You will then create a Windows application that will use your data and build a data-centric application that will allow the user to store any amount of data.

Refer to Figure 8-2 for the database diagram pertaining to this section's example.

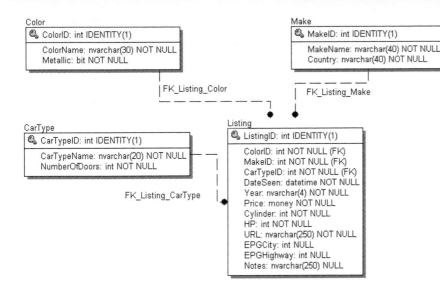

Figure 8-2
Car tracker application database diagram

Color

🔑 ColorID: int IDENTITY(1)

ColorName: nvarchar(30) NOT NULL
Metallic: bit NOT NULL

Make

🔑 MakeID: int IDENTITY(1)

MakeName: nvarchar(40) NOT NULL
Country: nvarchar(40) NOT NULL

| FK_Listing_Color

| FK_Listing_Make

CarType

🔑 CarTypeID: int IDENTITY(1)

CarTypeName: nvarchar(20) NOT NULL
NumberOfDoors: int NOT NULL

FK_Listing_CarType |

Listing

🔑 ListingID: int IDENTITY(1)

ColorID: int NOT NULL (FK)
MakeID: int NOT NULL (FK)
CarTypeID: int NOT NULL (FK)
DateSeen: datetime NOT NULL
Year: nvarchar(4) NOT NULL
Price: money NOT NULL
Cylinder: int NOT NULL
HP: int NOT NULL
URL: nvarchar(250) NOT NULL
EPGCity: int NULL
EPGHighway: int NULL
Notes: nvarchar(250) NULL

Creating a Database Using Visual C# 2005 Express Edition

Before using data, we need a place to store the data. You'll learn how to create a database in Visual C# 2005 Express Edition. You'll also see how easy it is for you to create all of the tables we need to satisfy the needs of our car tracker application because the SQL Server team did a wonderful job of integrating the tools into Visual Studio.

TO CREATE A DATABASE USING VISUAL C# 2005 EXPRESS EDITION

1 Start **Visual C# 2005 Express Edition**.

2 Create a new Windows application and name it **CarTracker**.

3 You will now create the database that will hold all the tables for the application. In the Solution Explorer, right-click the **CarTracker** project, select **Add**, and then select **New Item**.

4 In the Add New Item dialog box, select **SQL Database** from the Visual Studio Installed Templates. Type in the filename **CarTracker.mdf** and click the **Add** button. By doing so, you'll create a database and attach the database file (**CarTracker.mdf**) to your CarTracker project.

5 You will then see a Data Source Configuration Wizard. Don't pay attention to this dialog box just yet; you'll learn about it soon. Just click **Cancel** for now.

MORE INFO

SQL Server is well integrated because Visual Studio provides a great SDK for other components to plug into the IDE.

MORE INFO

The .mdf file extension is used by the SQL Server family of products. The .mdf contains the entire database; this means all tables and other elements that can exist in the database are located in that one file. The only thing that is not part of the .mdf file is the log information, which is in a .ldf file. It is created whenever you create the database. The file has an .ldf extension and is used to store the database log information. You can see this file by clicking the Show All Files icon in the Solution Explorer.

6 The Solution Explorer should now contain a new item within your project: the new database file called **CarTracker.mdf** as shown in Figure 8-3.

7 You will now start to add tables to your database. To do this, you can either double-click the **CarTracker.mdf** file or right-click **CarTracker.mdf** and then select **Open**. This will cause Visual Studio to connect to the SQL Server 2005 Express instance installed on your machine.

The Database Explorer should appear on the left side of the screen where the toolbox usually opens up, as shown in Figure 8-4. If you do not see the Database Explorer, go to the View menu, Other Windows, Database Explorer.

Figure 8-3
Solution Explorer with the newly created CarTracker.mdf database file

Under the database name, you should see a list of database elements represented by folder icons. Although you will not recognize most of them, you will see two elements that are already familiar to you: the database diagram and the tables. You will use both of these elements shortly.

Figure 8-4
Database Explorer with the CarTracker database connected

You'll know that you're connected to the database when you see the database icon with an electric cord look-alike. When you're disconnected, you will see the database icon with a red X. However, seeing a red X does not necessarily mean that you're disconnected. You might have been disconnected earlier, but the Database Explorer was never refreshed. To verify the state of the connection to your database, you should click the **Refresh** button in the Database Explorer toolbar.

8 Right-click on your database named **CarTracker.mdf** in the Database Explorer and select **Close Connection**. You should now see the red X near your database name.

You're now disconnected. To reconnect, you can do three different things. You can double-click your database name (e.g., **CarTracker.mdf**) in the Database Explorer, you can click the Refresh button, or you can right-click on the filename in the Database Explorer and select **Modify Connection. . .**. If you select the Modify Connection route, you will see a dialog box like the one shown in Figure 8-5.

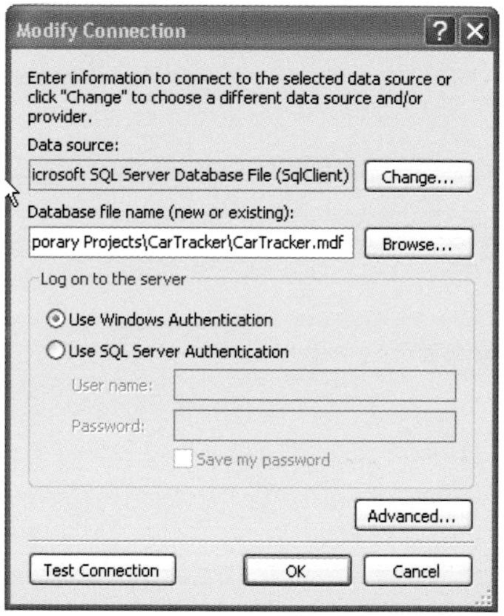

Figure 8-5
The Modify Connection dialog box will let you reconnect to your CarTracker database

9 Because it's a good practice to test your connection, you can click the Test Connection button and it will verify the connection currently specified. It's also verifying that SQL Server 2005 Express Edition is ready and able to receive connections from your applications.

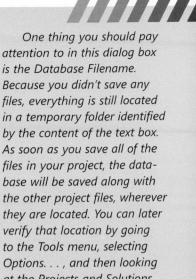

One thing you should pay attention to in this dialog box is the Database Filename. Because you didn't save any files, everything is still located in a temporary folder identified by the content of the text box. As soon as you save all of the files in your project, the database will be saved along with the other project files, wherever they are located. You can later verify that location by going to the Tools menu, selecting Options. . . , and then looking at the Projects and Solutions node in the tree. On the right panel in this dialog box, you can determine where your projects are stored by looking at the first text box called Visual Studio Project Locations.

10 Click **OK** to reconnect to your database.

> **NOTE**
>
> **Currently, you have only one database in your projects, but it's not unusual to need to connect to and get information from two or more databases. That's why Database Connections in the Database Explorer is there as a tree, for it's representing each database as a node in that tree. You have only one node in the tree, which is your CarTracker database.**

Creating Tables in Your Database

Now you'll create all tables and relationships needed for the CarTracker application. Using the information found in Figure 8-2, you'll create tables, primary keys, identities, and foreign key relationships in the CarTracker database, and you'll do all of this without leaving Visual Studio.

TO CREATE TABLES IN A DATABASE

1 Let's start with the Color table. In the Database Explorer, right-click on the table's folder icon and select **Add New Table**. You should now see an empty grid on the designer surface, which is called the Table Designer. You will also see that a new toolbar has appeared, which is called the Table Designer toolbar. This toolbar has all the tools necessary to help you create a table without writing a single SQL query.

2 You'll now add a column to the Color table. Type **ColorID** in the Column Name field of the Table Designer. Select **int** as the Data Type and uncheck the **Allow Nulls** check box because this column will be the primary key in this table. A primary key cannot be null since it is part of the uniqueness of a row in the table.

3 Before you add the second column in the Color table, you'll set this column as the primary key. To do so, you need to click the **Set Primary Key** icon in the Table Designer toolbar.

> **NOTE**
>
> **From this point onward, for every tree control and every control that is a group (i.e., has a + sign), the word *expand* will be used instead of repeating the words *click on the + sign*.**

The database diagram shown in Figure 8-2 illustrates that you also need this column to be an identity; therefore, you need to modify that property in the Column Properties window right below the Table Designer. Scroll down until you see the Identity Specification group. Click on the **plus sign** (+) located to the left of the words *Identity Specification* to expand this group. Now click in the **(Is Identity)** field and set it to **Yes**. Leave both the Identity Seed and Identity Increment set at 1 for now.

④ To add another column, click in the row under the ColorID column name. Add the two remaining columns based on the diagram shown in Figure 8-2. You can set the size of the ColorName nvarchar to 30, by typing in the Data Type field. When done, your table should look like the one shown in Figure 8-6.

dbo.Table1: T...RTRACKER.MDF)*		
Column Name	Data Type	Allow Nulls
🔑 ColorID	int	☐
ColorName	nvarchar(30)	☐
▶ Metallic	bit	☐
		☐

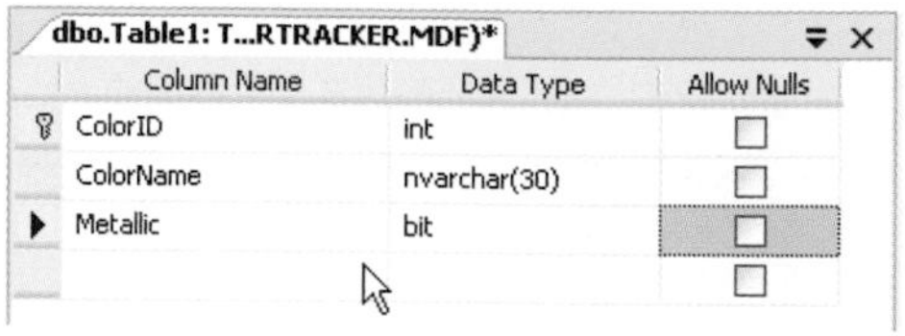

Figure 8-6
Table Designer with all of the columns for the Color table

⑤ Now that you're done with the design, you need to add the table to the database. To do this, you need to save the table. Click the **Save** icon or press **Ctrl+S**. When the Choose Name dialog box appears, as shown in Figure 8-7, name your table **Color** and then click **OK**.

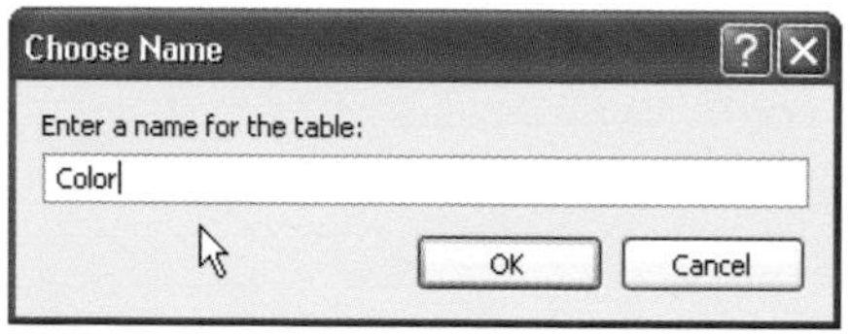

Figure 8-7
The Choose Name dialog box showing the Color table name

Choose Name [?][X]

Enter a name for the table:

Color|

[OK] [Cancel]

⑥ Expand the **Tables** folder in the Database Explorer to view the list of existing tables in the database; the new Color table should appear. When you expand the **Color** table to view the list of columns, all three columns that you just created should appear, as shown in Figure 8-8.

⑦ Close the Color table in the Table Designer by clicking the **X** near the Solution Explorer.

Figure 8-8
Database Explorer with the Tables folder and Color table expanded

⑧ Click the **Save All** icon in the toolbar to save your project. Make sure the project name is CarTracker and click the **Save** button.

⑨ Before creating other tables, read this step completely. Now that you have the knowledge to create a table, create all remaining tables (ColorType, Make, and Listing) using the same techniques you've just learned. Make sure that all tables and *all* of their columns are recreated exactly the same way in your tables as shown in Figure 8-2. Don't worry about establishing the relationships, for you'll create those in the following exercises. Between each table creation, save your new table immediately and make sure it appears in the Database Explorer. Then close the table in the designer surface as shown earlier in step 7 of this section.

Creating Relationships Between the Tables

You have created tables, but they don't have any relationships. You'll now add those relationships and make sure your database has data integrity to cover the basis of orphaned rows. Like many other elements in Visual C# 2005 Express Edition, there's more than one way to create those relationships. One is more visual than the other, and you'll start with this more visual approach so as to stay focused on the main idea of the book, which is being productive.

Before you're able to create the relationships visually, there is a prerequisite to add to your project: a database diagram. It might not look exactly as the one shown in Figure 8-2, but it will be similar.

TO CREATE RELATIONSHIPS BETWEEN TABLES

 Go to the Database Explorer and right-click the **Database Diagrams** node located above the Tables node. Select **Add New Diagram**. A dialog box will appear indicating that SQL Server 2005 Express Edition doesn't have all of the database objects it needs if you want to create database diagrams.

② Click **Yes** to have SQL Server create the components it needs to obtain a database diagram. When it's done creating, you should be asked which tables you want to add to your diagram in the Add Table dialog box.

③ Select all of the tables you created and then click **Add**. It should take less than a minute for your diagram to appear. Click the **Close** button to indicate to Visual Studio that you have all the tables you need.

④ Click the **Save All** button or press **Ctrl+Shift+S**. You'll be asked to save your diagram and choose a name. Name your diagram **CarTrackerDiagram**.

 If you don't see your database diagram, first go to your **Database Diagrams** node, expand it, and then open the diagram by double-clicking on it. You should see the designer surface with all of your tables.

> **TIP**
> Depending on your resolution, the view might be tight. If you want to view more of the diagram, you might need to unpin or close some windows, such as the Solution Explorer or the Properties window; you can return these items to your screen by going to the View menu and selecting Solution Explorer or the Properties window. You can also change the zoom value by changing the value in the Zoom drop-down list.

Let's focus on one relationship that we need to create. When you look at Figure 8-2, you'll see that the ColorID column is present in the Listing table because there's a relation to the Color table. The line between both tables is a foreign key (FK) relationship. You need to have this relationship established or otherwise you'll have orphaned nodes in the Listing table whenever a Color row is deleted. This means that you have to establish a relationship between the primary key table and the foreign key table. In this case, it means you need to create a relationship from the Color table toward the Listing table.

6 In the database diagram, click on **ColorID** in the Color table where you see the small yellow key.

7 Look at Figure 8-9 to see where you should be at the end of this manipulation. Hold the left button down and drag **ColorID** toward the Listing table; you should see a line appear as you drag. Align your mouse cursor so that it's over the column with which you want to create the relationship—in your case, over the ColorID field in the Listing table. When you see a small + appear, then drop it.

Figure 8-9
Creating the foreign key relationship between the CarType and Car tables

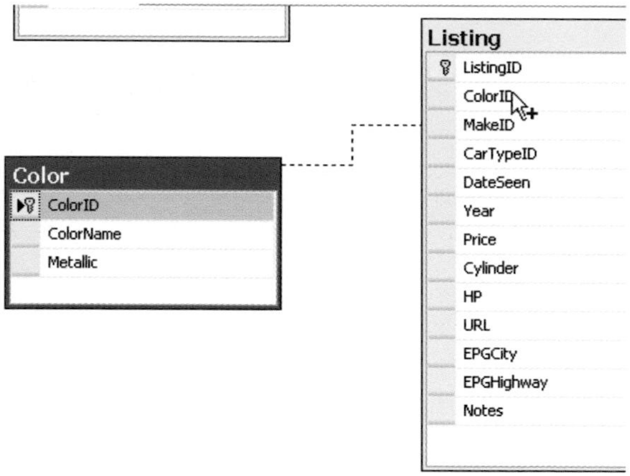

8 If you correctly selected and released the mouse once you were over ColorID in the Color table, you should see a Tables and Columns dialog box that asks you to confirm the creation of the FK relationship. It's important for each table that ColorID is the column name that appears to link both tables in that dialog box. If the primary key and foreign key tables are correct and the selected column names are correct, then click the **OK** button.

9 You should then see the Foreign Key Relationship dialog box shown in Figure 8-10.

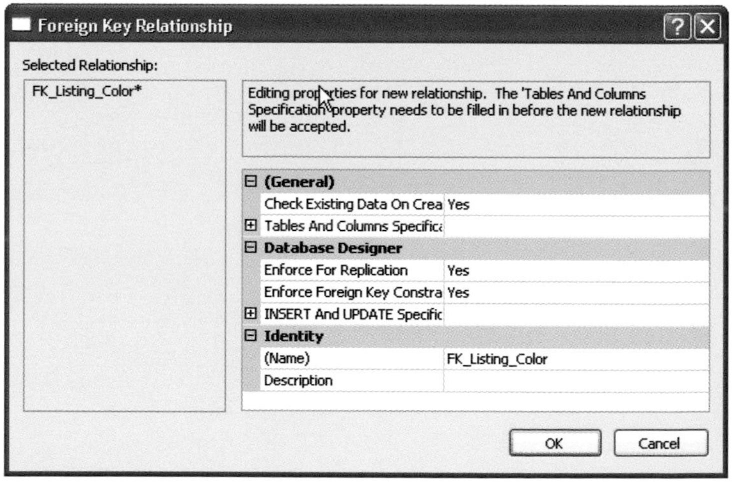

Figure 8-10
Foreign Key Relationship dialog box for the Listing to Color tables

Microsoft Visual C# 2005 Express Edition: Build a Program Now!

Although you can change some properties within this dialog box, just click **OK** for now. See Figure 8-11 to view the diagram with the new relationship created.

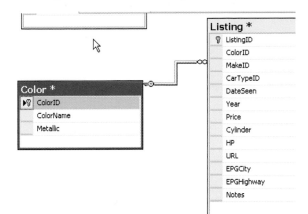

Figure 8-11
Modified diagram showing the new FK relationship between the Listing and Color tables

The first thing to note on the diagram is the infinity symbol ∞ located close to the Listing table and the yellow key located close to the Color table. The infinity symbol on the Listing table indicates the table's cardinality. It indicates that, in this relationship, the Listing table can contain many rows with information coming from the matching primary key table. The yellow key indicates from which table the primary key is coming.

I rearranged the diagram so that the two tables are close together. You can rearrange your tables any way you want by dragging them by the title bar (i.e., where the table name is displayed). This is sometimes necessary to do when you create relationships so that you do not end up with an unusual-looking diagram. I suggest that you put your Listing table in the middle of your other tables because it will be easier to create relationships this way. You can also rearrange the tables on your diagram at any time by right-clicking anywhere except on a table on the diagram's designer surface and selecting **Arrange Tables**. You can also have the labels for every relationship appear on the diagram by right-clicking the diagram's designer surface and selecting **Show Relationship Labels**, as shown in Figure 8-12.

MORE INFO

To reinforce the concept of establishing relationships between tables, let me give you another way of looking at the relationship in this exercise. There are two reasons why the ColorID column is in the Listing table as an FK. The first reason is that it is used for a normalization and design principle because you don't want to have duplicate data. The second reason is that it is used for data integrity reasons and, more specifically, for the orphaned rows problem. Let's look at it with some sample data. Suppose there is a Color row called Dark Blue and the Listing table contains six different ad definitions that are Dark Blue. If you remove the Dark Blue color from the Color table, it would mean that those six ads would have orphaned data. That is why you created a foreign key relationship: to make sure that if an application or a user tries to remove data in the Color table, a process within SQL Server 2005 would prevent this by validating that there are no "kids" left behind in the Listing table before allowing the deletion to occur in the Color table.

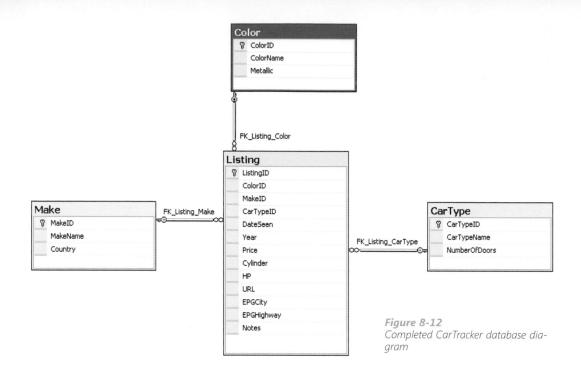

Figure 8-12
Completed CarTracker database dia-gram

 Now create the other FK relationships by using either Figure 8-2 or the following table.

Column	Primary Key Table	Foreign Key Table
MakeID	Make	Listing
CarTypeID	CarType	Listing

Table 8-4
List of foreign key relationships to create

MORE INFO

You can always go back and review the properties of any relationship by double-clicking on the line or by right-clicking and selecting Properties from the context-sensitive menu.

When finished, the content of your diagram should resemble the content shown in Figure 8-12. Make sure your relationships are arranged properly by looking at where the infinity symbols and yellow keys are located and also by looking at the previous table for verification.

12 Click the **Save All** button or press **Ctrl+Shift+S** to commit the changes to the database. Click **Yes** when asked if you want to save.

Entering Data in SQL Server Tables Using Visual Studio

Now that you have created all of your tables and relationships, you'll start inserting data in your tables and verifying that your constraints ensure the data integrity of your database.

Let's start by adding data in all tables. You'll first add rows into the Color table.

TO ENTER DATA IN SQL SERVER TABLES USING VISUAL STUDIO

1 To start entering rows in the Color table, right-click the **Color** table in the Database Explorer and select **Show Table Data**. Your designer surface should have a grid like the one shown in Figure 8-13.

Color: Query(...RTRACKER.MDF)	dbo.CarTrack...TRACKER.MDF)*	⚏ ✕
ColorID	ColorName	Metallic
NULL	NULL	NULL

◄◄ ◄ [0] of 0 ► ►► ►⊠ ⊙

Figure 8-13
Empty Color table in the table data grid

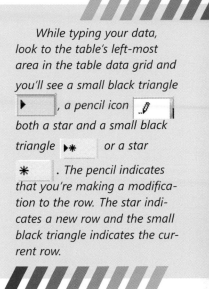

While typing your data, look to the table's left-most area in the table data grid and you'll see a small black triangle ▶, *a pencil icon* 🖉, *both a star and a small black triangle* ▶✳ *or a star* ✳. *The pencil indicates that you're making a modification to the row. The star indicates a new row and the small black triangle indicates the current row.*

2 Let's add the first color. Click in the **Color Name** field, type **Dark Blue**, and then press the **Tab** key to go to the next column. Type **true** in the **Metallic** field. Because that column type is a bit, its values can only be either true or false because a bit type is a binary type. When you're done, press the **Tab** key to go to the next row.

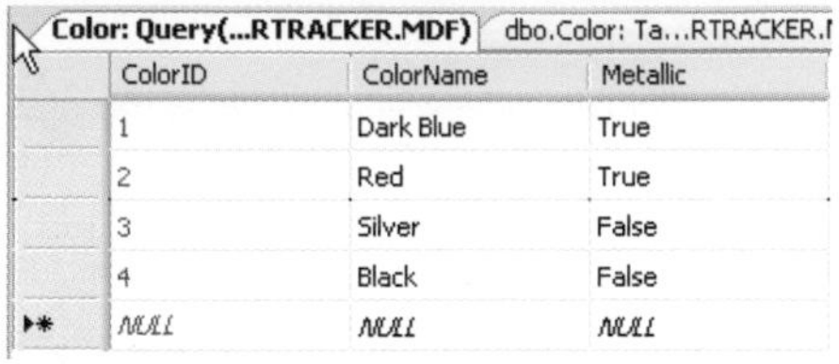
ColorID	ColorName	Metallic
1	Dark Blue	True
2	Red	True
3	Silver	False
4	Black	False
NULL	NULL	NULL

Figure 8-14
Color table with four new rows of data

For all columns that you created as an identity, don't type the data because the field will automatically be generated by SQL Server 2005 Express Edition whenever the row is created in the table. If you try to type data in an Identity column, you will not be allowed to do so. When in an Identity column, it states that the cell is read-only near the navigation bar at the bottom of the Table Designer.

3. Add three more car colors—**Red**, **Silver**, and **Black**—and set Red as **Metallic** and the other two colors as **Non-metallic** (i.e., false). When done, the table should look like the one shown in Figure 8-14.

4. Add the following data to the Make and the CarType tables.

Make Table

MakeName	Country
GoodRoadster	Germany
SmallCar	France
BigSUV	USA
ReliableCar	Japan

CarType Table

CarTypeName	NumberOfDoors
Roadster	2
SUV	5
Hatchback	5
Sedan	4
Coupe	2

You might not have realized that by giving a type to your data, you actually added data integrity verification to your database. Try modifying one of the Color rows by changing the Metallic column to read *Helloworld* instead of true or false. You'll get an error message telling you that the Metallic field is of type Boolean.

To show how data integrity is preserved using the foreign key constraints, you'll add two Listing rows. You will enter more rows when using your Windows Form application.

5. Right-click on the **Listing** table, select **Show Table Data**, and add the following two rows.

Listing Table

ColorID	MakeID	CarTypeID	DateSeen	Year	Price	Cylinder	HP	URL	EPGCity	EPGHighway	Notes
1	1	1	08/11/2005	2005	42500	6	240	http://www.litwareinc.com/	20	28	This is my dream car, follow regularly.
4	3	2	07/30/2005	2003	39775	8	340	http://www.cpandl.com/	10	15	Too much gas

6 You'll now verify that one of your foreign key constraints is working correctly. Open the Make table by right-clicking on the **Make** table and selecting **Show Table Data**.

7 Let's try to delete the first row by clicking on the left-most field where the pencil usually appears. The row should be selected and all fields should be blue. Right-click and select **Delete**.

8 A dialog box should appear on your screen inquiring whether you really want to delete the row. Click **Yes**.

9 You should receive a dialog box error message stating that the row was not deleted because of the foreign key constraint that reads as follows: **Error Message: The DELETE statement conflicted with the REFERENCE constraint "FK_Listing_Make."** This statement affirms why the foreign key constraint was created, which was to avoid orphaned rows. Figure 8-15 depicts what the error dialog box looks like and what kind of information is provided to help you debug the problem, if necessary. In this case, it's not a problem but a feature of your creation!

10 Click **OK** to exit this dialog box.

11 Test your other constraints related to the Listing table by trying to delete the first row of the CarType table. You should receive a similar error message.

Figure 8-15
Error dialog box showing the foreign key relationship preventing the deletion of a row from the Make table

MORE INFO

You can navigate through the table by using the navigation controls at the bottom of the grid. These controls will allow you to do things such as move to the first and last row, move to the previous and next entry, move to a new record, or directly type in the row number.

Microsoft Visual C# 2005 Express Edition

No rows were deleted.

A problem occurred attempting to delete row
Error Source: .Net SqlClient Data Provider.
Error Message: The DELETE statement conflicted with the REFERENCE constraint "FK_Listing_Make". The conflict occurred in database "D:\MY DOCUMENTS\VISUAL STUDIO 2005\PROJECTS\C#\CHAPTER8\CARTRACKER\CARTRACKER\CARTRACKER.MDF", table "dbo.Listing", column 'MakeID'.
The statement has been terminated.

Correct the errors and attempt to delete the row again or press ESC to cancel the change(s).

OK

Now that you have all of your domain tables loaded with some data, you'll now learn to use the database in a Windows Forms application. You'll learn about ADO.NET and about databindings with Windows Form controls.

What Are ADO.NET and Databinding?

If you want more information about SQL and Transact-SQL, you should download the SQL Server 2005 Express documentation. You can find this information at the following link: http://go.microsoft. com/fwlink/?LinkId=51842. SQL Server 2005 Express documentation is designed to help you answer most questions you might have, but it might also refer you to the SQL Server 2005 documentation. You can download it at http://go.microsoft.com/fwlink/ ?LinkId=51843.

You rarely enter all data manually using Visual Studio. You typically let the user do it or you do it through an application. You can also either import data from another source or create the new data using SQL scripts, but this is a more advanced concept that will not be covered in this book.

This section will focus on how to build Windows applications that can connect to and receive data from a SQL Server 2005 Express Edition using ADO.NET. The following is a formal, official definition of ADO.NET from the MSDN online library:

*ADO.NET provides consistent access to data sources, such as Microsoft SQL Server, as well as data sources exposed through **OLE DB** and **XML**. Data-sharing consumer applications can use ADO.NET to connect to these data sources and retrieve, manipulate, and update data.*

ADO.NET cleanly factors data access from data manipulation into discrete components that can be used separately or in tandem. ADO.NET includes .NET Framework data providers for connecting to a database, executing commands, and retrieving results. Those results are either processed directly or placed in an ADO.NET DataSet object in order to be exposed to the user in an ad-hoc manner, combined with data from multiple sources, or remoted between tiers. The ADO.NET DataSet object can also be used independently of a .NET Framework data provider to manage data local to the application or sourced from XML.

The ADO.NET classes are found in System.Data.dll and are integrated with the XML classes found in System.Xml.dll. When compiling code that uses the System.Data namespace, reference both System.Data.dll and System.Xml.dll.

I wanted to present the long and formal definition of ADO.NET because it contains elements that you'll learn about while working with the Car Tracker application. I also chose it because I would like you to refer back to it whenever you're working with ADO.NET. Here is a less formal definition that I think summarizes what ADO.NET is all about.

You can say that ADO.NET is the .NET Framework way of accessing and programmatically manipulating databases. With ADO.NET you can also manipulate other sources of data like XML sources.

New to ADO.NET 2.0 are new ways of accessing data from different sources. In Visual C# 2005 Express Edition, you are limited to the following data sources: databases (SQL Server Express and Microsoft Access databases), Web services, and custom objects. It is much easier (i.e., there is less code) to manipulate data in ADO.NET 2.0, especially when using all of the tools included in Visual Studio 2005. There are many new wizards and other tools that make the experience of working with databases a pleasant one. Visual Studio 2005 covers numerous common scenarios with its tools and wizards, but it's also very powerful when used programmatically without the use of the visual tools. You will learn the basics in this book, but there's nothing preventing you from learning more about databinding and ADO.NET and from unleashing powerful applications.

Before proceeding any further, let's talk about the Car Tracker application. The main goal of the application is to track car ads over the Internet. As you have your database ready to go, you now need to consider what will be included in this application. In reality, what you need is simply a way of displaying the ads, adding new ads, modifying/deleting existing ads, and searching through the ads using a series of drop-down boxes that allow you to narrow your search based on certain criteria. These search criteria will come directly from the domain tables (i.e., separate drop-down controls for the car type, color, make, and so forth).

When using drop-down controls or any other controls with data that you know exist in your database, you don't want to populate the data by hand. You want to use the databinding capabilities of a control. **Databinding** is an easy and transparent way to read/write data and a link between a control on a Windows Form and a data source from your application.

ADO.NET takes care of a great deal of activity behind the scenes (it's even better in .NET Framework 2.0), as well as managing the connection to the database. Managing the connection doesn't stop at opening and closing the connection, but also concerns itself with finding the database with which you're trying to connect. When a connection is opened, it means your application can talk to the database through ADO.NET method calls. All exchanges (send/receive) of data between your application and the database are managed for you by ADO.NET. The data itself is also managed by ADO.NET through diverse mechanisms: read-only forward navigation, navigation in any direction with read-write, field evaluation, and so forth. And the beauty of it is that you usually don't have to write a lot of code to enjoy those nice features.

> Visual C# Express allows you to work with Microsoft Access databases, but working with SQL Server 2005 Express Edition gives you all the benefits of the Enterprise quality of SQL Server 2005, with the only downside being a reduced set of features.

NOTE
Not all Windows Form controls are "databinding aware." When they are aware, they have a DataBindings property.

The Car Tracker Application Development

NOTE

The Data Sources window might end up somewhere else in your IDE. Because your IDE is entirely customizable to your liking, you can customize your windows and tabs to appear wherever you feel they are most productive for you.

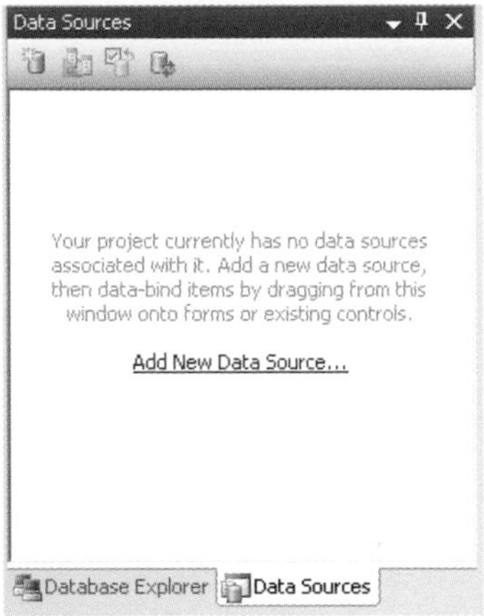

Figure 8-16
The Data Sources window

You'll now proceed to the development of the Car Tracker application. First, you need to create a dataset that will provide you with all the databinding you need for the Car Tracker application. Now that your tables are established, you can configure the dataset with all of the elements you've just added to your database.

Before creating a dataset, you must learn what a dataset is. A dataset is an in-memory representation of one or more tables and is used to store the rows you retrieve that match the query you sent to the database. You can then add, delete, or update rows in memory. When the user is done, you can submit, save, or commit the changes to the database. The CarTrackerDataSet.xsd is called an XML Schema Definition file. The .xsd file ensures that the data will be structured and respect the schema. This file will be used later in the project when we discuss databinding.

To create a dataset, you'll learn to use the Data Sources window. This window gives you access to all of the data sources you have configured in your application. See Figure 8-16 to see where the Data Sources window is located. If you don't see the Data Sources window, you can access it by clicking on the Data menu and selecting Show Data Sources. If Show Data Sources does not appear on the Data menu, be sure you have closed all of the CarTracker table data grids and Form1 is visible.

TO CREATE A DATASET

1. In the Data Sources window, click the **Add New Data Source** link or click the **Add New Data Source** button in the toolbar. The Data Source Configuration Wizard appears.

2. The first screen of the Data Source Configuration Wizard allows you to choose the data source type you want to create. You can choose a database, a Web service, or one of your objects. You've just built a database for the Car Tracker application, so you're going to choose that Data Source Type. Select **Database** and then click **Next**.

In the next screen, you will choose your data connection. CarTracker.mdf should already be selected. When you created the CarTracker SQL Server Express database in your project, a data connection was created for you. You can click the **plus sign** (+) in the bottom of the dialog box to see what the connection string looks like. This connection string defines how your application will connect to the database.

Click **Next** on the Choose Your Data Connection screen.

The next screen in the wizard inquires whether you want to save this connection string in the application configuration file. As you saw in the previous screen, you know where your database is stored. Yet you might change your mind and deploy the file somewhere else. If you do that, you don't want to modify the source code and recompile it. Putting the connection string in your application configuration file is actually a best practice. It gives you the advantage of only modifying the file and restarting the application without recompilation so as to automatically pick up the changes in your connection string and connect to that new location.

The application configuration is stored in an XML file named using the application's executable name and adding **.config** at the end of the executable filename. In our application, the file is named CarTracker.exe.config, although you only see app.config while working in Visual Studio. If you want to save the connection string, you are also asked to provide a variable name under which it will be saved in the file.

4 Make sure the **Yes, Save The Connection As** check box is selected and then click **Next**.

5 In the next screen, you'll select all the tables from the database that will be in your dataset and name your dataset. In your case, you will need all of the tables, so expand the Tables node and select all tables. Leave the DataSet Name set to CarTrackerDataSet and then click **Finish**.

The result of your dataset configuration is an .xsd file or a XML Schema Document, and it will define the internal structure of your dataset. Remember that a dataset is an in-memory representation of one or more tables from your database. ADO.NET will use this schema file when working with your application. When running the application, the user will be able to add, delete, or modify rows in the dataset (in the computer's memory). The changes will remain in memory until the user commits the changes back to the database, which in our example is the CarTracker.mdf file.

6 In the Solution Explorer, double-click the .xsd file named **CarTrackerDataSet.xsd**. As shown in Figure 8-17, the result of the dataset creation is similar to the database diagram you created earlier. Your diagram might be different depending on your screen resolution and how you customized your IDE.

Figure 8-17
*Graphical representation of
the CarTracker dataset*

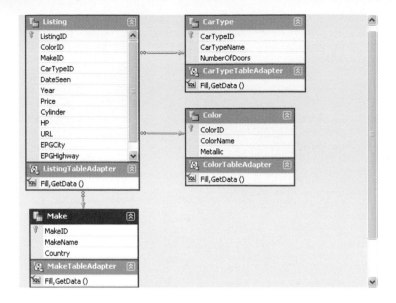

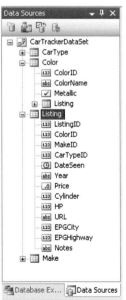

Figure 8-18
*View of the Color and Listing
dataset tables from within
the Data Sources window*

There are some notable differences, however. You'll see the same columns that you have created in your physical database, but in the bottom of each table, you will see methods: Fill, GetData(). These methods are particular to the dataset, and the ADO.NET-generated code by Visual Studio will use them to databind data to your Windows Form controls—controls that do not exist yet!

7 Return to the Data Sources window and expand the dataset tables. You'll see the in-memory representation of your tables, and you'll also see that each column has a small icon that gives you its type. These icons may look familiar to you because they are similar to the controls in the toolbox. Refer to Figure 8-18 for a quick glance at the Color and Listing dataset tables and their column types.

8 Close the graphical representation of your dataset by clicking the **X** in the corner of the designer surface.

9 In the Solution Explorer, double-click your **Form1.cs** file to open the designer surface for Form1.

In the Data Sources window, select the **Listing** node in your dataset and click on the drop-down arrow point that's next to the word *Listing*. You will be presented with two choices: DataGridView or Details. DataGridView brings all of the dataset fields into a table or grid format with multiple rows, while Details brings the dataset fields in one row at a time with all fields as individual controls. For our example, select **Details**.

You'll also see that each member of the dataset has the same drop-down arrow, which allows you to change which controls will be dropped onto the form when it is dragged. Allowing you to choose controls prior to dragging the dataset table onto the form prevents you from having to lay out the UI yourself piece by piece.

 Change the ColorID, MakeID, and CarTypeID to the ComboBox type by clicking on the drop-down arrow next to each column and selecting **ComboBox**.

 Select the **Listing** node by clicking on it, and then drag and drop it onto the designer surface on Form1.

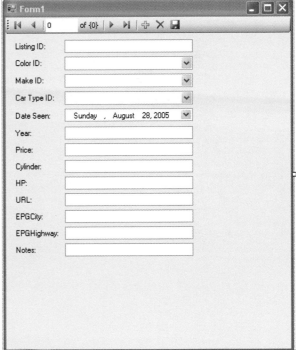

You'll now modify the form size like you did in previous chapters by modifying the form's Size property. Change the form size so that its **Width** is **450** pixels and its **Height** is **550** pixels.

Move all of the controls so that the first label is almost in the top-left corner just beneath the tool strip. See Figure 8-19 to determine how the controls should approximately be placed.

WARNING
You may need to scroll to see all of the controls depending on your screen resolution.

Figure 8-19
Resized Car Tracker form after moving all of the controls

When working with local database files, it is necessary to understand that they are treated like any other content file. For desktop projects, it means that, by default, the database file will be copied to the output folder (i.e., bin) each time the project is built. After pressing F5, here's what it would look like on disk:

CarTracker\CarTracker.mdf
CarTracker\Form1.cs
CarTracker\Bin\Debug\CarTracker.mdf
CarTracker\Bin\Debug\CarTracker.exe

At design time, CarTracker\CarTracker.mdf is used by the data tools and wizards. At run time, the application will use the database under the bin\debug folder. As a result of the copy, many people have the impression that the application did not save the data to the database file. This assumption occurs because there are two copies of the data file involved. This also happens when looking at schema/data through the Database Explorer. The tools are using the copy in the project folder and not the file in the bin\debug folder. The following are a few ways to work around this copy behavior:

1. If you select your database file in the Solution Explorer window, you will see a property called Copy To Output Directory in the Properties window. By default, it is set to Copy Always, which means that data files in the project folder will be copied to the bin\debug folder on each build, thus overwriting the existing data files if any. You can set this property to Do Not Copy and then manually place a copy of the data file in the bin\debug folder. In this way, on subsequent builds, the project system will leave the database file in the bin\debug folder and not try to overwrite it with the one from the project. The downside to this method is that you will still have two copies. Therefore, after you modify the database file using the application, if you want to make those same changes within the project, you will need to copy the changes to the project manually and vice-versa.

2. You can leave the data file outside the project and create a connection to it in Database Explorer. When the IDE asks you to bring the file into the project, simply say no. In this way, both the design time and run time will be using the same data file. The downside to this method is that the path in the connection string will be hard coded, and it will therefore be harder to share the project and deploy the application. Before deploying the application, make sure to replace the full path in the settings with a relative path. If you want to read more about the relative path versus the full path (plus a bit more about this copy behavior), read the following article: http://blogs.msdn.com/smartclientdata/archive/2005/08/26/456886.aspx. You'll see that I took portions of that article and modified them so that they fit our application.

As you can see, many things have just happened. Let's start by looking at the designer surface. All of the fields from the dataset have been added as controls, and labels were also added based on the name of the field in the dataset. This feature is called smart caption. Visual Studio uses Pascal or Camel casing as a mechanism to insert a space in labels when using smart captions. When you drop the dataset fields onto the form, smart caption looks at each field's casing. When it finds an uppercase letter or an underscore character (i.e., _) following a lowercase letter, it inserts or replaces the _ with a space. An exception to this rule can be seen in the EPGCity and EPGHighway fields. When you use uppercase letters for an acronym Visual Studio cannot distinguish that these are two words and therefore doesn't split them apart. You'll have to split these two fields manually.

You will also notice that a tool strip has been added that contains almost the same buttons you used while working with the database table designer.

15 Read the blue Important sidebar to the left. With this copy behavior in mind, I suggest that you use Approach #1, even though you'll have to perform some manual steps. If you want to debug your application from within Visual Studio, it's preferable to use this solution or you will not be able to see the changes applied to your database file. The database file will always come back to the initial one from your project, which is similar to resetting the whole database to what it is inside Visual Studio.

16 Select the **CarTracker.mdf** database file in the Solution Explorer and change the Copy to Output Directory property to **Do Not Copy** in the Properties window.

17 Press **F5** to build and run your application. You'll get an exception message because the file won't be copied in the bin\debug directory. Also, on the form load event when your code tries to fill the dataset, it won't find the database at the place specified by the connection string. Therefore, you get an SQLException stating that it's not able to attach to the database. Click the **Stop Debugging** button or press **Shift+F5** to stop debugging.

18 Using Windows Explorer, go into your project directory (it should be located at My Documents\Visual Studio 2005\Projects\CarTracker\CarTracker\) and copy the **.mdf** and **.ldf** files into the bin\debug directory under CarTracker.

 19 In Visual C# Express, press **F5** to build and run your application again.

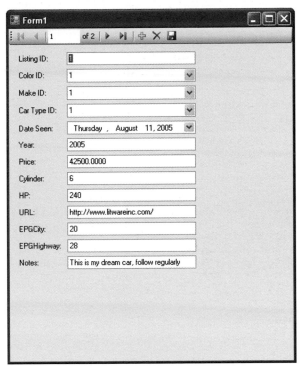

You should see the two records that you've inserted manually into the Listing table. You should be able to navigate using the tool strip and also modify, insert, and delete a record. See Figure 8-20 for a snapshot of your Car Tracker application at run time.

 20 Change the URL of the row at position 1 to end with **.net** instead **.com**.

 21 After changing the URL for the record, press the **disk icon** to commit the changes to the database.

22 Close the Car Tracker application and restart it by pressing **F5**. You should now see the first row with the modified URL ending in .net. Close the application again.

23 To verify that you are working with a design time and a run time version of the CarTracker database, open the **Listing** table and select **Show Table Data** from within the Database Explorer. The first row should contain a URL column ending in .com and *not* in .net. Point proven! The database file in Visual Studio is now de-coupled with the one your application is using at run time. Read the More Info note on the next page to learn how to make the data the same in both the design and run time.

Figure 8-20
Execution of the Car Tracker application

Component Tray

When you dragged the Listing dataset table onto the designer surface, you probably saw that four items were added in the gray area below the designer surface. This section of the designer surface is called the component tray. This is the section that Visual Studio uses for nonvisual controls. In your case, it added an instance of the CarTracker dataset, a Listing table adapter, a Listing binding source, and finally a Listing binding navigator.

Let's describe them individually.

■ **Binding Source** You can think of a binding source as a "broker" or a layer of indirection.

It can also be viewed as an intermediary between a data-bound control on your form and a data source, such a a dataset. A binding source provides currency management and notifications services (events). The binding source has many methods to facilitate, such as sorting, filtering, navigating, and editing of data from its data-bound controls to the data source. It's also linked tightly to the next component: the binding navigator. When you see a binding navigator, you're assured of getting a binding source.

■ **Binding Navigator** The binding navigator is a means to enable navigation and data manipulation. It has a UI component or, more specifically, a tool strip with buttons to facilitate the functionalities provided by the binding source.

■ **Typed Dataset** Although you know what a dataset is, you may not know that it's a strongly typed object. It contains data tables of the DataTable type that constitute the in-memory representation of your database tables. These data tables also have a special data adapter called the table adapter. There is a table adapter for each data table.

■ **Table Adapter** A table adapter is a data access object. It connects to the database (e.g., SQL Server 2005 Express Edition), executes the queries, and fills a data table with data when it returns from SQL Server. Therefore, it's the central point for all data access on an individual table. There is one table adapter per table in your data source. A table adapter can have more than one SELECT query.

How Do I Get More Meaningful Information on My Form?

Let's return to our CarTracker project. As you can see, the ColorID, MakeID, and CarTypeID combo boxes are there, but they are displaying the ID and not the name associated with the ID. This is not helpful for the user because an ID doesn't have any meaning to the user and he/she might not be able to easily add or modify rows without having a human-readable format for those columns. Consequently, you need to make sure the data is displayed in a humanly readable way and that the ID is stored in the row whenever the user modifies the information.

There's an easy way to accomplish this, which you will do now for your three combo boxes.

TO DATABIND WITH DOMAIN TABLES

 In the Data Sources window, select the **Color** table from the dataset, drag it onto the form's designer surface over the ColorID combo box, and drop it.

You'll see that another table adapter (**colorTableAdapter**) and another binding source (**colorBinding-Source**) were added to the component tray. If you go to the ColorID combo box and click on the smart tag triangle, you'll see the Data Binding Mode information box appear, as shown in Figure 8-21. You'll notice that your drag-and-drop action bound the combo box control with the ColorBindingSource. Because of this action, whenever the combo box displays, it will display the color names instead of ColorID. When the user picks a color from the combo box, the associated value member that will be used in the row will still be the ColorID, specifically, the ColorID associated with the ColorName. Wonderful, isn't it? And no lines of code were used.

Figure 8-21
ColorID combo box smart tag information showing Data Binding Mode

ComboBox Tasks

☑ Use data bound items

Data Binding Mode

Data Source	colorBindingSource
Display Member	ColorName
Value Member	ColorID
Selected Value	listingBindingSource - Color

Add Query...

Preview Data...

 Repeat the same process for the Make and CarType dataset tables and the corresponding MakeID and CarTypeID combo boxes.

3 Build and run your application and then look at each combo box. You now have real color names and not merely ColorIDs; the same is true for CarType and Make. The combo boxes are also populated with all of the values coming from those tables and not simply the value for that specific row. Click on the drop-down arrow and you'll see all other potential values. Close the application.

4 On the form, remove the "ID" part from the **Color ID**, **Make ID**, and **Car Type ID** labels.

5 You will now enlarge the Notes field by making it a multi-line text box. Select the **Notes** text box and change the Multiline property to **true**. Also change the **MaxLength** to **250**, the **Size:Height** to **50**, and the **Size:Width** to **250**.

6 Delete the **ListingID** text box and its label.

MORE INFO

This intelligent databinding is a new Visual Studio feature called Smart Defaults. Smart Defaults looks in the dataset table to see whether there's a column of type string by either the ID or the primary key. If so, it tries to use this one for the databinding.

7 Size and reposition the controls on the form so that it resembles the form shown in Figure 8-22; it does not need to be an exact duplicate. It will be good practice to bring back UI design concepts from Chapter 5 and also good preparation for Chapter 9. Change the Text property of the form to "Car Tracker".

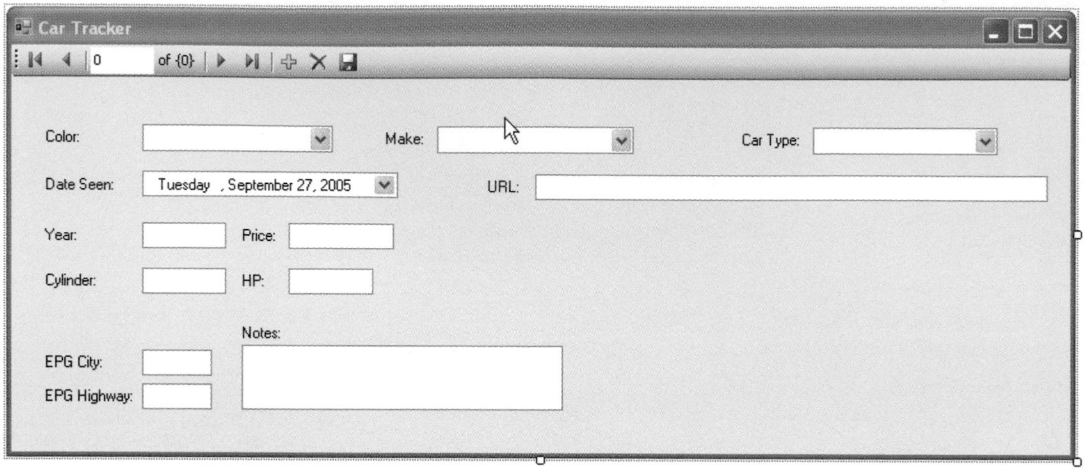

Car Tracker
0
of {0}
Color:
Make:
Car Type:
Date Seen:
Tuesday , September 27, 2005
URL:
Year:
Price:
Cylinder:
HP:
Notes:
EPG City:
EPG Highway:

Figure 8-22
New visual aspects of the Car Tracker application

8 In the Solution Explorer, rename form1.cs to **Main.cs**. When asked if you want to rename all references in this project, click **Yes**.

9 Select the form and change the BackColor property to **Highlight**.

Everything is nearly complete for this application, but the research capabilities are lacking. Currently, the only way to search is to scan through all of the rows until you find the correct one. This is not difficult now because you have only two rows in your Car Tracker database. Yet, if you had 500 rows, the Scan method would not be effective at all! Therefore, you'll implement search capabilities by adding queries to your application by using the Dataset Designer.

10 In the Data Sources window, select **CarTrackerDataSet**. Right-click and select **Edit DataSet with Designer**.

11 Select the **Listing** data table, and then select the **ListingTableAdapter** section at the bottom of the data table.

- When you look in the Properties window, you'll see that four types of queries were automatically generated by Visual Studio: SELECT, INSERT, DELETE, and UPDATE. They are the queries that helped you have a fully workable application without writing a single line of code. When you read about table adapters earlier, you learned that you can have multiple queries with a table adapter because it is the central point of data access. You will thus add search capabilities to your application by adding queries to the table adapters and by using parameters from the UI. First, you will add the ability to search for listings that have a certain color.

Figure 8-23
Adding new queries to a table adapter

12 Right-click the **ListingTableAdapter** section and select **Add Query. . .** as shown in Figure 8-23.

This will bring you to the TableAdapter Query Configuration Wizard. This wizard will help you add another SELECT query that will use parameters to refine your search. You can also create a SELECT query and turn it into a stored procedure or use an existing stored procedure. As its name implies, a stored procedure is one that is stored in SQL Server and contains SQL statements, along with other programming constructs, that use a language called T-SQL or Transact-SQL. A new feature to SQL Server 2005 Express Edition is that stored procedures can also be coded in managed languages, such as C# and Visual Basic. Stored procedures are executed on the server. Since you're using SQL Server 2005 Express Edition, this will be of no concern because the SQL Server and the application are executed on the same machine.

13 Select **Use SQL statements** and click **Next**. When asked which type of SQL query you want to use, choose **SELECT which return rows** and then click **Next**. Note that you could have added any SQL query type you wanted.

14 You are now presented with an edit window in which to add your SQL statement that will perform a search for all of the listings that contain a particular color. Refer to Figure 8-24 to see the SQL command edit window. Click on the **Query Builder. . .** button to get a visual view of the query.

15 You will now add the Color table to the diagram so that you'll be able to base your search on a particular color. To add the Color table, simply right-click in the diagram area and select **Add Table. . .** The Add Table dialog box appears as shown in Figure 8-25. Select the **Color** table and click the **Add** button. When the Color table has been added to the diagram, click the **Close** button.

TableAdapter Query Configuration Wizard

Specify a SQL SELECT statement
The SELECT statement will be used by the query.

Type your SQL statement or use the Query Builder to construct it. What data should be loaded into the table?

What data should the table load?

```
SELECT ListingID, ColorID, MakeID, CarTypeID, DateSeen, Year, Price, Cylinder, HP, URL, EPGCity,
EPGHighway, Notes FROM dbo.Listing
```

Query Builder...

< Previous   Next >   Finish   Cancel

Figure 8-24
SQL command edit window ready to customize the user's search

Figure 8-25
The Add Table dialog box

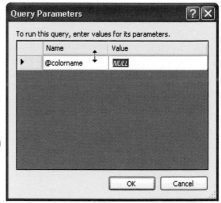

16 In the SQL code pane of Query Builder, append the following SQL code that will help in the filtering process:

```
WHERE      (Color.ColorName LIKE '%' + @colorname + '%')
```

17 Before you proceed with your new query, make sure it will give you the results you're expecting. Click the **Execute Query** button to display the Query Parameters dialog box, as shown in Figure 8-26.

18 Try replacing the word *NULL* with **blue** and then click **OK**. The Results pane of Query Builder should display only one row. Using the word **black** should return the black car row. Simply enter the letter **b**, and you should get both the blue and the black rows. Once you're satisfied with your query, click **OK** in Query Builder.

Figure 8-26
Query Parameters dialog box with prompt to enter a color name value

19 On the Specify a SQL SELECT Statement screen of the wizard, click **Next**. It's time to add your query to the application.

 20 A screen appears that will prompt you to name the methods that your query will generate. Those methods will be available after this creation from the Listing table adapter. Refer to Figure 8-27 to view this screen containing the two new method names. For both names you basically need to add what your filter is. In your case, you can add ColorName since you filtered by that in your WHERE clause. When done, click **Next**.

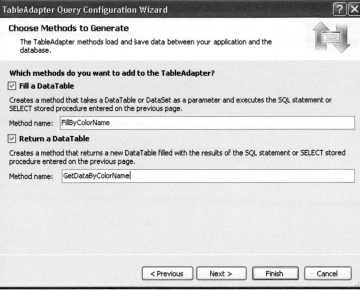

Figure 8-27
Dialog box with prompt to rename the methods used to increase search capabilities

 21 After processing for a few seconds, the computer should come back with a results screen informing you that your Select statement and your new Fill and Get methods are ready to use. Click the **Finish** button.

Look at the table adapter section of the Listing data table. Your new methods will be added there.

 22 Repeat steps starting at step 12 and add another query to the ListingTableAdapter for the CarType table. Use the following WHERE clause:

```
WHERE (CarType.CarTypeName LIKE '%' + @cartypename + '%')
```

Name the fill and get data methods **FillByCarTypeName** and **GetDataByCarTypeName**.

 23 Repeat steps starting at step 12 and add another query to the ListingTableAdapter for the Make table. Use the following WHERE clause:

```
WHERE (Make.MakeName LIKE '%' + @makename + '%')
```

Name the fill and get data methods **FillByMakeName** and **GetDataByMakeName**.

You're almost done now, but you still have to bind those new queries to controls on your form. On any data-bound control on your form, you can select **Add Query...** from the smart tag menu. In your case, you want to add search capabilities to the whole form and not simply to a particular control.

24 Go to the component tray, click the **ListingTableAdapter** smart tag, and select **Add Query. . .** You'll see a Search Criteria Builder dialog box that will prompt you to create a new query or pick an existing one. Since you just built three new sets of methods, you merely need to select one. Select the **Existing Query Name** option and then select **FillByColorName** as shown in Figure 8-28.

Search Criteria Builder

Choose an existing query or enter a new query below. A ToolStrip will be added to the form to run the query. To edit an existing query or use stored procedures use the Configure command on the TableAdapter in the DataSet Designer.

Select data source table:

CarTrackerDataSet.Listing

Select a parameterized query to load data:

○ New query name: FillBy

◉ Existing query name: FillByColorName(colorname)

Query Text:

```
SELECT    Listing.ListingID, Listing.ColorID, Listing.MakeID, Listing.CarTypeID, Lis
              Listing.URL, Listing.EPGCity, Listing.EPGHighway, Listing.Notes
FROM      Listing INNER JOIN
              Color ON Listing.ColorID = Color.ColorID
WHERE     (Color.ColorName LIKE '%' + @colorname + '%')
```

Sample: SELECT ColumnName1, ColumnName2 FROM   Query Builder...
           TableName WHERE ColumnName1 =
           @ParameterName

              OK   Cancel

Figure 8-28
*Search Criteria Builder with the
FillByColorName method selected*

25 Click the **OK** button. You'll see that a tool strip has been placed at the top of the form with a search button that will call your method when you click it, thereby giving you a way of searching by certain criteria. This was accomplished by only typing in the three WHERE clauses for your specific queries.

26 Repeat step 24 and add the **FillByCarTypeName** and **FillByMakeName** queries, which will add two more tool strips.

27 Now add a tool strip container to the form like you did in Chapter 6. Set the Dock property to fill the form. In the smart tag menu, select **Re-Parent Controls** to place all of your tool strips on the top panel and all of your other controls in your content panel. If necessary, use the Document Outline window to view and adjust the hierarchy of objects on the form.

28 When you're through moving controls, extend the top panel by clicking the grip and pulling it down so that it becomes two tool strips wide.

29 Make sure your application looks like the one shown in Figure 8-29. Press **F5** to see the results of your work. Type "blue" in the colorname tool strip and click **FillByColorName** to see if it returns blue color car listings. Experiment with the other features of the application.

Figure 8-29
Final Car Tracker application screen

Car Tracker application window showing navigation toolbar, search toolstrips (cartypename: / FillByCarTypeName, colorname: / FillByColorName, makename: roads / FillByMakeName), and data fields: Color: Dark Blue, Make: GoodRoadster, Car Type: Roadster, Date Seen: Thursday, August 11, 2005, URL: http://www.nicecars.net, Year: 2005, Price: 42500.0000, Cylinder: 6, HP: 240, EPG City: 20, EPG Highway: 28, Notes: This is my dream car, follow regularly.

This was a simple application that you can probably modify to handle more information, such as car pictures. But there is nothing that you can't add by yourself now! Here's a list of other things you can do if you want to continue to work on this application:

- Add validations for user input, such as making sure the year of the car is not greater than the current year + 2
- Add pictures in the databases and on the form
- Add a sold check mark
- Add three forms to add data in the domain tables (CarType, Make, Color)
- Add more information in the listing, such as contact information
- Make the URL clickable
- Save an ad as a text file

In Summary...

That was a big chapter with a lot of material! Let's review what you've learned. You were first introduced to databases and database concepts. You learned what constituted a database and what you usually find within a database. You learned about data integrity and how it is related to the primary key and the foreign key.

You then used Visual C# 2005 Express Edition to create a database and tables and then populated them with some initial data using various tools in Visual C# 2005 Express Edition. You implemented all of the foreign key relationships without leaving Visual Studio and validated them as well.

After entering your data manually, you learned how to allow a user to enter data more easily by developing a sample Car Tracker application that uses ADO.NET and databinding.

Lastly, you learned about the new components of ADO.NET 2.0 and how, with little or no code, you can develop a fully working data-centric application. You've only been introduced to a brief part of ADO.NET, for it's a vast subject. If you want to learn more, try looking at some code or samples on MSDN. A good place to begin is the 101 samples for Visual Studio 2005. Pay particular attention to the data access and Windows Forms samples. Here's the link: *http://go.microsoft.com/fwlink/?linkid=51659*.

In the next chapter, you will develop the final application of this book—the Weather Tracker application. You'll learn new concepts such as deployment, consuming Web services, user settings, and much more in a complete application with all of the necessary validations.

Chapter 9

Build Your Own Weather Tracker Application Now!

You have now reached the last chapter of the book and have learned quite a few new concepts along the way. In this chapter, you'll dot the i's and cross the t's by developing a full application. You will be working with new processes in this chapter, but you will also need to draw on what you've learned in previous chapters to create the final product. You've been developing other applications throughout the book, but you may not have performed all of the validations based on the steps or on my recommendation. You will put it all together with this application.

IMPORTANT

This chapter uses a United States weather Web service. I expect that this Web service will be available and function as described in this chapter. However, since this Web service is on the Internet, it is possible that this Web service might change or might not be available. If you don't have an Internet connection or if the weather Web service is not available, the application will let you know by displaying a message. If there are any changes or corrections for this chapter (or in the book), they will be collected and added to a Microsoft Knowledge Base article. To view the list of known corrections for this book, visit the following article:

http://support.microsoft.com/kb/905040/

Features of the Weather Tracker Application

In this section, you'll become acquainted with the features used to create version 1.0 of the Weather Tracker application. This application contains the following features in version 1.0:

- Starts and resides as an icon in the notification area of the Windows Taskbar
- Configures optional user settings from the notification area icon in the context menu
- Refreshes all weather data on demand from the context menu in the notification area
- Uses a Web service for the data (weather)
- Stores and persists user settings using XML
- The application will minimize and not close when the user clicks the Close button in the title bar. The application will only close when the user selects Exit on the context menu.
- Contains a splash screen on startup
- Contains an About box from the context menu
- Displays the current temperature using the weather icon as follows: a temperature above 100 degrees is displayed in red; any negative temperature is displayed in blue; normal temperature is displayed in black

The application will not contain the following features in version 1.0:

- Will not work for more than one city at a time
- No graphical gauge controls for wind, pressure, temperature, and so forth
- Conversions between metric units and English units

The High-Level Plan

For the Weather Tracker application, the user will briefly see the splash screen and then it will go directly to the notification area in the Windows Taskbar and display the current temperature. If the temperature is above 100 degrees F, the temperature will be displayed in red starting at 00. If the temperature is below 0 degrees F (negative degrees), the temperature will be displayed in blue. Otherwise, the temperature will be displayed in black. If a problem occurs, a red NA will show up in place of the temperature reading.

If the user right-clicks the icon in the notification area, it will open a context menu with choices to open the Main form and retrieve the current weather. The current weather will have an icon and provide all of the weather data that the Web service can provide.

If the user selects Refresh Weather Info from the context menu from the notification area icon, it will automatically trigger a call to the weather Web service to update both types of weather data. This will be done asynchronously and will start by updating the current weather. If the user select Options from the context menu, an Options dialog box will be displayed. The user will be able to change the ZIP code where weather data should be retrieved. If the user selects About from the context menu, it will display an About dialog box.

In this chapter, I will use a different approach than used in previous chapters. As long as you are using the same components that I specify, you may personalize your application as far as size, color, and other attributes are concerned. I'll also present my solution as well at different steps along the development; therefore, if you like what you're seeing, you may proceed with your application from the companion content provided. I will also post a great deal of code and explain the sections that are linked to the features described above.

To produce the application in this chapter, an incremental approach will be used in which you will implement one feature, integrate it with the rest of the application, and then test it. You will then move to the next feature until completion.

The Main form user interface (UI) will contain all of the weather information that you'll display to the user. Refer to Figure 9-1 to see what the Main form will look like when finished.

Creating the Application User Interface

The Main form user interface (UI) will contain all of the weather information that you'll display to the user. Refer to Figure 9-1 to see what the Main form will look like when finished. At the moment, the form does not have any controls to display the weather information. As you learned in the last chapter, you will use databinding to bind the controls to the weather data. You'll recall that when creating the data source, you had a choice of Database, Web Service, and Objects. In this application, you will use a Web service as a data source, and the fields you will display on the form will be data-bound to the Web service dataset.

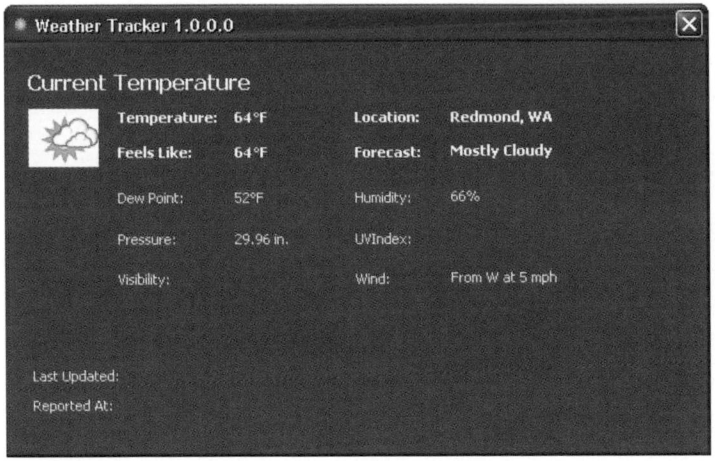

Figure 9-1
View of the Main form in the Weather Tracker application

TO CREATE A DATA SOURCE FOR A MAIN FORM CONTROL

1 Start Visual C# 2005 Express Edition and create a new Windows Application project. Name the application **Weather Tracker**.

2 In the Solution Explorer, rename Form1.cs to **Main.cs**. When you do this, Visual C# will ask you if you want to perform a rename of all references to Form1 in the project. Click **Yes** to accept.

3 Using the Properties window, change the properties for the Main form using the following table:

Property	Value
Size:Width	550
Size:Height	350
BackColor	System:MenuHighlight
ForeColor	Web:White
Font	Tahoma 8 Bold
Icon	Sun.ico
MinimizeBox	False
MaximizeBox	False
StartPosition	CenterScreen
FormBorderStyle	FixedDialog
ShowInTaskBar	False
DoubleBuffered	True
WindowState	Minimized

NOTE

All icons or image files in this chapter will be located in a folder named Images under the Chapter9 folder where you installed the companion content. The default location is \My Documents\Microsoft Press\VCS 2005 Express\.

MORE INFO

DoubleBuffered helps to reduce or prevent flickering when the form is redrawn. The form control is using a secondary buffer to update the form's graphics data, whereby a quick write to the displayed surface memory is then performed, reducing the chances of flickering. If DoubleBuffered is not enabled, then progressive redrawing of parts of the displayed form occurs, creating the flickering.

Adding Notification Area Capabilities

Now that you have established the Main form, you'll add the notification area capabilities. Let's talk about terminology. If an application uses an icon located in the notification area (the area on the Windows Taskbar where the clock normally appears), this icon is called a notify icon and is implemented with a NotifyIcon control. The icon can have a context menu with different actions. Your icon will have a context menu with the following choices: About, Refresh Weather Info, Options, Open, and Exit.

TO CREATE A NOTIFYICON CONTROL

1 In the Toolbox from the Common Controls group, drag a **NotifyIcon** on the form. It appears in the
component tray. Name the control **notifyWeather**.

2 Change its text property to **Weather Tracker**.

3 In the Toolbox from the Menus & Toolbars group, drag a **Context Menu Strip** onto the form and
name it **cmsNotify**.

4 Using the smart tag on the cmsNotify control in the component tray, select **Edit items . . .** The Items
Collection Editor appears.

5 In the Items Collection Editor, change the cmsNotify control's properties using the following table:

Property	Value
BackColor	System:Gradient InactiveCaption
ShowImageMargin	False

6 From the Select Item And Add To List Below drop-down list on the left, select **MenuItem** and click the
Add button. Change the control's properties using the following table:

Property	Value
(Name)	tsmiAbout
Text	About . . .
ForeColor	System:MenuHighlight

7 From the Select Item And Add To List Below drop-down list, select **Separator** and click the **Add** button. Change its ForeColor property to **System:MenuHighlight**.

From the Select Item And Add To List Below drop-down list, select **MenuItem** and click the **Add** button. Change the control's properties using the following table:

Property	Value
(Name)	tsmiRefresh
Text	Refresh Weather Info
ForeColor	System:MenuHighlight

 From the Select Item And Add To List Below drop-down list, select **Separator** and click the **Add** button. Change its ForeColor property to **System:MenuHighlight**.

 From the Select Item And Add To List Below drop-down list, select **MenuItem** and click the **Add** button. Change the control's properties using the following table:

Property	Value
(Name)	tsmiOptions
Text	Options ...
ForeColor	System:MenuHighlight

 From the Select Item And Add To List Below drop-down list, select **Separator** and click the **Add** button. Change its ForeColor property to **System:MenuHighlight**.

 From the Select Item And Add To List Below drop-down list, select **MenuItem** and click the **Add** button. Change the control's properties using the following table:

Property	Value
(Name)	tsmiOpen
Text	Open...
ForeColor	System:MenuHighlight

From the Select Item And Add To List Below drop-down list, select **MenuItem** and click the **Add** button. Change the control's properties using the following table:

Property	Value
(Name)	tsmiExit
Text	Exit
ForeColor	System:MenuHighlight

You're finished adding items to the context menu strip. The Items Collection Editor should look like Figure 9-2.

Figure 9-2
Items for the context menu

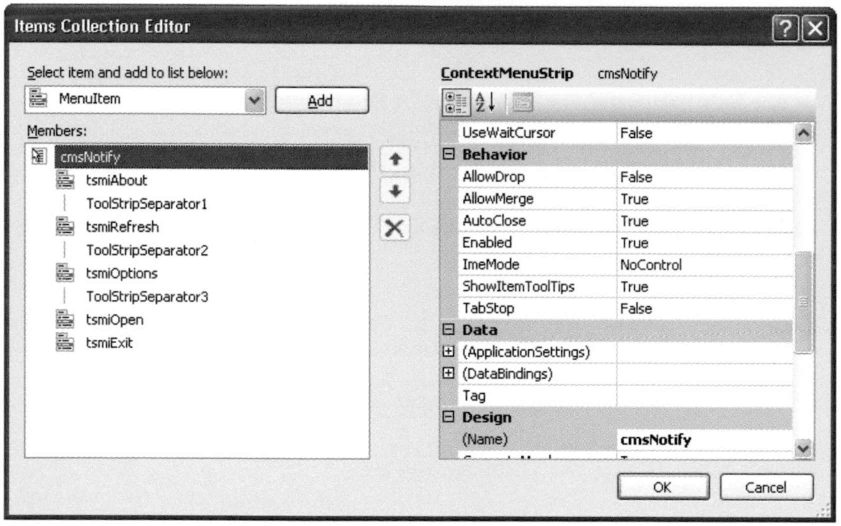

Items Collection Editor

Select item and add to list below:

MenuItem   Add

Members:

- cmsNotify
  - tsmiAbout
  - ToolStripSeparator1
  - tsmiRefresh
  - ToolStripSeparator2
  - tsmiOptions
  - ToolStripSeparator3
  - tsmiOpen
  - tsmiExit

ContextMenuStrip   cmsNotify

UseWaitCursor	False
□ **Behavior**	
AllowDrop	False
AllowMerge	True
AutoClose	True
Enabled	True
ImeMode	NoControl
ShowItemToolTips	True
TabStop	False
□ **Data**	
⊞ (ApplicationSettings)	
⊞ (DataBindings)	
Tag	
□ **Design**	
(Name)	**cmsNotify**

OK   Cancel

 Click **OK** to close the Items Collection Editor.

You now need to associate the context menu strip with the notifyWeather control, which is fairly easy to do.

Select the **notifyWeather** control in the component tray. In the Properties window, change the ContextMenuStrip property to **cmsNotify**.

Let's say you are currently acting as the user. In order for you to be able to click on the application when it's in the notification area, your notifyWeather control needs an icon. The icon will later become dynamically generated by your application, and the icon will become the current temperature. Therefore, you now need to associate a temporary icon with the application, otherwise you would not be able to select it in the notification area.

16 In the Properties window for nofityWeather, set the Icon property to **otheroptions.ico**. This file is located in a folder named Images under the Chapter9 directory where you installed the companion content.

 17 Press **F5** to execute the application.

You should see this icon in your notification area: . If you right-click on this icon, you should see the context menu shown in Figurte 9-3.

When you are finished, the only way to stop the application is to click the blue Stop Debugging button in the Visual Studio toolbar. You will now add another way to stop the application.

Figure 9-3
Context menu of the
notifyWeather control

TO STOP AN APPLICATION

1 Select the **tsmiExit** control from the Properties window's drop-down list.

2 Click on the **event** icon (yellow lightning) in the Properties window and then double-click the **click** event. The Code view appears.

3 Edit the tsmiExit_Click event handler and add the Shutdown method as shown in the following code. A Shutdown method is created because you always want to make your code re-usable, and a Shutdown method will enable you to do this.

```
1  private void tsmiExit_Click(object sender, EventArgs e)
2  {
3      this.Shutdown();
4  }
5
6  private void Shutdown()
7  {
8      if (notifyWeather.Visible)
9      {
10          notifyWeather.Visible = false;
11      }
12      Application.Exit();
13 }
```

The first instruction of the Shutdown method will verify if the notifyWeather control is visible; if it is, make the notify icon disappear from the notification area. The last line will terminate the application. You will now be able to select the Exit menu choice from the context menu to terminate the application; you won't need to use the Stop Debugging button. You can try your application by pressing **F5** to verify whether the Exit menu choice works as expected..

Now you can exit from your application, but you don't have a way to open the Main form, which will have the weather information. To do this, you will want to link the double-click event of the notifyWeather control icon in the notification area to the action of opening the Main form in the middle of the screen.

4 In Design view, select the **notifyWeather** control in the component tray. In the events list of the Properties window, double-click the **MouseDoubleClick** event. Edit the notifyWeather_ MouseDoubleClick event handler and add the Restore method as shown in the following code.:

```
14 private void notifyWeather_MouseDoubleClick(object sender, MouseEventArgs e)
15 {
16     this.Restore();
17 }
18
19 private void Restore()
20 {
21     if (this.WindowState == FormWindowState.Minimized)
22     {
23         this.WindowState = FormWindowState.Normal;
24     }
25     this.Visible = true;
26 }
```

Again, a private method called Restore() was created in case you need it elsewhere in your application.

The first line of code in the Restore method is there because it is impossible to know in which context your method will be called. In your case, when you created the form, you set the WindowState property to mini-mized and ShowInTaskbar to false so that the form starts minimized and the user doesn't see it. When you start the application, the first time the user selects the Open... menu choice (you'll code this soon) or dou-ble-clicks the notifyWeather control, the user won't be able to see the form if you only have set its Visible property to true. Therefore, you need to verify in which WindowState the form appears. If it's still minimized, you need to set it to Normal so that the focus is on the Main form.

5 Press **F5** to test the changes. Double-click the **notifyWeather** icon in the notification area and the Main form should appear.

Now let's see what happens if the user clicks the Close button (red X). If you close the application by using the Close button, it closes permanently. Yet, our design requirements state that the application should simply minimize back to the notification area when the user clicks the Close button. Therefore, you'll now intercept an event that occurs just before the form is closed and just before the form object is deleted, which is an event called the FormClosing event. By using a FormClosing event, you can extract the reason for the form's closing and in this way intercept the event when the user clicks the Close button.

 In Design view, select the **Main** form. Go to the events list in the Properties window and double-click the **FormClosing** event. Add the following code to the Main_FormClosing event handler.

```
27 private void Main_FormClosing(object sender, FormClosingEventArgs e)
28 {
29     if (e.CloseReason == CloseReason.UserClosing)
30     {
31         e.Cancel = true;
32         this.Hide();
33     }
34 }
```

MORE INFO

If you want to learn more about why a form might be closing, you can search the Help system by entering the following keywords: CloseReason enumeration.

Part of the event is the FormClosingEventArgs, which contains the arguments that accompany the event notification as well as the reason why the form is closing. If the user is closing the form, setting the Cancel property to true will stop the closing process and prevent the form from closing. The next instruction is a call to the Hide method. The Hide method is simply a synonym for setting the Visible property to false. The form will simply be hidden.

MORE INFO

The UserClosing event would also be called whenever the user presses Alt+F4 or if the user selects Close from the Form Control menu (the menu that appears when you click on the left corner where the icon is usually located).

When the user selects the Exit choice from the context menu, the FormClosing event will be raised; however, the reason given will not be UserClosing. Instead it will be ApplicationExitCall, and therefore the application will continue the closing process.

 You'll now add the code for the Open . . . menu choice. To write the code for this event, select **cmsNotify** in the component tray and then double-click on the **Open . . .** menu choice on the context menu strip. The click event handler will be created, and you'll call the Restore method to handle the form's visibility, which is done by the this.Restore() code. You will add code to make sure the form has the focus so that it ends up on top of any other displayed windows. Add the following code to the tsmiOpen_Click event handler:

```
35 private void tsmiOpen_Click(object sender, EventArgs e)
36 {
37     this.Restore();
38     this.Focus();
39 }
```

Now, test the application with the following test scenario:

- Start the application by pressing **F5.** Right-click on the notify icon and select **Open . . .** The Main form should appear in the middle of your screen. Minimize the Main form by clicking the **Close** button. Once it is minimized, double-click the notify icon. You should again see the Main Form. Terminate the application by selecting the **Exit** menu choice.

Adding the Splash Screen and About Dialog Box

Since you have done these procedures in Chapter 6, I won't spend too much time on this section. You'll just add forms that are almost finished from the companion content. Follow these steps to add the SplashWeather.cs form and AboutWeatherTracker.cs form to your project.

TO ADD A SPLASH SCREEN AND ABOUT DIALOG BOX

1 In the Solution Exoplorer, right-click the **Weather Tracker** project, select **Add**, and then select **Existing Item**. The Add Existing Item dialog box apears.

2 Browse to the SplashAbout folder under the Chapter9 companion content. By default the companion content is located at \My Documents\Microsoft Press\VCS 2005 Express\.

3 Select the **AboutWeatherTracker.cs** file and, while pressing the **Ctrl** key, select the **SplashWeather.cs** file.

4 Click **Add** to add the AboutWeatherTracker and SplashWeather forms to your project in Solution Explorer.

Using the following table, set the specified properties on the SplashWeather form. Images are located in the Images folder under Chapter9 of the companion content.

Control Name	Control Type	Property	Value
SplashWeather	Form	BackgroundImage	mountain.jpg
SplashWeather	Form	BackgroundImageLayout	Stretch

Using the following table, set the specified properties on the AboutWeatherTracker form. Images are located in the Images folder under Chapter9 of the companion content.

Component	Property	Value
LogoPictureBox	Image	Sunset.jpg

Now you need to attach these two forms to the rest of the application.

TO ATTACH FORMS TO AN APPLICATION

1 To attach the splash screen, begin by opening the code for **Main.cs** and modify the constructor so that it looks like the following:

```
1 public partial class Main : Form
2 {
3   SplashWeather splashScreen = new SplashWeather();
4   public Main()
5   {
6     InitializeComponent();
7     splashScreen.Show();
8     Application.DoEvents();
9   }
```

2 The previous step will display the splash screen, but you need to close it and make it disappear. Open the **Main.cs** form in design mode and select the form. Click the **events** button (yellow lightning) at the top of the Properties window and double click the **Load** event.

Add the following code to the Main_Load event handler.

```
10 private void Main_Load(object sender, EventArgs e)
11 {
12     //Splash screen business.
13     Thread.Sleep(2000);
14     splashScreen.Close();
15 }
```

 Place your cursor within the "Thread" text. You should see a familiar yellow and red smart tag. This smart tag is there to let you know that the Thread class is in the System.Threading namespace and that you don't have it in your using directives at the top of Main.cs. Move your mouse over the smart tag, click the down arrow, and then select **using System.Threading**; to add it to your list of using directives.

 To attach the About dialog box, you need to tie it to the context About . . . menu choice. Go to your **Main.cs** form in design mode.

 Select **cmsNotify** in the component tray and double-click the **About . . .** menu choice in the context menu strip. Add the following code to the tsmiAbout_Click event hander.

```
16 private void tsmiAbout_Click(object sender, EventArgs e)
17 {
18     aboutScreen.ShowDialog();
19 }
```

 At the top of Main.cs, just below SplashWeather splashScreen = new SplashWeather();, add the following line of code:

```
20 AboutWeatherTracker aboutScreen = new AboutWeatherTracker();
```

 In the Solution Explorer, right-click the **Weather Tracker** project and select **Properties** to open the Project Designer.

9 On the Application tab, click **Assembly Information** and set the assembly information for the project. This information will fill the splash screen and About dialog box fields.

10 On the Application tab, change the application icon to **Sun.ico**. Click the ellipsis (**...**) button next to the Icon drop-down list. Select the **Sun.ico** file in the Chapter9 Images folder.

Adding the Options Dialog Box

You now have three forms. You will add the final Options dialog box form that will appear when the user selects the Options... menu choice in the context menu from the notify icon.

Figure 9-4
The Options dialog box

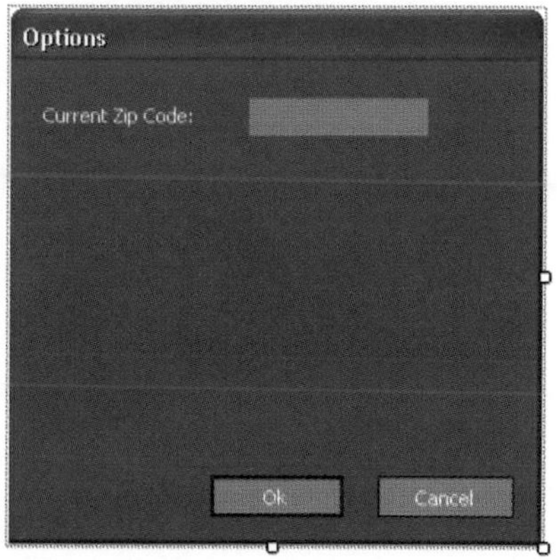

TO ADD THE OPTIONS DIALOG BOX FORM

1 In the Solution Explorer, right-click **Weather Tracker,** select **Add**, and then select **Windows Form**.

2 From the templates, select **Windows Form**, name the form **Options.cs**, and then click **Add**.

3 Using the following table, set properties and add controls to the Options form so that it looks like the form shown in Figure 9-4.

Component	Control Type	Property	Value
Options	Form	Font	Tahoma 8
Options	Form	BackColor	System:MenuHighlight
Options	Form	StartPosition	CenterScreen
Options	Form	ForeColor	Web:White
Options	Form	ControlBox	False
Options	Form	FormBorderStyle	FixedDialog
Options	Form	MaximizeBox	False
Options	Form	MinimizeBox	False
Options	Form	Text	Options
txtCurrentZipCode	Textbox	AcceptReturn	True
txtCurrentZipCode	Textbox	BackColor	System:InactiveCaption
lblCurrentZipCode	Label	Text	Current Zip Code:

Continued on the next page

Continued from the previous page

Component	Control Type	Property	Value
btnOk	Button	BackColor	System:InactiveCaption
btnOk	Button	FlatStyle	Popup
btnOk	Button	Text	Ok
btnCancel	Button	BackColor	System:InactiveCaption
btnCancel	Button	Text	Cancel
btnCancel	Button	FlatStyle	Popup
Options	Form	AcceptButton	btnOk
Options	Form	CancelButton	btnCancel

TO HOOK UP THE FORM TO THE CONTEXT MENU

1. Display the **Main** form in design mode.

2. Select **cmsNotify** in the component tray, and double-click the **Options . . .** menu choice in the context menu.

3. Add the following line of code to the tsmiOptions_Click event handler:

```
1 private void tsmiOptions_Click(object sender, EventArgs e)
2 {
3     optionsForm.ShowDialog();
4 }
```

4. At the top of Main.cs, just below AboutWeatherTracker aboutScreen = new AboutWeatherTracker();, add the following line of code:

```
Options optionsForm = new Options();
```

5. Press **F5** to run the application. You should see your splash screen. Use the context menu on the notify icon to open the **About** dialog box and the **Options** dialog box. When finished, exit the application.

You are now finished with this part of the project. Be sure to save your project. It is time to add the meat of the project: using Web services.

NOTE

At this point in the chapter, the current project state is saved in the Chapter9 companion content in a folder named Weather Tracker UI. To add the Web service functionality, you can continue with your own project or use the project in Weather Tracker UI.

Using Web Services

You have constructed a nice shell, but the shell is rather empty at this moment. You need to access weather data in order to populate the shell. To accomplish this, you will learn to consume Web services. But first: what is a Web service?

A Web service is an application that runs on a Web server, such as Internet Information Services (IIS). A Web service has a series of exposed public methods that an application can call. There are numerous examples of Web services on the Internet. You can use Web services that perform a variety of operations, such as finding a ZIP code, viewing a map, buying movie tickets, looking for information on search engines such as MSN or Google, and accessing weather information like your application will soon do. In the .NET world, there are classes and wizards available to help you consume Web services.

Web services use XML to send messages and return results. All objects are serialized (the messages are sent as a series of bits and pieces over the Internet) and are then de-serialized on the other side back into objects. The beauty of XML Web services is that they can be hosted and consumed on any operating system and developed in any language. Because they use a series of standardized protocols and rules, XML Web services promote interoperability and efficiency. The future of the transacted world over the Internet lies in big part with the success of Web services.

In this project, you will use a weather data Web service. You will need to tell Visual Studio where this Web service is located so that it can add a Web reference to your project that points to this service. Follow the steps below to accomplish this task.

TO ADD WEB SERVICES TO YOUR PROJECT USING VISUAL STUDIO

1 You'll need to register for the free weather Web service to obtain a username and password to authenticate yourself. In fact, you'll use that information to retrieve the weather data. Otherwise your experience will be limited. Go to *http://www.ejse.com/WeatherSignup/Signup.aspx* to register and receive your login information.

2 In the Solution Explorer, right-click on the project name and then select **Add Web Reference . . .** The Add Web Reference dialog box appears.

3 In the URL text box, enter the URL of the weather Web service, *http://www.ejse.com/ WeatherService/Service.asmx*, and click the **Go** button.

4 If you are connected to the Internet and the weather Web service is available, you will see a list of methods that are exposed to you, the pro- grammer. Refer to Figure 9-5 to view the results.

5 Change the Web Reference name to **WeatherWebService** and click the **Add Reference** button. It will take some time as Visual Studio creates all of the necessary files for you to consume that Web service.

6 Under the Web References folder, you should now have a small globe icon with the name you just gave to that Web service. This is a Web reference that points to the weather Web service discovered at that URL. You can now connect and execute the methods on this Web service.

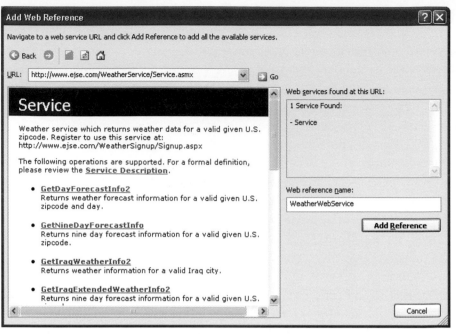

Figure 9-5
List of exposed methods from the weather Web service

Figure 9-6
The weather Web service added to the project

7 Click on **Show All files** in the Solution Explorer toolbar and expand the weather Web service refer- ence. You'll find that three items were created by Visual Studio: a file called Reference.map, a file called Service.wsdl, and another called Service.disco. Refer to Figure 9-6 to see what Solution Explorer should look like. The weather Web service is the heart and soul of this application, without which you simply have a nice shell without content.

Reference.map is an XML file that contains the URL of that Web service. It is produced by a tool called wsdl. exe. WSDL stands for Web Services Description Language. The reference.map file is linked to a proxy file called reference.vb. The proxy file is a local representation of the Web service on the Internet that enables you to call methods in your projects without having compilation error or run time problems. It also enables you to have IntelliSense in Visual Studio when using Web services. The proxy file is a copy of a class on the Web server where the Web service is hosted. The .wsdl file is an XML file describing the Web service and what it has to offer. Finally, the .disco file is an optional file for discovering the Web service.

In Chapter 8, "Managing the Data," you learned that you could create data sources from a Web service, a database, or an object. In this section, that's exactly what you'll benefit from. You will see how re-using tools and components allows you to be more productive. You will use the same techniques used in the previous database sections except that this time you will be binding data coming across the wire from all parts of the globe.

You will now call the public Web methods and obtain the information you need. This is where the fun begins. As you have previously done with the database and with databinding, you will now execute the same procedures for the Web service. Go to the Data Sources window by selecting Show Data Sources on the Data menu. You'll notice that you already have a weather Web service data source. It will therefore be easy to drop the weather information you will need to see on your form.

Your regular Web browser can be used to try a Web service without writing a line of code. You can usually point your Web browser to the Web service address and invoke its methods. This is an excellent way to learn what a Web method needs and what its output looks like. Please note that it's not possible to talk to all of them in this way. As an example, try a regions Web service that returns a list of all states in the U.S.: http://www.synapticdigital.com/webservice/public/regions.asmx. Click on the listByCountry method, type in USA in the yellow text box, and click Invoke. In a separate browser, you will obtain the list of states in the U.S.

TO ADD WEATHER INFORMATION TO YOUR FORM

1 First, make sure you are viewing the Main form on the designer surface.

2 In the Data Sources window, expand the **WeatherWebService** node, and you'll see that there are five different types of data that the Web site can retrieve. They are all datasets.

3 Expand the **WeatherInfo** node and change all element types (except IconIndex) in that dataset from TextBox to Label by clicking the down arrow on each element and selecting **Label** from the drop-down list.

4 Set IconIndex to **PictureBox**. If the picture box type is not available, you can add it. In the drop-down list, click the **Customize** choice. In the Options dialog box, you'll see a drop-down list with possible data types. Integer should be selected by default because Visual Studio recognizes that the field returned by the Web method is an integer; if not, select **Integer**. Just below you should have a series of

check boxes representing a list of associated controls, which means a list of controls with which an integer can be associated. If you scroll down, you should see the PictureBox control. Click in the check box beside PictureBox and then click **OK**. Now for IconIndex, select the **PictureBox** type from drop-down list.

5 In the Data Sources window, select the **WeatherInfo** node and change the data representation from a DataGridView to **Details** by selecting it in the drop-down list. When finished, the Data Sources window should look like Figure 9-7.

Figure 9-7
The WeatherInfo data in the weather Web service

Drag and drop **WeatherInfo** onto the Main form designer surface. A WeatherInfoBindingSource and a WeatherInfoBindingNavigator is added to the component tray.

7 Select **WeatherInfoBindingNavigator** in the component tray and change its Visible property to **false**. (You might need to click on the **Properties** button at the top of the Properties window to see the list of properties.)

8 You can't see the boundaries of all the controls on the form. To help with layout, select all of the controls on the form by creating a large selection rectangle around them with your mouse. In the Properties window, set the BorderStyle from None to **FixedSingle**. Black borders should appear around all controls. Once the form is done, we'll set the BorderStyle back to None.

9 On the PictureBox control, set the Name property to **pbCurrentTemp**, set the BackColor property to **Web:White**, set the Size. Width to **55**, and set Size.Height to **45**.

10 Delete the **Icon Index** label.

11 Add a Label control and set the Text property to **"Current Temperature"**.

12 Change the text of the "Temprature:" label to **"Temperature:"**.

13 Change the name of the label to the right of "Temperature:" to **lblTemperatureCurrent**. The label is identified with a red box in Figure 9-8.

14 Using Figure 9-8 as a guide, size and position the controls on the form. If you want, adjust the font size and style of the labels.

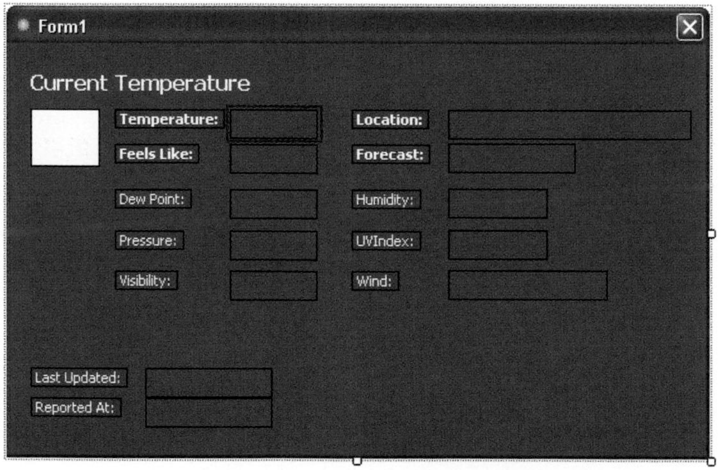

Figure 9-8
Layout of the current weather information

User Settings

For the Weather Tracker application to work, you will need to specify your weather Web service registration information. Your username and password will be saved in the application settings. The application settings are settings stored in an XML file and persist from one execution to another. The current ZIP code will also be saved here.

TO CREATE USER SETTING ENTRIES

 In the Solution Explorer, right-click the **Weather Tracker** project and select **Properties**. The Project Designer appears.

Figure 9-9
Application settings in the Project Designer

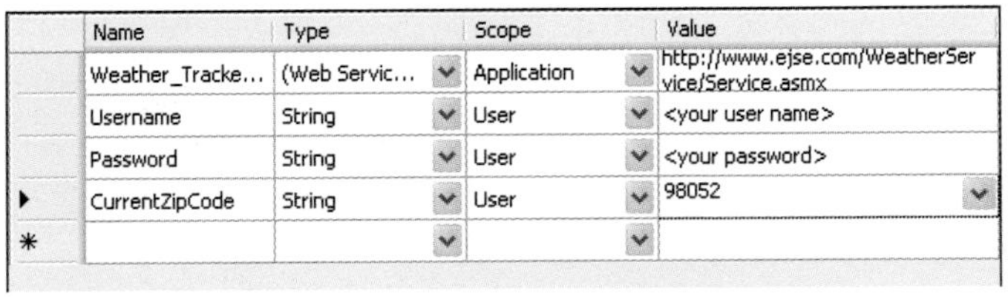

 In the Settings tab, add entries for **Username**, **Password**, and **CurrentZipCode** as shown in Figure 9-9. (You will need to specify your own username and password.)

Name	Type	Scope	Value
Weather_Tracke...	(Web Servic...	Application	http://www.ejse.com/WeatherService/Service.asmx
Username	String	User	<your user name>
Password	String	User	<your password>
CurrentZipCode	String	User	98052

All entries are strongly typed (i.e., real .NET type) and set to string type. You might be alarmed by the fact that Username and Password are in clear text. In your case, you don't need a great deal of security because the weather Web service is a free service. If you had to, you could encrypt those settings to make them more secure.

3 Save your project and close the Project Designer.

Working in the Background

If you try to run your form now, you won't get anything from the Web service. This process differs from your work with databases, in which a great deal of code was completed for you so you could retrieve the data and populate the fields. When dealing with a Web service, you must do more of the actual coding to get the data into the form. Let's talk about how you'll do this.

First, talking to a Web service can be a long process. A long process typically means only a few seconds (perhaps up to 30 seconds), but you can't leave the user with a blocked UI while your application is retrieving information. You therefore need a way of saying to your application: "Go get this information and let me know when you have it." This programming technique is called multithreaded programming with call backs. In .NET Framework 2.0, this type of programming is simplified by creating a new class called the BackgroundWorker class. As its name implies, it works in the background on a task; what's not implied is that it will let you know when it has completed the task.

TO PERFORM A TASK IN THE BACKGROUND

1 Open the **Main** form in design view.

2 Go to the **Toolbox**. In the Components section, select the **BackgroundWorker** control and drag it onto your form. It doesn't have a design time portion, so it will be added to the component tray. Rename it **backgroundCurrentWorker**.

3 At the top of the Properties window for backgroundCurrentWorker, click the events icon (yellow lightning) and then double-click the **DoWork** event.

4 At the top of Main.cs, add the following using statements to the existing using statements.

```
1 using Weather_Tracker.Properties;
2 using Weather_Tracker.WeatherWebService;
```

5 Add the following code to the backgroundCurrentWorker_DoWork event handler.

```
3 private void backgroundCurrentWorker_DoWork(object sender, DoWorkEventArgs e)
4 {
5     // This method will execute in the background thread created by the
6     // BackgroundWorker component
7     int desiredZipCode = (int)e.Argument;
8     Service weatherService = new Service();
9     e.Result = weatherService.GetWeatherInfo2(
10         Settings.Default.Username,
11         Settings.Default.Password,desiredZipCode);
12 }
```

The DoWork event handler is where the call to the weather Web service is performed. You will start by calling the GetWeatherInfo2 method exposed by the Web service. When you invoke the GetWeatherInfo2 method, it runs in a separate context so that it doesn't block the application UI. Otherwise, the application might appear to hang.

The GetWeatherInfo2 method takes three parameters (username, password, ZIP code) and returns a WeatherInfo result. How do you know what parameters you need and the return value? You can look at the WSDL (pronounced WISDLE) file to understand. Also, when you added the weather Web service, Visual Studio generates the appropriate IntelliSense.

6 Add the following startBackgroundTaskCurrentDay method.

```
13 private void startBackgroundTaskCurrentDay()
14 {
15     try
16     {
17         // Execute the background task only if it's not already working
18         if (!backgroundCurrentWorker.IsBusy)
19         {
20             this.UseWaitCursor = true;
21             this.backgroundCurrentWorker.RunWorkerAsync(
22                 int.Parse(currentZipCode));
23         }
24     }
25     // Normally an exception handling class or logging would be used,
26     // but we'll just use a message box.
27     catch (FormatException)
28     {
29         MessageBox.Show("Invalid conversion from string to int",
30             "Parse Zip Code Exception");
31         throw;
32     }
33     catch (Exception)
34     {
35         MessageBox.Show("Fatal Error!",
36             "Fatal error starting background task");
37         throw;
38     }
39 }
```

The startBackgroundTaskCurrentDay method starts the BackgroundWorker. The first thing you need to do is verify whether the BackgroundWorker is already busy with a previous call; if you don't do this, you'll end up with an InvalidOperationException. Simply verifying whether the BackgroundWorker is busy ensures that you won't get that exception when calling the RunWorkerAsync method. In fact, this is the only exception that this method can raise. A quick look at the documentation can confirm this.

Executing the RunWorkerAsync method is submitting a request to start an operation asynchronously, which raises the DoWork event. An event handler with the following name format is invoked: <your background-worker variable>_DoWork. In your case, the backgroundCurrentWorker_DoWork method is executed when the DoWork event is raised.

7 Switch to Design view and select **backgroundCurrentWorker** in the component tray.

8 In the events list in the Properties window, double-click the **RunWorkerCompleted** event.

9 Add the following code to the BackgroundCurrentWorker_RunWorkerCompleted event handler.

```
40 private void backgroundCurrentWorker_RunWorkerCompleted(object sender,
RunWorkerCompletedEventArgs e)
41 {
42     if ((e.Error == null))
43     {
44         this.UseWaitCursor = false;
45         WeatherInfo weatherInfo;
46         weatherInfo = (WeatherInfo)e.Result;
47         weatherInfoBindingSource.DataSource = weatherInfo;
48         pbCurrentTemp.Load(@".\Images\" +
49             weatherInfo.IconIndex.ToString() + ".gif");
50         // If web service returned weather info, then
51         // update notify icon
52         currentTemperature = this.ExtractTemperature();
53         this.CreateIcon((int)Math.Round(currentTemperature));
54     }
55     else if ((e.Error.Message.IndexOf("503") > 0))
56     {
57         MessageBox.Show(
58             "Weather Web service is unavailable, retry later!\n" +
59             "Retry later using the Refresh Weather Info menu.",
60             "Weather Web service unavailable");
```

```
61        }
62        else if ((e.Error.Message.IndexOf("timed out") > 0))
63        {
64            MessageBox.Show(
65                "Unable to retrieve the data in the time allowed\n" +
66                "Retry later using the Refresh Weather Info menu.",
67                "Weather Web service Timeout");
68        }
69        else
70        {
71            MessageBox.Show(
72                "Problem with Weather Web service! Error message:\n" +
73                e.Error.Message + " \nRetry Later!",
74                "Weather Web service problem");
75        }
76 }
```

If the Web service was available and your parameters were good, the method you invoked is then working in a different context and on its own. When it is finished with its business, you will be notified that the method has completed because a RunWorkerCompleted event will be raised.

To retrieve the results, you must have an event handler with the following name: <your backgroundworker variable>_RunWorkerCompleted. In this method, you have a parameter of type RunWorkerCompletedEventArgs that contains everything you need to obtain the results. If an exception was raised in the DoWork event handler, you'll be able to retrieve it by checking the Error property, which is of type Exception. If there is no error, then you must retrieve the results yourself. Remember that the Results property will give you an element of type Object, which by itself will not help you. You need to assign it a variable with the same type that the Web service method used to spit out the results.

In your case, if you look into the method signature for GetWeatherInfo2, WeatherInfo is the type of results it is producing. Therefore, you need to declare a variable of that type. If you recall, when you dragged the WeatherInfo dataset onto the designer surface, you automatically created databound controls for all of those fields. Thus, you simply need to assign that WeatherInfo variable as the DataSource for your BindingSource, and you will have a link between what's coming from the Web service and the controls on your form.

Now, you also have a picture box on the designer surface that will serve to display an icon portraying the current forecast. The info is returned to you as an index: the iconIndex property. You need to load an image file from your hard drive into the picture box you dragged onto the designer surface using the index as the filename.

What happens next is the creation of the icon that will appear in the notification area representing the current temperature.

You may be wondering: What is the link between the index and the filename, and who is creating that link? This is a convention used by many weather providers on the Internet; therefore, this is something that will work with many services if you want to add some later.

TO ADD SUPPORTING BACKGROUND CODE

 At the very top of Main.cs, add the following using statements.

```
1 using System.Net;
2 using System.Runtime.InteropServices;
```

 At the top of the class, add the following lines just below Options optionsForm = new Options();.

```
3 public static double currentTemperature;
4 public static string currentZipCode = Settings.Default.CurrentZipCode;
```

The first line of code is declared as a public static field named currentTemperature. A static field simply means that it doesn't belong to any particular instance of that class, but that there is only one for the entire class. The currentZipCode code found in the next line is also a static field. It's initialized from the user settings, but it will change once you complete the Options form.

3 Add the following ExtractTemperature method.

```
5 private Double ExtractTemperature()
6 {
7     if ((this.lblTemperatureCurrent.Text.Length == 0))
8     {
9         return int.MinValue;
```

```
10        }
11     else
12     {
13        //  Returning only the number portion ignoring the
14        //  the F.
15        return Double.Parse(
16             this.lblTemperatureCurrent.Text.Substring(0,
17             this.lblTemperatureCurrent.Text.IndexOf("°")));
18     }
19 }
```

The ExtractTemperature method extracts the temperature from the lblTemperatureCurrent label and returns it as a number.

 Add the following UpdateWeather method.

```
20 public void UpdateWeather()
21 {
22     try
23     {
24        this.tsmiRefresh.Enabled = false;
25        this.tsmiOptions.Enabled = false;
26        this.startBackgroundTaskCurrentDay();
27        this.tsmiRefresh.Enabled = true;
28        this.tsmiOptions.Enabled = true;
29     }
30     catch (WebException)
31     {
32        MessageBox.Show(
33             "Web service currently unavailable.\n" +
34             "Retry later using the Refresh Weather Info menu.",
35             "Web Exception");
36        this.tsmiRefresh.Enabled = true;
37     }
38     catch (Exception ex)
39     {
40        MessageBox.Show(
41             "Unknown problem. Error message:\n" +
42             ex.Message + "please, retry later!", "Unknown error");
43        this.tsmiRefresh.Enabled = true;
44     }
45 }
```

The UpdateWeather method initiates the update of the weather data by calling the startBackgroundTask-CurrentDay method you added earlier. The weather data needs to be updated when the ZIP code is changed or when the Refresh Weather Info menu choice is selected on the context menu of the notify icon. The UpdateWeather method also enables or disables menu choices on the context menu as appropriate.

Completing the Core Weather Tracker Functionality

In the next sections, you will add more code to obtain a working version of the Weather Tracker application. This includes creating the icon, verifying connectivity, verifying weather Web service availability, and other tasks.

In this section, you will add code to create and destroy the icon in the notification area. You can review the code, but I won't discuss it in much detail because GDI+ and COM "interop" are subjects that are too advanced for this book. However, you may want to refer to the comments within the code.

TO ADD CREATE AND DESTROY NOTIFICATION ICON CODE

1 In Main.cs, add the following CreateIcon method.

```
1 private void CreateIcon(int temperature)
2 {
3     string displayString;
4     Bitmap drawnIcon;
5     SolidBrush brushToDrawString;
6     Color iconColor;
7     Graphics iconGraphic;
8     FontFamily fontFamily = new FontFamily("Arial");
9     Font IconFont = new Font(fontFamily, 11,
10         FontStyle.Regular, GraphicsUnit.Pixel);
11
12     if ((temperature == int.MinValue))
13     {
14         displayString = "NA";
15         iconColor = Color.Red;
16     }
17     else if ((temperature > 100))
18     {
```

```
19          iconColor = Color.Red;
20          displayString = ((temperature - 100)).ToString();
21      }
22      else if ((temperature < 0))
23      {
24          iconColor = Color.Blue;
25          displayString = ((temperature * -1)).ToString();
26      }
27      else
28      {
29          iconColor = Color.Black;
30          displayString = temperature.ToString();
31      }
32
33      // Start by creating a new bitmap the size of an icon
34      drawnIcon = new Bitmap(16, 16);
35
36      // To draw the string we need a brush
37      brushToDrawString = new SolidBrush(iconColor);
38
39      //  Creating a new graphic object so that we
40      //  can call the drawstring method with our
41      //  temperature or NA if there is no temp.
42      iconGraphic = Graphics.FromImage(drawnIcon);
43
44      //  Now we are drawing the temperature string onto
45      //  graphic and therefore on the bitmap.
46      iconGraphic.DrawString(displayString, IconFont,
47          brushToDrawString, 0, 0);
48
49      //  We are getting ready to convert the bitmap into
50      //  an icon and to set the notifyWeather.Icon with
51      //  this newly created icon
52      IntPtr hIcon = drawnIcon.GetHicon();
53      Icon customMadeIcon = System.Drawing.Icon.FromHandle(hIcon);
54      notifyWeather.Icon = customMadeIcon;
55
56      // Now that we're done manipulating the new icon
57      // we need to destroy the unmanaged resource,
58      // otherwise we'll have a handle leak.
59      DestroyIcon(hIcon);
60 }
```

2 Add the following DestroyIcon method.

```
61 //  The GetIcon method generated an unmanaged handle
62 //  that we need to take care of otherwise there
63 //  will be a handle leak.
64 [DllImport("User32.dll")]
65 public static extern bool DestroyIcon(IntPtr hIcon);
```

Once the application starts to load, you'll verify that the user has a valid and established Internet connection. To verify this, you'll make a simple HTTP request to the Microsoft Web site. If you receive an HTTP OK (e.g., 200) code back from the Web server, it means that you successfully accessed the Web page you requested. If an exception is raised, it's because you have encountered a problem or the Microsoft.com Web site is down, which is quite rare. If a valid Internet connection is not detected, a message will be displayed.

You'll also verify that the weather Web service is up and running even before making a call to it. Again, if the Web service is not up and running, a message will be displayed.

TO ADD VERIFICATION CODE

1 In Main.cs, add the following VerifyConnectedToInternet method.

```
1 private Boolean VerifyConnectedToInternet()
2 {
3     try
4     {
5         WebRequest request =
6             WebRequest.Create("http://www.microsoft.com/");
7         HttpWebResponse response =
8             (HttpWebResponse)request.GetResponse();
9         if (response.StatusCode == HttpStatusCode.OK)
10             return true;
11         else
12             return false;
13     }
14     catch (Exception)
15     {
16         return false;
17     }
18 }
```

Add the following VerifyWebService method.

```
19 private Boolean VerifyWebService()
20 {
21     try
22     {
23         WebRequest request = WebRequest.Create(
24             "http://www.ejse.com/WeatherService/Service.asmx?op=GetWeatherInfo2");
25         HttpWebResponse response =
26             (HttpWebResponse)request.GetResponse();
27         if (response.StatusCode == HttpStatusCode.OK)
28             return true;
29         else
30             return false;
31     }
32     catch (Exception)
33     {
34         return false;
35     }
36 }
```

TO FINISH THE MAIN FORM

 In Main.cs, locate the existing Main_Load event handler.

 Modify Main_Load to look like the following.

```
1 private void Main_Load(object sender, EventArgs e)
2 {
3     // Splash screen business.
4     Thread.Sleep(2000);
5     splashScreen.Close();
6
7     //Changing the title of our main form with the
8     //application name and the version
9     this.Text = aboutScreen.AssemblyTitle + " " +
10         aboutScreen.AssemblyVersion;
11
12     //Creating temporarily the NA icon.
```

```
13      this.CreateIcon(int.MinValue);
14
15      if (!VerifyConnectedToInternet())
16      {
17          MessageBox.Show(
18              "Your computer doesn't seem to be connected " +
19              "to the Internet or your Internet connection " +
20              "is not working properly!");
21          this.tsmiOptions.Enabled = false;
22          this.tsmiRefresh.Enabled = false;
23      }
24      else if (!VerifyWebService())
25      {
26          MessageBox.Show(
27              "Web service is currently unavailabled.\n" +
28              "Retry later using the Refresh Weather Info menu.",
29              "Web Service Not available");
30          if ((currentZipCode == String.Empty))
31              this.tsmiRefresh.Enabled = false;
32          else
33              this.tsmiRefresh.Enabled = true;
34      }
35      else
36      {
37          tsmiRefresh.Enabled = false;
38          this.UpdateWeather();
39      }
40  }
```

The Main_Load event handler is the starting point for Weather Tracker. In this code, the My construct is used to build the title of the application by using its name and the version stored in the assembly parameters in the same manner that the About dialog box uses this information. Next, a red NA (not available) icon is drawn in the notification area that will remain until the Web service returns with positive results, in which case the temperature will be drawn as an icon. If a connection to the Internet cannot be verified or the weather Web service cannot be verified, a message is displayed and the appropriate menu choices in the notify icon context menu are disabled. If everything is working as expected, the process for obtaining the weather data is started.

 In Design view, select **cmsNotify** in the component tray. In the context menu strip, double-click the **Refresh Weather Info** menu choice.

Add the following code to the tsmiRefresh_Click event handler. This code initiates an update of the weather data when the Refresh Weather Info menu choice in the context menu is selected.

```
41 private void tsmiRefresh_Click(object sender, EventArgs e)
42 {
43     this.tsmiRefresh.Enabled = false;
44     this.UpdateWeather();
45 }
```

5 In Design view, select all of the controls on the Main form. Set the BorderStyle property to **None**. (You might need to click the **Properties** button at the top of the Properties window to see the list of properties.)

All of the weather forecast images need to be copied from your companion content to the same folder where the Weather Tracker application is located. You need to create a folder called Images and copy all of the *.gif weather image files into this folder.

TO ADD WEATHER ICONS

1 In the Solution Explorer, right-click the **Weather Tracker** project, select **Add**, and then **New Folder**. Name the folder **Images**.

 Using Windows Explorer, copy the *.gif images (1.gif through 47.gif) from the companion content to the Images folder you just created. (The default location is \My Documents\Visual Studio 2005\Projects\Weather Tracker\Weather Tracker\Images.)

3 In the Solution Explorer, right-click the **Images** folder, select **Add**, and then **Existing Item**. The Add Existing Item dialog box appears.

4 In the Files Of Type drop-down list, select **Image Files**.

5 Make sure you are looking in the Images folder and select all of the .gif files. To select all the files, you can press **Ctrl+A** or you can use **Shift+click**.

6 When all of the .gif files are selected, click the **Add** button to add the images to the Weather Tracker project.

 In the Solution Explorer, select all of the .gif files. First, select **1.gif** and then, while pressing the **Shift** key, select the last .gif file.

With all the .gif files selected, in the Properties window, set the Copy To Output Directory property to **Copy Always**, as shown in Figure 9-10. Make sure the Build Action property is set to **Content**.

Figure 9-10
Weather icons added to the project

Testing Weather Tracker

Before running the Weather Tracker application, verify that you have successfully completed the following:

■ You have an Internet connection.

■ You have registered for the free weather Web service.

■ You have specified your username and password in the application settings.

Now you will see if your application works. Press F5 to run Weather Tracker. If you have any build errors, review the errors in the Error List window and fix them. If necessary, you can review the completed application in the Complete folder. When you run the application, you should see your splash screen and then see a red NA in the notification area indicating that the current temperature has not been retrieved. Right-click the NA icon in the notification area and select Refresh Weather Info in the context menu. If the weather Web service is available, you should see the current temperature for the Redmond, Washington, area in the notification area. (Be patient, depending on the current Web service load you might have to wait a few moments.) When you double-click the temperature in the notification area, you should see detailed weather information as shown in Figure 9-11. Right-click the temperature to see the context menu. When finished, exit the application.

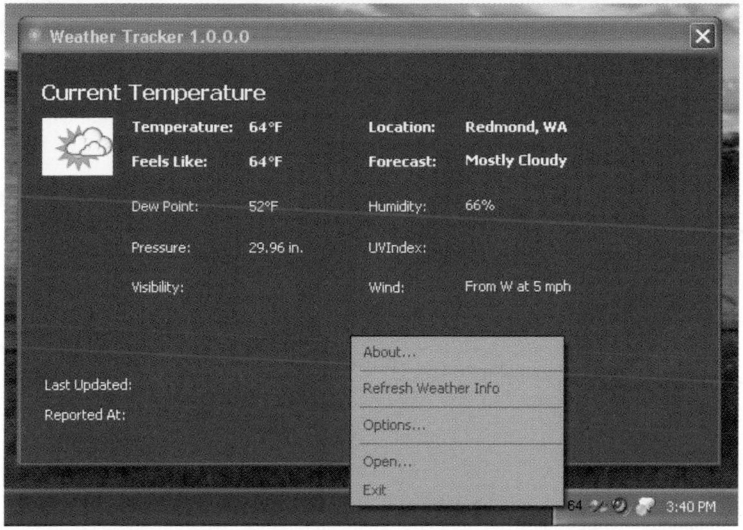

Figure 9-11
The Weather Tracker application displaying weather data from a Web service

Working with the Options Dialog Box

Currently, the ZIP code is set to a particular value and that really isn't our intent. Therefore, you will use the Options dialog box and let the user enter the ZIP code they want to monitor. The ZIP code will be persisted to disk so that, whenever the user restarts the application, it will be restored to the last ZIP code they specified. Remembering the user's settings from one execution to another will provide the user with a better experience.

You will also perform some checking to verify the ZIP code entered by the user. You will verify that the ZIP code is a number and within a specific range. You will use the error provider control to display appropriate text if the ZIP code is empty or not within range.

The error provider control is used to display error information to the user. For example, if the user enters invalid information in a text box, an error icon is displayed next to the control indicating that an error has occurred. By default, the error icon is a small red circle with an exclamation point. When the user clicks the error icon, an error description is displayed to explain what is wrong to the user. You can change how the error is presented. For example, you can use a different error icon and you can make the error icon blink. Once a user addresses the error, you set the error description to an empty string to make the error icon disappear.

TO VALIDATE USER INPUT

1 Open the **Options** form in Design view.

2 From the Toolbox in the Components group, add an **ErrorProvider** control to the form. The control will appear in the component tray.

3 Name the control **ErrorProviderCurrentZipCode**.

4 Double-click the **OK** button.

5 Add the following code to the btnOk_Click event handler.

```
1 private void btnOk_Click(object sender, EventArgs e)
2 {
3     if (ValidateZip())
4     {
5         UpdateCurrentInfo();
6         this.DialogResult = System.Windows.Forms.DialogResult.OK;
7         this.Close();
8     }
9 }
```

6 Add the following ValidateZip method.

```
10 private bool ValidateZip()
11 {
12     int zipNumber;
13     bool ValidZipCode = true;
14     if (txtCurrentZipCode.Text != String.Empty)
15     {
16         zipNumber = int.Parse(txtCurrentZipCode.Text);
17         if (!(zipNumber > 999) && (zipNumber <= 99950))
18         {
19             ErrorProviderCurrentZipCode.SetError(
20                 this.txtCurrentZipCode,
21                 "Invalid Zip Code, enter a valid US zip code " +
22                 "(Between 1000 and 99950)");
```

```
23              ValidZipCode = false;
24          }
25          else
26          {
27              ErrorProviderCurrentZipCode.SetError(
28                  this.txtCurrentZipCode, "");
29          }
30      }
31      else
32      {
33          ErrorProviderCurrentZipCode.SetError(
34              this.txtCurrentZipCode,
35              "Invalid Zip Code, enter a valid US zip code " +
36              "(Between 1000 and 99950)");
37          ValidZipCode = false;
38      }
39      return ValidZipCode;
40 }
```

The ValidateZip method ensures that the ZIP code text box is not empty and checks that the ZIP code is greater than 999 and less than or equal to 99950. If not, an error is displayed using the SetError method of error provider control. In the call to SetError, the txtCurrentZipCode text box is specified, which indicates that the error is associated with the txtCurrentZipCode control. If the ZIP code appears to be valid, the ValidZip method returns True; otherwise, it returns False.

 Switch back to the **Options** form in Design view.

8 Select the **txtCurrentZipCode** text box.

9 In the Properties window, click the **events** icon (yellow lightning) to display the events list.

10 Double-click the **KeyDown** event.

11 Add the following code to the txtCurrenZipCode_KeyDown event handler.

```
41 private void txtCurrentZipCode_KeyDown(object sender, KeyEventArgs e)
42 {
43     if ((e.KeyCode < Keys.D0) || (e.KeyCode > Keys.D9))
44     {
```

```
45          //  Determine whether the keystroke is a number from the keypad.
46          if ((e.KeyCode < Keys.NumPad0) || (e.KeyCode > Keys.NumPad9))
47          {
48              //  Determine whether the keystroke is a backspace.
49              if ((e.KeyCode != Keys.Back))
50              {
51                  if ((e.KeyCode != Keys.Enter))
52                  {
53                      MessageBox.Show("Only numeric characters please!");
54                  }
55              }
56          }
57      }
58 }
```

This code checks the user's keystrokes as they type in the ZIP code. If the keystroke is not a number, a message box is displayed.

TO SAVE SETTINGS

1 In Options.cs, add the following UpdateCurrentInfo method.

```
1 private void UpdateCurrentInfo()
2 {
3     if (this.txtCurrentZipCode.Text != Settings.Default.CurrentZipCode)
4     {
5         Settings.Default.CurrentZipCode = this.txtCurrentZipCode.Text;
6         Main.currentZipCode = this.txtCurrentZipCode.Text;
7         Settings.Default.Save();
8     }
9 }
```

2 Place your cursor within the "Settings" text. You should see a familiar yellow and red smart tag. This smart tag is there to let you know that the Settings class isn't listed in your using directives at the top of Options.cs. Move your mouse over the smart tag, click the down arrow, and then select **using Weather_Tracker.Properties**; to add it to your list of using directives.

The UpdateCurrrentInfo method saves the user's ZIP code back to the application settings.

Testing Weather Tracker

Now you will test the Options dialog box. Press F5 to run Weather Tracker. Once the splash screen disappears, right-click the icon in the notification area and click Options. In the Options dialog box, test the ZIP validation code. For example, try to type alphabetic characters and try to type an invalid ZIP code. Figure 9-12 shows the error provider control when an out-of-range ZIP code is entered.

When finished, type in a valid ZIP code and click OK. Right-click the notify icon and select Refresh Weather Info. Wait for a few moments and open the main form. You should see weather data for the new ZIP code.

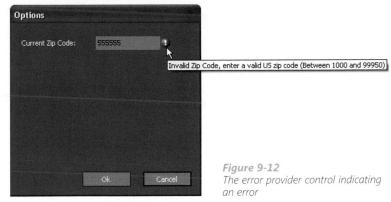

Figure 9-12
The error provider control indicating an error

You should be proud of yourself. You've developed an application with numerous complex features, and it works! The Weather Tracker application accomplishes the basic features established at the beginning of the chapter. There is plenty of room for enhancement. In fact, if you look in the Chapter9 folder of the companion content, you will find an enhanced version. If you want, check out this enhanced version and maybe step through the code to see how it works. The enhanced version includes the following capabilities:

- Displays weather data for the current day, as well as a three-day forecast.

- Includes an Options dialog box with many more controls and settings.

- Uses a ZIP Code Web service, which allows a user to select from a list of ZIP codes.

- Uses a State/Provinces Web service, which allows a user to search for a ZIP code by city.

- Allows users to select temperature unit, Celcius or Fahrenheit.

- Uses a Timer control to automatically refresh the weather data at regular intervals (e.g., every 10 minutes). The user can change this interval.

Now it's time to learn how to distribute Weather Tracker or another application.

And Now, Just ClickOnce!

A new technology for deployment called ClickOnce is now available with .NET Framework 2.0. It's a fantastic feature that let's you customize how your tool gets onto other people's machines. It's very easy—almost as easy as deploying Web applications, which often only entails copying files onto a server. ClickOnce allows you, the developer, to distribute your application via a robust and reliable mechanism. You can deploy on Web servers, file servers, or onto a CD/DVD. You can add the .NET Framework to your distribution package along with SQL Server if your application needs it. ClickOnce handles rollback and uninstall well, and it's a charm to push new updates. In your case, you'll deploy to a CD/DVD.

TO PACKAGE AND PUBLISH YOUR APPLICATION

1 To ensure that all of the *.gif files representing the weather icons are included with the installation, make sure the Build Action properties is set to **Content** for all of the *.gif images in the Solution Explorer. (This process was described earlier in the chapter.)

2 Rebuild the application completely by clicking **Rebuild Solution** on the Build menu.

3 In the Solution Explorer, right-click the **Weather Tracker** project and select **Properties** to open the Project Designer.

Figure 9-13
Publish tab in the Project Designer

Publish Location
Publishing Location (web site, ftp server, or file path):
publish\
Installation URL (if different than above):

Install Mode and Settings

○ The application is available online only

◉ The application is available offline as well (launchable from Start menu)

- Application Files...
- Prerequisites...
- Updates...
- Options...

Publish Version

Major:	Minor:	Build:	Revision:
1	0	0	0

☑ Automatically increment revision with each publish

[Publish Wizard...] [Publish Now]

4 Click the **Publish** tab. You should see a screen that looks like the one shown in Figure 9-13.

5 Click the **Application Files** button to see the list of files that will be included in the installation. All of the *.gif files should be listed. Click **OK**.

You now want to select the prerequisites for your application. When the installer runs on the user's machine, it will check for the presence of these items. If they are not present, the installer will by default download them from Microsoft.com or another source that you have configured.

Click the **Prerequisites** button. In the Prerequisites dialog box, select the **.NET Framework 2.0** and **Windows Installer 3.1** check boxes. Make sure the **Download Prerequisites From The Component Vendor's Web Site** option is selected. Click **OK**.

Click the **Publish Wizard** button.

The first page of the wizard appears, as shown in Figure 9-14, asking you to specify a location to publish the application.

Click the **Browse** button. In the Open Web Site dialog box, select **File System** on the left, and then select a location on your computer where you want to publish your application. I suggest you create a new folder named **Weather Tracker**. You can use the Create New Folder icon in the upper left to create a new folder. When finished, click the **Open** button and then click **Next**.

On the next page, select how the user will install the application. It could be a Web site, a UNC share on a network, or a CD or DVD. Select the **From A CD-ROM Or DVD-ROM** choice and click **Next**.

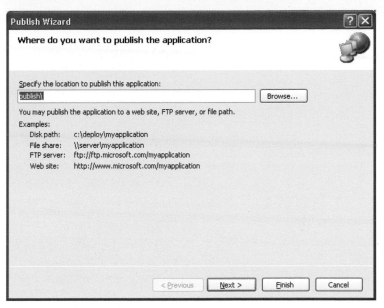

Figure 9-14
Publishing Wizard's first page

The next page asks whether you want your application to look for updates every time it starts. Because you are deploying on a CD or DVD, you won't have your application check for updates. Select the default **The Application Will Not Check For Updates** choice and click **Next** to continue.

Click **Finish** to publish your application.

After a few moments, setup files will be created at the folder location you selected earlier. To test the installation, double-click the Setup.exe file. During the installation, a shortcut will be added to the Programs menu. To uninstall the application, use Add Or Remove Programs in the Control Panel.

Once the installation works as expected, you can deploy your application by simply burning the installation files onto a CD or DVD.

ClickOnce has more features, but this short demonstration can get you started creating your own installations.

NOTE

During the installation, if you get an error message that the application validation did not succeed or another error message, try re-publishing your application and testing again.

NOTE

Every time you publish your application, the publish version number (not the application version number) will be incremented—that is, it will become version 1.0.0.0, 1.0.0.1, and so on.

Congratulations on getting this far! I hope you've learned a lot and had some fun developing applications using Visual C# 2005 Express Edition. If you like what you've learned (and I certainly hope so), then your education is just beginning. There's so much more to see and try. This book provided a small sample of the types of applications you can create. My advice to you is to continue thinking of fun projects you can create! You'll be surprised at how much you can accomplish. In my opinion, developing an application is one the greatest feelings of accomplishment. People are proud of their applications and you will be, too!

If you happen to create an application that's useful to you, chances are that it could be useful for others as well. In the end, you might be helping people by providing them with the fruits of your labor. You can also join development projects for fun and help others in the process while learning a great deal. Visit GotDotNet Workspaces *(http://www.gotdotnet.com/ workspaces/)* for a sample of cool project examples.

In September 2005, I started writing a column on MSDN that will be devoted to programming for fun. The column is called Coding4Fun and can be found at *http://msdn.microsoft.com/coding4fun/*. Part of this column on MSDN pertains to improving the Weather Tracker application you created here, so be sure to look for this feature. You can also visit my blog at *http://blogs.msdn.com/ppelland/*. I haven't updated my blog for a while because I've been busy writing this book as well as helping to ship Visual Studio 2005, but rest assured that in the near future, I will have some updates (I normally blog at least 4-5 times a week). You can use my site as another location to keep informed about cool stuff in the Express products line.

Until then, happy developing!

Glossary

A

argument A variable that is passed to a subprogram

B

black box testing Functional testing of a computer program to see that it performs correctly

breakpoint A pause or stopping place in a program, intentionally inserted to help with debugging

C

class The basic building block of OO programming; it defines the fields, properties, methods, and events of an object

compiler A computer program that translates the instructions written in one computer language into output in another computer language; compilers translate source code into some type of machine language that can be executed by a computer

console application An application that is run from a command prompt with no Windows or Web interface

context-sensitive menu A menu that provides different choices to the user depending on when it is accessed

controls Components of a Graphical User Interface, such as text boxes or buttons

D

data member Data encapsulated within a class or object

database A collection of data that is stored in files using a systematic structure

databinding An easy and transparent way to read/write a link between a control on a Windows Form and a data source from your application

debugger A computer program used to find the defects in another program

DLL (Dynamic Link Library) A binary application library file format in Microsoft Windows

E

encapsulation Hides private methods of a class or object; ensures that an object cannot be changed

event A software message that indicates something has happened in the program

execution engine Development tool for executing programs

F

FCL (Framework Class Libraries) A set of pre-written code for common programming tasks

H

hyperlink A reference in a hypertext document to another document or location

I

icon A small image or picture used to represent a program, file, or other object

IDE (Integrated Development Environment) Computer software tools that help developers write computer programs

inherit Objects are created that are specialized types of existing objects and can share and extend their behavior without having to re-implement it

instance A manifestation of a class

J

Jscript An Active Scripting Engine; the Microsoft version of JavaScript

M

method Procedure or function; a piece of code associated with a class or object

Microsoft .NET A software development platform developed by Microsoft

O

override A class or object may replace a behavior it has inherited

P

Perl A programming language that supports both procedural and object-oriented programming

programming language A method for providing instructions to a computer

property A quality of an object

Python An object-oriented computer programming language

R

reference The address of the memory space used to store information about a variable

S

Screen Tip Short, context-sensitive information provided at the point where the cursor is held

splash screen An image that appears on the screen while a program is loading; it provides information to the user about the loading process and disappears once the program is loaded

SQL Server 2005 Express Edition A version of SQL Server 2005 designed to help developers build applications by providing a powerful database that is also free and easy to use

string A sequence of characters or words

T

toolbar A row or section of clickable icons that activate different functions of a program

U

user interface (UI) The means by which users interact with a computer program

V

variable A structure that holds information temporarily for use later in a program

Visual Basic 2005 Express Edition A streamlined version of Visual Basic that provides hobbyists, students, and novices an easy-to-use Windows programming and development tool

W

Windows application Computer software that provides various functions for the user, such as word processing, database, or spreadsheet

Index

F

FCL. *See* Framework Class Libraries (FCL)
FK. *See* Foreign key (FK)
FlatStyle, 180
Font, 83, 179
ForeColor, 83, 179
Foreign key (FK), 132, 134–135
Foreign Key Relationship dialog box, 142
Form
    add weather information to, 183–185
    finish main, 195–197
    hook up to context menu, 180
FormBorderStyle, 83, 93, 179
Form control, 12, 169
Form properties, 49
Fortran, 4
Framework. *See* .NET Framework
Framework Class Libraries (FCL), 3

G-H

Getting Started, 28–29
GetWeatherInfo2 method, 187, 190
Google, 181
GotDotNet Workspaces, 206
Help. 33-37
Help menu, link About box to, 90–92
Hyperlink, 29–30

I

IBM SQL PL, 136, 148
Icon(s)
    alternative way to complete action, 29
    change main form, 85
    for entering data in table, 145
    error, 199
    modify browser form, 108
    NotifyIcon, 168–173
    pencil, 145
    personalize application with, 102–103
    ShowIcon, 93
    weather, 197–198
    yellow lightning, 76
IDE. *See* Integrated Development
    Environment (IDE)
Identity increment, 132
Identity seed, 132
IIS. *See* Internet Information Service (IIS)
Image, 106
Immediate Window, 116, 125

Immutable, 133
Inherits, 6
Instance, 52
Integrated Development Environment (IDE)
    components of, 28–31
    customizing, 39–40
    defined, 25
IntelliSense, 11, 59–66, 95, 187
    auto-using statements, 66
    code snippets, 63–64, 78
    and Ctrl+Spacebar, 60
    and period/left parentheses, 60–61
    select from list of options in, 62
    WriteLine method, 61
IntelliSense Filtering, pre-selecting "most
    recently used," 62
Internet. *See* Web services
Internet Information Service (IIS), 181
Invalid Zip code, 203
Items Collection Editor, 172

J-L

Java, 4
Label, 72
Lisp, 4
ListBox, 73
Local Help, 35
Locals, 114–117

M

Main form
    create data source for, 168–169
    finish, 195–197
    view of, in Weather Tracker application,
      168
MainFormToolStripContainer, 98
Main Toolbar, 28, 30
ManipulateStrings method, 120–122
MaximizeBox, 93, 179
Maximize Button, 27
.mdf file extension, 137
Menu Bar, 28–30
Menu strip, add dotted grip to, 98
Methods, 5, 7. *See also entries for individual
    methods*
Microsoft Access, 149
Microsoft.com Web site, 53, 194, 204
Microsoft Developer Network (MSDN),
    30, 206
Microsoft Developer Network Really Simple
    Syndication, 28, 30

Microsoft Office Excel, 123
Microsoft Office Outlook, 96
Microsoft SQL Server 2005 Express Edition,
    20–21
Microsoft Transact-SQL (T-SQL), 136, 148
Microsoft Update, 16, 22
Microsoft Virtual PC 2004, 17
Microsoft Visual Studio 2005 Express
    Edition
    add Web services to project using,
      181–183
    applications to build with, 10
    enter data in SQL Server tables using,
      145–148
    getting help, 33–37
    side-by-side installation, 16
    use of Pascal or Camel casing, 154
Microsoft Visual Studio 2005 Express
    Edition documentation, 33–37
Microsoft Windows AntiSpyware Beta, 16
Microsoft Windows application, 26–27
Minimize box, 93, 179
Minimize Button, 27
Modal Form, 92
Modify Connection dialog box, 13
"Most recently used," 62
Most Valuable Professionals, 37
MSDN. *See* Microsoft Developer Network
    (MSDN)
MSDN Express Library, 20–21
MSDN Feeds, 30
MSDN Help page, 17
MSDN Library, 35. *See also* Help
MSDN Online, 36–37
MSDN RSS (Microsoft Developer Network
    Really Simple Syndication), 30
MSDN Visual C# RSS Feed. *See* Microsoft
    Developer Network Really Simple
    Syndication (MSDN Visual C# RSS
    Feed)
MSN, 181
Multithreaded programming with call
    back, 186
myPosition, 120

N

Namespace, 46–47
Naming variable, 54
Natural key, 133
Navigate box, 92–95

Navigation buttons, modify behavior of,
    105–106
Navigation tool strip, add new controls
    to, 106
.NET Framework
    classes and wizards available in, 181,
      186
    ClickOnce, 204
    components of, 3
    defined, 2–4
    derived from Object class, 7
.NET Passport Sign-in, 2
New Project dialog box, 31–32, 41
Normalization rules, 129
Notification area, 169–173
Notification icon code, create and destroy,
    192–194
NotifyIcon, 169–173
Null, 132
NumericalUpDown, 74

O

Object class, 7
Object-oriented programming (OOP)
    concepts in, 7–9
    defined, 4
    more information about, 54
    terminology for, 67
Online Help Settings choices, 34
OOP. *See* Object-oriented programming
    (OOP)
Options dialog box, 30, 179–180, 199
Oracle PL/SQL, 136
Out-of-range Zip code, 203
Output, 116
Override, 6–7

P

Pascal, 4, 154
Password, 187
Pencil icon, 145
% symbol, 160
Period/left parentheses, 60–10
PK. *See* Primary key (PK)
Primary key (PK), 132
Private method, 174
Product Table, 130
Programming language, 3
Programming paradigm, 4
Progress bar, 99

What do you think of this book?
We want to hear from you!

Do you have a few minutes to participate in a brief online survey? Microsoft is interested in hearing your feedback about this publication so that we can continually improve our books and learning resources for you.

To participate in our survey, please visit:
www.microsoft.com/learning/booksurvey

And enter this book's ISBN, 0-7356-2229-9. As a thank-you to survey participants in the United States and Canada, each month we'll randomly select five respondents to win one of five $100 gift certificates from a leading online merchant.* At the conclusion of the survey, you can enter the drawing by providing your email address, which will be used for prize notification only.

Thanks in advance for your input. Your opinion counts!

Sincerely,

Microsoft Learning

Microsoft | Learning

Learn More. Go Further.

To see special offers on Microsoft Learning products for developers, IT professionals, and home and office users, visit:
www.microsoft.com/learning/booksurvey